TO Rick Fr[illegible]

Enjoy

[illegible]

Sept 22, 04

Lawyers, Judges and Journalists

The Corrupt and the Corruptors

By

Robert B. Surrick

ISBN: 1-4107-6033-2 (e-book)
ISBN: 1-4107-6032-4 (Paperback)

This book is printed on acid free paper.

Author's Website
Surrickbook.com

Printed in Canada

ACKNOWLEDGMENTS

There is always the risk when mentioning some, others are left out. I shall therefore keep this short and limited to those immediately involved with this project. First, my high school classmate whom I met again at our fortieth class reunion, Dort Perks, now going by Dottie Sheppard, formatted, spell checked and advised. It would not have been finished but for her. Val Loiacono was a constant inspiration, telling me over and over again that the project was worthwhile and should be finished. Chris Wojcik gave me space and quiet and put up with my cluttering her house. David Shaw, an English teacher in Chesapeake, VA offered advice and carefully proofed the text. Susan Ellis Green taught me that midnight in the garden of good and evil is not only in Savannah. Most of all, I want to acknowledge the unwavering support and final proofing by my son, Craig, who has always gone the extra mile for his old man.

Lastly, I want to thank several journalists who made suggestions. I accepted most but will deviate from the accepted use of capital letters. I believe the use of capital letters for courts, justices, judges and boards helps emphasize the importance of who and what I am writing about.

DEDICATION

This book is dedicated to:

Sam Klein, quintessential lawyer, honorable and decent man

and

Dechert Price and Rhoads, a law firm with enormous talent and even greater heart who stood by me when the need was the greatest

and

Most of all, my children Bart, Laura and Craig

CONTENTS

Title **Page**

I BELONG 1
THE MEANING OF ARGO V GOODSTEIN 6
VARIATION ON A THEME 12
LOSING YOUR VIRGINITY, ... 19
ONWARD AND UPWARD? 23
"I WOULD BE CHIEF JUSTICE BUT FOR THAT NIGGER" 29
THE O'BRIEN LETTER 35
STOP THE WORLD 37
RICHARD A. SPRAGUE 42
WHY DID HE DO IT? 46
CROSSING THE RIVER STYX 51
PROTECTING THE POLITICALLY POWERFUL 57
THE VOTE AND THE XYZ PETITION 63
LARSEN CASTS A CRUCIAL VOTE 70
STONEWALLING AT ITS FINEST 75
LARSEN STRIKES BACK 80
"NEPOTISM WILL NEVER DIE" 88
A $750,000 FIX 93
SOMEONE HAS IT ALL WRONG 96
A SHAMEFUL DEAL 102
RICHARD SPRAGUE REDUX 105
I WON THE GAMBLE — OR DID I? 108
A SECONDARY MOTIVE? 113
THE POLS LOSE ONE 117
HERE WE GO 122
PREPARING FOR THE GOOD RUN 128
LARSEN BEGINS HIS FALL 131
THE CANDIDATE 135
LASHING SURRICK TO THE RACK 138
THE GOOD RUN 141
THE RACE TO THE FINISH LINE 147
PENNSYLVANIA, LAND OF GIANTS 151
A VERY GOOD RUN 155
LASHED TO THE RACK 159

JUSTICE STOUT 164
LASHED TO THE RACK 166
LASHED TO THE RACK 171
THE LAST HURRAH 175
MERIT SELECTION OF JUDGES 181
LASHED TO THE RACK 185
LASHED TO THE RACK 189
ADRIENNE CALLS IT QUITS 193
THE ROLE OF THE SUPREME COURT IN THE COMING MEDICAL MALPRACTICE CRISIS 196
LASHED TO THE RACK 199
DE NILE REVISITED 203
LASHED TO THE RACK 206
THE DISCIPLINARY BOARD OF THE SUPREME COURT 210
MAYBE — JUST MAYBE 212
HOW SWEET IT IS 215
LASHED TO THE RACK 218
A FEDERAL FIASCO 220
LASHED TO THE RACK 224
A GOOD GUY 227
THE RUMBLE REACHES THE LITTLE GUYS 230
LASHED TO THE RACK 233
STAN THE MAN 237
THE PENNSYLVANIA TRIAL LAWYERS ASSOCIATION 239
THE INQUIRER STRIKES BACK 244
THE ONSET OF THE DARK AGES 246
ONLY THE GOOD DIE YOUNG 252
REFORM—PENNSYLVANIA STYLE 257
SIR, HAVE YOU NO SHAME? 262
SELLING OUR SOULS 264
MORE OF THE BIG CHILL 268
THE SPREAD OF THE PENNSYLVANIA MODEL 271
"SOMEBODY IS GOING TO DIE" 273
THE NATIONAL TENSION 276
THE LAST HEARING? 279
PATLA BUYS A GOVERNOR 283
THE CRISIS SPREADS 285
PRESIDENT BUSH ENTERS THE FRAY 288

FEAR IS THE FOOD THAT NOURISHES POLITICS 290
MAY I MAKE MY POINT 296
MEDICAL MALPRACTICE VERDICTS 300
THE BARBARIANS ENTER THE GATES 302
WILL YOU PICK UP THE TORCH? 305
EPILOGUE 307

PREFACE

For many reasons that will become apparent in due course I deeply regret being a participant in this saga. On the other hand, I know of no other way to tell this story of lawyers and Judges slouching to Gomorrah other than to relate what I saw and heard while practicing law for almost forty years. In the beginning, I had a ringside seat but was soon catapulted into the ring.

In 1993, 1995 and 1997, as a candidate in statewide races for the highest Courts in Pennsylvania, my campaigns took me to every city, town, and hamlet in the Keystone State. My message was simple and succinct. For more than one hundred years, the citizens of our nation's fourth most populous state had been subjugated and abused by the coal barons, by the steel moguls, by the railroad operators, and most recently, by the lawyers and a corrupt Supreme Court. In these campaigns, I pledged that, if elected to the Supreme Court, I would do my utmost to clean up that Court and the lower Courts under its supervision.

Pennsylvania has been our nation's laboratory for economic and social trends over this period. While campaigning, I viewed the carnage left by robber barons such as the Morgans, the Fricks, the Mellons, the Carnegies, the Hills, and the Rockefellers. I saw the open scars from strip mines, the ghost-like abandoned steel towns, the once forested hills and valleys now stripped bare, and the empty rail yards. But the most permanent and serious injury inflicted has been the inculcation of fear in our citizens: Fear of the loss of a job for failure to toe the company or party line; fear of the company store which stripped the worker of his hard earned wages; fear of the law enforcement and court systems; and fear of political, judicial or corporate power. This fear has been cemented, even to the present day, by the brutal crushing of dissent and stifling of free speech. From the mass hangings of the Mollie Maguires, to the silencing of the once proud *Philadelphia Inquirer*, to the end of the right, indeed, duty, of lawyers to speak out against judicial corruption, we have been taught that there is a great deal more to fear than fear itself.

Pulitzer prizewinner Edmund Morris, in *Theodore Rex,* described the rape of Pennsylvania through the eyes of just sworn-in President Theodore Roosevelt. As the funeral train carrying the casket of assassinated President McKinley from Buffalo to Washington climbed over the mountains and snaked through the valleys of Pennsylvania, Morris analyzed the plight of Pennsylvania as Roosevelt saw it:

Roosevelt knew that nowhere in America was the threat (of violence) *more real than in the Pennsylvania coalfields-the bituminous region he had just entered, and the anthracite region to the east and south. Valley after valley, as the train snaked through, disclosed communities as squalid as any these people could have fled in Europe. Thousands of sooty shacks on stilts, with pigs tied below; gutters buzzing with garbage; mules clopping to the mine heads, hock deep in fine gray dust. Beneath that dust, men were scrabbling in wet, gassy gloom, earning a dollar and change for every ton of coal they hacked.*

. . .

In cash, they would realize about a third of that. Their wage packets were subject to compulsory deductions for rent, fuel, medical bills and food supplied at inflated prices by the company store. As a group, they aged and ailed faster than any other workers in American industry.

. . .

The Allegheny forest began to recede on both sides, leaving only stumps. Soon there was nothing but a fringe of trees on the highest ridges, beyond the reach of any who saw. Stumps, stumps and more stumps perforated the landscape, like arrows snapped off in death agony. Most were blackened...There were no saplings to be seen.

. . .

Governor William Stone of Pennsylvania was waiting on the platform with an honor guard, but Roosevelt stayed aloof behind drawn blinds. Harrisburg was notoriously the most corrupt seat of state government in the nation.

Later, in describing the United States Senate as Roosevelt saw it, Morris wrote:

What held them (the senators) together was their collective dedication to politics as a profession. Conscience, not corruption, kept the average senator in office. He worked seven days a week, assisted by one secretary and one typist, for five thousand dollars a year… Venality was a constant temptation, but only the most unscrupulous senators, men such as Matthew Quay and Boies Penrose of Pennsylvania, fattened at the public trough.

As I read this dreadful description of Pennsylvania and its leaders through Roosevelt's eyes, a comment of Abraham Lincoln's came to mind. When asked if Pennsylvania's Simon Cameron, his Secretary of War, was a thief, Lincoln dryly responded that he didn't think Cameron "would try to steal a hot stove." Cameron, you will perhaps recall, coined the phrase, "You scratch my back and I'll scratch yours."

It can be truly said, based upon our history, we have come to the corruption now permeating our judicial system as part of a continuum.

In my early years, the 1950's, the interaction between what was then a small community of lawyers and the general public was infrequent. In those days, the judiciary was essentially scandal-free.

Today, ubiquitous lawyers impact the lives of every man, woman and child in our society. As a result, we are again on the cutting edge of a social problem that could turn out to be more harmful to our citizens than the raw power of the "malefactors of great wealth" with their combinations or trusts that controlled corrupt governors and legislators. In thirty-five years of practice, I witnessed, first hand, the hijacking of a judicial system by a group of lawyers who embraced the creed of the fictional Gordon Gekko in the movie, *Wall Street*, and the very real junk bond king Michael Millken, that "greed is good." As in all social change, it didn't happen all at once-it was incremental. Those who saw it coming and tried to warn others were crushed. The First Amendment was washed away in a torrent of lawsuits that chilled and then silenced the media. The Pennsylvania Supreme Court made clear that any lawyer who spoke out against judicial corruption would be committing "professional suicide."

As a result, silence hangs over Pennsylvania as the pillage taking place in our legal system is becoming a way of life for both the predator and victim. Will the problem be exported to other states? Already, lawyers in other states and on the national level hear the cash register ringing. The battle over the so-called Patient Bill of Rights had less to do with the patient than the ability of lawyers to reach into the deep pockets of doctors and hospitals. Proliferating multi-million dollar verdicts in medical malpractice lawsuits are driving doctors out of practice and their insurers into bankruptcy while hospitals close their doors. The health care delivery system is in crisis. Product liability lawsuits have put manufacturers such as Piper and Lycoming of the small aircraft industry out of business. In the process, the Pennsylvania Supreme Court, once one of the most highly regarded in the country, has become a national disgrace.

Finally, if there is a God, Dante's inferno will be reserved for a long line of leaders, entrusted with the integrity of the law and our Courts, who, in their own self interest or out of fear of retaliation, either went along with the corruption or turned their heads. In the enduring words of British statesman/philosopher Edmund Burke:

> *It is necessary only for the good man to do nothing for evil to triumph.*

And triumph it did.

OVERVIEW

There have always been scoundrels, the corrupt and the corrupters, in government. But they almost always inhabited the executive and legislative branches. But now, the third estate, the judicial system, has been poisoned. When lawyers take an oath, they swear to take no cause for lucre or malice. This book is about lucre, malice, and unchecked power. I will name names and focus on the emergence of leaders in the legal system who were, and are, men and women without moral direction; leaders who took an oath to uphold the law who would, and will, without hesitation, break the law. Unfortunately, there is no mechanism to check the misuse of power and abuse of office by Justices and Judges whose absence of reverence for the Rule of Law is palpable. While this book is centered in Pennsylvania, the corrupt and the corrupters I write about are in every state.

This story is about the use of the judicial system as a weapon to destroy the core First Amendment protections of a free press. This didn't happen by accident. It was brought about by lawyers who saw money and power in an unholy alliance with Justices and Judges to silence investigative reporting by the print media.

It is also about a man who saw clearly the degradation of the judicial system and tried to tell the world about it. Because those in control of the judicial system were threatened, they stripped this man of his constitutional rights and tried to destroy him.

How can this happen in a country where for centuries the Rule of Law has been revered and honored? In a few short years, how did the third estate become corrupted, probably beyond redemption? The question is simple but the answers are more complex. I will attempt to set forth below several of the root causes of the collapse of one branch of government. Obviously, there are other causes but this is what I see. Then, in the chapters that follow, we will examine the death of our basic constitutional right of free speech for all lawyers because of the denial of that basic right to one lawyer. And the story of the demise of the print media as an instrument of investigation of the abuses of power and privilege in the third estate will be told. Lastly, I will outline the ascendancy of a group of lawyers, the so-called trial lawyers, who hijacked the judicial system.

There are three basic causes for the collapse of integrity in the legal system. They are money, money and money.

Judges are now paid too much money. For decades lawyers who had independent means were attracted to an office that carried community respect. There also were lawyers who did not put money as their first priority. Lawyers who revered the law and understood the need for a system where rights could be adjudicated with dignity and integrity were willing to serve. Political leaders often picked a quality lawyer because many didn't seek after the office. The successful argument of the so-called reformers that we can't attract good people to the bench because of the poor pay produced exactly the opposite result. The office became attractive to the marginal lawyer and a plum for the politicians to reward the loyal. It, therefore, is no wonder that as the pay for judges dramatically increased, the number of judges found guilty of corruption or ethical lapses in every state increased proportionally.

Lawyers are now driven by money. Not too many years ago courts served only one purpose—to adjudicate the rights of those in dispute. But class action litigation and the opening of the floodgates of product liability and medical malpractice litigation have turned the court systems into cash machines. Enter the trial lawyers. As they perfected their methods of extracting large sums of money from those with deep pockets, they became more organized. As they became more organized, they had more money to lobby for legislation that would create or enlarge causes of action. To make sure their money chase would continue, they worked and spent millions to put Judges on the bench at all levels who saw the courts as they did—a marketplace where the nimble could get very rich.

Because lawyers make so much money, many are attracted to what was once a profession. When I started practicing in Delaware County in 1961, there were five hundred thousand residents in the county and one-hundred-and-thirty-eight lawyers. Forty years later, there are still five hundred thousand residents but now over fifteen hundred lawyers. In 1972 there were twelve million citizens of Pennsylvania and thirteen-thousand-five hundred lawyers. That translates to one lawyer for every nine hundred citizens. In 2002, there were still twelve million citizens but the number of lawyers had quadrupled to fifty-five thousand or one lawyer for every two hundred citizens.

It was inevitable that a group of lawyers would band together to enrich themselves—to scratch each others' backs. The first order of business was to gain control over the judicial system. In Pennsylvania they found an ally in an obsessively ambitious Supreme Court Justice who, for his own purposes, gave them the keys to the judicial kingdom.

With these keys, they poured through the gates like the hordes led by Genghis Khan. They gave themselves the high sounding name of the Pennsylvania Trial Lawyers Association (PATLA), but money and power were their Gods. Have the trial lawyers become a powerful force in your state? Of course they have and they will grow even stronger as they buy legislators and judges at every level.

This tale is not pretty. Those who want or need to believe that the judicial system works will be shocked. Discovering the extent and depth of the problems should trouble those more sanguine. I will raise questions about the conduct of many lawyers and Judges. The chore of assigning guilt and/or responsibility, I leave to you. It is my fervent hope that this book will cause many good and decent lawyers and Judges to come out of the denial closet and say "we are mad as hell and aren't going to take it anymore."

One last thought before we begin. This is not a memoir. It is a narrative of a number of events involving lawyers, Judges, journalists and the Courts. Despite some setbacks along the way, I have otherwise enjoyed a full, rich, life. Everybody should be so lucky.

I BELONG

June 22, 1961

My first trial, and the "jury was out." In lawyer talk, this means the jury was deliberating after the close of evidence, closing speeches by counsel, and the charge, or jury instruction, from the Judge.

While wandering the halls in the courthouse on this late Wednesday afternoon following Judge Curran's charge to the jury, my mind raced over the last six months and all that had happened. Last November, the exquisitely agonizing wait for the results of the Pennsylvania Bar examination was over. Not only did I pass, I passed by a comfortable margin. Only forty-eight percent of those law school graduates who took the exam passed that year. That was about average. Then there was the six-month clerkship with Hodge, Hodge and Cramp at fifty dollars a month. We had purchased a two bedroom Cape Cod at 113 Sandy Bank Road in Media the previous September. With Jean (whom I had married during law school) working, we were getting by.

The clerkship was new territory for me. I pored over the firm files to see how a lawsuit was prepared for trial. I spent endless hours in the courtroom watching how it was done. Countless nights were spent in the law library researching the law for the partners. Other rookies were researching at night and we would trade stories. Just as in law school, I avoided those who seemed to know it all. It couldn't be that easy. As the months passed, I began to shed some of the uncertainty and find confidence in my ability to understand what was really important. I loved the courtroom. It was tradition, theater, and competition. The drama was exhilarating. The battle of wits between the lawyers was excruciating as a single slip could doom a case. The timelessness of the law and majesty of the proceedings began to creep into my soul. I revered the Judges. I was all business. No foolishness. Straight as the proverbial arrow, I was on my way.

Toward the end of my clerkship, I began to attract clients. I was involved with the local Republican Party and coaching Little League baseball. I also was an officer in the National Guard with C Company in Chester. One day a C Company sergeant approached me about a relative who was charged with assault and robbery. His name was Phil Profitt. I agreed to meet with him. He turned out to be a good-looking young man who was very persuasive in his protestations of innocence. It seemed a drunken merchant seaman was rolled on the docks in Chester, and Profitt was in the vicinity. I believed his story. I agreed to take the case that was scheduled for trial the Monday after I was to be admitted to the bar.

On Friday, June 23, 1961, John Cramp, my brother-in-law and senior partner in the firm, moved my admission to the Delaware County Court in Courtroom 1. It was packed with lawyers and relatives of those being admitted. I dressed conservatively, with a white pin-collar shirt, rep tie, dark summer suit with vest, and highly polished wing-tip shoes. As I stood before the bar of the court with the other inductees, I listened to the President of the Bar Association speak of the long traditions of the bar, where a lawyer's word was his bond. I was filled with emotion as I realized that I now belonged to a noble profession. I would give my utmost to uphold the honor of this sacred trust. I belonged! That afternoon, with my head still spinning, my wife Jean took me to lunch on the toney Philadelphia Main Line and bought me a handsome leather trial lawyer's briefcase. I was in love with life. It just can't get any better.

On Monday morning, with Phil Profitt in tow, I went into Courtroom 1, where President Judge Henry Sweeney was calling the criminal trial list. When he called *Commonwealth v. Phillip Profitt*, I answered "Trial" in a firm and confident voice and was assigned to Courtroom 4 before Judge Thomas A. Curran. The new lawyers with whom I was inducted on Friday looked at me with a touch of envy as I motioned for my client, seated in the body of the courtroom, to go to Courtroom 4.

When I arrived in Courtroom 4, Herb Hayes, Judge Curran's court clerk, told me that Judge Curran was in conference in his chambers behind the courtroom with Clem McGovern, the District Attorney. At that time, no one seemed to find fault with the District Attorney meeting privately with a Judge behind closed doors to discuss the cases on the list. A few minutes later, I was summoned to Judge Curran's chambers where McGovern shook hands with me and noted it was customary for a lawyer to win his first case. We reviewed the case, and McGovern finally indicated he would recommend to Judge Curran, who was sitting right there, no jail if my client would plead guilty to simple assault to avoid the likelihood of jail on the robbery charge. I asked for a moment to meet with my client, and Judge Curran agreed. He was sure I would take the offer, which would remove a case from his list.

I went into the hall to talk to Profitt who, to my surprise, balked at a guilty plea, saying he was innocent and would not plead guilty to anything. I went back to chambers and told Judge Curran and McGovern that my client refused to plead guilty. There was tension in the room. McGovern lectured me on my obligation to control my client, but I stood firm. In addition to my client's refusal to cave in, I had done my homework and believed I had a good defense. I played my trump card, *Mapp v. Ohio,* a case from the Supreme Court of the United States that had been decided the previous week. It created a new law involving search and seizure, which, if applied, would block evidence incriminating my client. Judge Curran snorted at my use of a case from the Supreme Court of the United States. He said it "didn't apply in Delaware County". After a great deal of heated discussion, Judge Curran, obviously angry with this upstart lawyer who didn't know his place, said he would dismiss the charges if my client would pay the court costs. In those days the jury could assess court costs on a defendant even after a not guilty verdict.

I again talked with my client. He stubbornly refused the offer. He would not pay the costs. I had no choice but to go back and demand a trial. McGovern and Judge Curran were furious. McGovern hissed at me, "You want a trial, young fella, you're gonna get a trial."

This case, which should have been a simple trial, spanned three days. Judge Curran openly aided McGovern, who used every trick in the book and then some. I stood firm and refused to be bullied. I doggedly cross-examined the police and called my witnesses and protected them as best I could. I truly believed in my client's innocence and told the jury why they should acquit him of all of the charges and put the costs on the county.

By this time, word was spreading in the courthouse about this rookie lawyer, trying his first case, and, believe it or not, trying it for court costs after refusing a dismissal offer. The robbery count with a potential jail sentence was now in play.

The jury finally reached a verdict. The courtroom was packed with county employees and lawyers who had heard about the case. Judge Curran entered the courtroom through a side door. The courtroom was dead silent as the jury returned and entered the jury box.

"Ladies and gentleman of the jury, have you arrived at your verdict?" asked the clerk.

"Yes we have," answered the foreman.

"How do you find?" asked Hayes.

"We find the defendant not guilty," answered the foreman.

"And how do you find on the costs?" asked Hayes. You could have heard a pin drop.

"Costs on the county," said the foreman, and the courtroom erupted.

I put my papers in my new briefcase and dared a glance at Judge Curran. His ruddy Irish face had turned an angry purple. He would never forget, and he would never forgive. In the flush of victory, I didn't stop to realize the long-term consequences of what had happened. All I knew was that I had entered the fraternity of trial lawyers and that I belonged.

The county newspaper, the *Chester Times*, covered the trial, and wrote:

...One of the defense counsels in the complicated case was Robert B. Surrick, 27, of Upper Providence.

The young attorney is the brother-in-law of John Cramp, assistant county solicitor and former county Republican chairman.

It was Surrick's first trial — and he acquitted himself well. The jury acquitted his client and ordered the county to pay the costs.

Judge Curran, in his charge to the jury, had explained about the placing of costs and said he saw no reason why the county should have to pay them in this case. The jury overruled the judge.

Surrick, who could pass for an Ivy League student or a budding movie actor, conducted his first case with confidence. He looked and acted every inch the pro.

Maybe it's obstinacy, maybe it's arrogance, but, upon reflection, I see in this case a foreshadowing of my lifelong refusal to go along to get along. I never learned to sell out my client, or my principles, to curry favor with the Judges, or to get along with the pols in the back room.
I belonged, at least for the moment.

THE MEANING OF ARGO V GOODSTEIN

May 1964 to May 1970

It was not just another trial. When it was over for better or worse, it defined me as a maverick.

Sidney Goodstein, a realtor and entrepreneur, owned a storefront building in the 6700 block on Market Street in Upper Darby that he was renovating. The construction included removing and replacing the floor in the vestibule. On July 11, 1960, James Argo, a blind peddler of brooms and mops, opened one of the clear glass double doors, stepped into the hole, and sustained serious injury when he and his brooms and mops crashed-landed in the basement. Argo engaged Garland (Bill) Cherry, who filed suit. Goodstein's insurance carrier assigned the lawsuit to Cramp and D'Iorio, and John Cramp assigned the case to me, with the note "sure winner!"

Bill Cherry was considered a rising star among trial lawyers. I had received equal attention for the trials I had handled. I disliked Cherry from our first meeting. He was a partner of Bobby Curran, whose father was the Common Pleas Judge with whom I was having serious continuing problems ever since my very first case. The elder Curran was a political power in Delaware County.

Cherry was without character. His creed was whatever works is alright. In short, he was very clever, very bright, a dangerous adversary, and slippery as he could be.

My research revealed that Argo's ability to win under Pennsylvania law depended upon his status when he entered the building. If he had been a trespasser, he had no rights, and no duty-of-care was owed to him by Goodstein. On the other hand, if he was a business visitor, someone Goodstein had expressly or impliedly invited in for mutual business purposes, Goodstein owed him the duty to make his property safe. The hole was obvious to a sighted person through the clear glass doors. But what duty is owed to a blind person who can't see the absence of a floor? It wasn't a "sure winner." It was a damn tough issue with all the sympathy on the side of a blind peddler trying to eke out a living selling brooms and mops door-to-door.

We went to trial in May 1964. The case was assigned to Judge Francis (Franny) J. Catania, who had been a political power in Ridley Township before his controversial nomination to the bench the year before. Catania had no experience as a trial lawyer. He was the protégé of Judge Curran. Even in Delaware County, where lawyers know to keep their mouths shut, there was opposition to the proposed Catania nomination because of his lack of courtroom experience. When the lawyers gathered in Courtroom 5 to vote on Catania's qualifications (newly elected Governor Bill Scranton had said he would not nominate anyone to a judicial vacancy who did not have county bar association approval), a bitter fight developed over whether or not the ballot would be secret. The politically powerful did not want a secret ballot; they wanted the intimidation factor to coerce the lawyers, many of whom had county jobs or township solictorships, into voting for Catania

In a very close vote about whether there would be a secret ballot, the motion for a secret ballot failed. As I grew more experienced in the ways of Delaware County politics, I came to wonder whether the votes on the secret ballot question had been counted properly.

In any event, on the next vote, this time on endorsing Catania, by a show of hands, political flunkies Steve McEwen and Bobby Curran stood in the back of the courtroom writing down the names of those lawyers who raised their hands against the inexperienced Catania. There were few — nowhere near the number that voted for a secret ballot. And so, the chunky Catania, with his slicked-back black hair, and politicians' smoothness, became a Judge.

Argo v. Goodstein was a hard-fought trial. Judge Catania was very short on trial practice but exhibited the coolness under fire that marked his rise to great power in Pennsylvania. There was no question that he wanted to help his mentor's son's partner, Bill Cherry. Cherry fought hard and was smooth as silk. The battle was a harbinger of things to come.

On May 19, 1964, the jury rendered its verdict in favor of James Argo for twenty-seven thousand five hundred dollars. In those days, that was serious money. It was one of the highest verdicts in the history of conservative Delaware County. I was crushed. I took it as a personal defeat.

I filed an appeal. It was ultimately argued before the state Supreme Court in late 1966. During oral argument, the Justices seemed to split all over the place. Chief Justice Bell, who never found a personal injury defendant he didn't favor, was in my corner. The great dissenter, Justice Michael Musmanno, was, as usual, willing to compensate any plaintiff for any injury, regardless of how it happened. Months later, the Supreme Court affirmed the verdict, and my angst deepened. It was a loss that I couldn't seem to handle. Losing to Cherry was galling.

A week after the Supreme Court decision, I saw a case in the Advance Sheets (early publication of Court Opinions) where the Supreme Court granted a new trial in a case where the Judge had communicated with the jury in the absence of trial counsel. Bells went off in my head. I remembered that Judge Catania had received a question from the jury and answered it without consulting counsel. I hadn't thought much about it when he put it on the record during the acceptance of the jury's verdict. There were two defendants, Sidney Goodstein and his company, Good Company, Inc., owner of record of the building. The jury had, by written question, asked about allocating a verdict between the defendants. Judge Catania, without consulting counsel, wrote a response telling them to put what they found as to one defendant on one verdict slip, and what they found as to the other defendant on the other slip.

The new law was an opening! I petitioned the Supreme Court for re-argument. At a very deep level, when I filed the Petition for re-argument, I knew that if I prevailed, I would have rendered a very public body blow to Judge Catania in one of his first trials.

The Supreme Court granted re-argument.

At re-argument, I urged a prophylactic rule that any communication between the Judge and jury in the absence of counsel was error, requiring a new trial. The Supreme Court accepted my argument, reversed their prior decision and granted a new trial. I had, for the moment, bested Bill Cherry. In the excitement of the moment, I overlooked the fact that I had also made Judge Catania look bad. Not only do trial Judges pride themselves on not being reversed, they hate to be reversed. This reversal, based solely on the communication between the trial Judge and the jury in the absence of counsel, inferred something sinister had taken place. A man of his macho Sicilian pride would surely take such a suggestion personally.

At re-trial in February 1968, I was thrilled to draw Judge John V. Diggins as the trial Judge. He was a great trial Judge and he knew it. A slight, bald man, he had wisdom and a sense of humor. I felt that I had the better of the law, and Judge Diggins would apply it precisely. Diggins would not slop around, as Judge Catania had, to Cherry's advantage. The trial went well. I put on quite a show and felt confident of victory.

The jury remained out all afternoon. Judge Diggins finally sent them, under the supervision of his court officers, to a local restaurant for dinner. I became anxious. Agro was a sympathetic figure and Cherry had milked the sympathy for all it was worth.

While the jury was out, Judge Diggins called me into the chambers behind the courtroom. We talked for a few minutes about his son, Johnny, who had been my friend in junior high. I had spent summers at the Diggins' summer home in Ocean City, New Jersey, and always felt that "the Judge" took a fatherly interest in me. For my part, I kept my distance, not wanting to gain advantage from the relationship. Then, out-of-nowhere, he looked at me sharply and said, "Bob, the long knives are out for you."

"What do you mean?" I asked.

"It means that your unwillingness to go along, your hard-headedness, even arrogance, has angered the wrong people. The plaintiff's lawyers can't stand you."

"Who? What specifically are you talking about?"

"That's it. No more! I've warned you. Please close the door when you leave."

I was stunned. I knew that my hard-charging ways made people nervous, or even angry, but I always thought that as long as I was scrupulously honest and played fair, I would be all right. I walked the courthouse halls pondering the warning until Diggins' Court Crier found me and told me the jury had a question.

The jurors, who had been brought back into the courtroom and seated in the jury box, asked whether or not a person could be a business visitor if the visit was only for that person's business, "or did it have to be bi-lateral?" It was the crux of the case. The answer would control the verdict.

I asked the judge to give a three or four word answer that to be a business visitor to whom a duty of care is owed, it had to be mutual.

Diggins refused my request and read to the jury a passage from Section 466.3(3) of the Trial Guide. When he started, I relaxed because the Section he was reading gave the answer I wanted — just with a lot more words. He suddenly stopped reading. I was startled. He had only given half an answer and that half wholly favored Cherry. He didn't read the last paragraph that sewed it up for me. What was going on?

"I object, your honor. I respectfully suggest that your honor left out the last paragraph."

"Mr. Surrick, the instruction is complete. The jury may retire again to deliberate."

For the second time in an hour, I was stunned.

I was even more stunned when, within five minutes, the jury returned with a verdict in favor of Argo for thirty-eight thousand dollars.

I again filed an appeal to the Supreme Court. In a five-to-two decision, the Supreme Court affirmed the verdict. On the issue of the truncated supplemental instruction by Judge Diggins, the Court said the entire section had been read in the original jury instruction at the end of the trial. What? The jury had asked that this instruction be clarified, and they had been given a misleading half of the whole. It went down very hard with me.

But the real meaning of that trial was not the result. It was the warning from Judge Diggins and the certain knowledge that I had made a powerful enemy in Judge Catania. I had thought playing the game straight was enough. I was wrong.

I was at the first of many crossroads where my future would be determined by my unwillingness to "play the game."

Holding my head high in defeat, I continued to strive to be the best lawyer I could be. But I was troubled. Was I beginning to see cracks in a judicial system that I revered. Were the cracks always there or was I becoming experienced enough to see the human frailty of our judiciary? Was the system deteriorating with the likes of the Catanias and Currans gaining power, or had it always been this way?

Trying not to think about it, I went about my quest to be the best I could be in what I saw as an ancient and honorable profession.

• • •

Judge Diggins went on to become President Judge and, later, a Senior Judge when he reached the constitutional mandatory retirement age of seventy. He sat as a Senior Judge on the Delaware County Court of Common Pleas until he died at ninety-six.

Judge Catania followed Judge Diggins as President Judge. While a Senior Judge, Diggins was fanatically protective of Catania, who amassed enormous power. A Sicilian, he became the Godfather over his Delaware County realm. As for me, he knew the meaning of the Old Country admonition that "vengeance is a meal that is best eaten cold."

Franny would wait patiently until I was vulnerable, and then strike.

VARIATION ON A THEME

January 1979

It was seven-thirty p.m. on a Wednesday night at the Towne House in Media. I was sitting in a booth in the bar with Dick Thornburgh, a candidate for the Republican nomination for governor. We had met the previous fall at a fundraiser held at the Racquet Club in Philadelphia. I had mentioned my concern about the deteriorating quality of the judiciary, and he had expressed similar concern. I felt very strongly that I had an obligation to leave the system better than I found it. Since I probably tried more cases and argued more appeals than any other lawyer in southeastern Pennsylvania, I was in a position to see what happens when the politicians start to put hacks, instead of quality lawyers, on the bench. We were getting hacks. In the last couple of years, I had become alarmed. Everything I believed about my profession was being called into question.

"Bob, I'm from western Pennsylvania. I just don't know this territory. The name Thornburgh is not a household name in this part of the world. I need your help."

"I don't know how much I can help but I'll do what I can. If you commit to cleaning up the judicial system, I'll give you all the help I can give you."

"Tell me about Delaware County."

I gave him the short version.

"The McClures have controlled this county for one hundred years. In the 1920's, John McClure took over control of the county Republican Party. He turned it into a machine every bit as corrupt and more monolithic than Mayor Curley's in Boston. Maybe you will remember in one election, Curley was re-elected mayor from his jail cell. McClure was twice prosecuted in the thirties for bootlegging but was acquitted each time. His control was total. He controlled the jobs for all the industry along the Delaware River. Sun Ship and Sun Oil were both in his pocket. You couldn't get a high school or even a grade school teaching job in Delaware County without your Republican Committeeman signing off. He controlled the courthouse jobs, the judges, the district attorney, everything. He owned the county.

I first met John McClure in 1961 after I ran for Republican Committeeman in Upper Providence and defeated the organization candidate two to one. He called me the next day and asked me to meet with him at his mansion in Chester. He told me that he admired fighters and that he was glad I was going to be part of, and have a future, in the Delaware County Republican Party. He was a very savvy politician.

When McClure died in the 1960's, Frank Snear became chairman of the Republican Party, but he was a figurehead. Franny Catania, the President Judge was really the power. Snear was compromised early on when a local lawyer rigged up a hotel room with a camera and had a hooker take Snear to the room. I saw the pictures. They were gross. Frank's wife, Dorothy, would have killed him if she ever found out. Fearing Dorothy more than the pols that set him up, Frank went along, after that, in order to get along.

By the time Snear died, John McNichol, the leader of Upper Darby, which is the largest municipality in the United States, was sharing power with the Catanias. John was the son-in-law of Sam Dickey, also known as 'Sammy Dick,' who ran the mob in the eastern end of the county. That's why the District Attorney of Delaware County is always from Upper Darby. In politics, he who controls the prosecutor controls the world. McNichol keeps a low profile.

Then there's Charlie Sexton, the leader of Springfield, the second largest municipality in the county. He's John McNichol's creation.

Another power is Jack Nacrelli, who runs Chester. People refer to him as "King Jack." Although Jack is white while Chester is mostly black, he nevertheless controls the city, lock, stock, and barrel. He produces big Republican numbers every election out of a city that should go Democrat. He's aligned with the Catanias."

I explained to Thornburgh what was happening in Delaware County: McNichol was moving on the Catania faction. The Catanias had it their way after McClure died by controlling Snear, but now the power was going to McNichol.

"Can you plug me in to these guys?" Thornburgh asked.

"Up to a point. I have no power. I know the players and they cut me slack because, at one time, I was part of the organization. I know where a lot of bodies are buried. My brother Barclay is now a Judge. But don't count on Barclay. He is a nice guy but has thrown in with John McNichol and the organization.

"I would like to meet Barclay."

"I just left him. He's in his chambers. Let's go now."

I quickly drained my beer and we left the Towne House and walked up Veteran's Square to the huge marble Grecian-style courthouse. We entered through the massive front doors into a darkened hallway that led to the elevators. The guard, used to seeing me there at night, merely looked up and nodded. Barclay was at his desk when we walked in. I told him I wanted to introduce him to Dick Thornburgh, the next governor of Pennsylvania. I could see the whites of Barclay's eyes. He knew that Thornburgh didn't have the support of the Delaware County Republican organization, and he didn't want to be seen in his presence, particularly in his Chambers. I told Barclay that no one saw us come in, and he seemed to relax a little.

Thornburgh, ignoring me, began to question Barclay. He acted as if he knew the players I had just clued him into, and Barclay gave answers along the lines of what I had told Thornburgh.

At the end of the discussion, Thornburgh said, "I need your help. Will you help me?" Again, Barclay's eyes were like a deer caught in the headlights. I took him off the hook.

"Barclay can't, Dick, because the Code of Judicial Conduct, as you well know, prohibits judges from engaging in political activity, but I can, and I will."

Barclay, recognizing that he was out of the woods, offered,

"you have to meet with Faith Whittlesey."

Faith was a newcomer and had been part of a so-called reform effort that had taken over County Council in 1977, when Barclay was elected a Common Pleas Judge. Reform, like revolution, is generally about who gets to drive the Mercedes.

"I think I can arrange that," I said. "How about Sunday afternoon? All the pols in Delco use Sunday for political meetings."

The next day, I called Faith and asked her if she would meet with Dick Thornburgh on Sunday. At first she refused because the organization was committed to Arlen Specter. I assured her that the meeting would be confidential. Not wanting to miss the opportunity to hedge a bet, she finally agreed.

On Sunday, I drove Thornburgh and Jay Waldman, his campaign manager, to Faith's house in Haverford Township. Waldman, with black, curly hair and horn-rimmed glasses, had been Thornburgh's top assistant when Dick was the United States Attorney for the Western District of Pennsylvania. Jay was brilliant, cocky, and arrogant with a serious mean streak. I made the introductions and said I was going for a walk. They met with Faith in her living room along with a couple of screaming infants. Faith's husband, Roger, had committed suicide a couple of years before, leaving Faith with two small children. She seemed a forlorn figure. In actuality, she was tough as nails. She later worked in the Reagan White House and became Ambassador to Switzerland. There were no flies on this very ruthless lady.

When Dick and Jay came out, they climbed into my station wagon and sat silently.

"Let's get out of here," Waldman finally said.

"What happened?" I asked.

Thornburgh looked lost in thought, but Waldman responded, "You won't believe that fucking bitch. She fucked around and fucked around with us. We asked what we needed to do to get support in Delaware County. She said that Dick, a prominent U.S. Attorney with a great record, a former First Assistant Attorney General of the United States, would have to go to that crook, John McNichol, 'as a supplicant.' That fucking bitch kept repeating 'as a supplicant,' and kept asking us if we 'knew what supplicant meant.'"

Waldman was wild-eyed. He and Thornburgh just had their asses handed to them, Delaware County style. He ranted and raved. He just couldn't understand how someone would agree to meet with them and then literally make fun of Dick, a very competent man who, Jay was certain, would be the next governor.

Several minutes later, with Waldman still on a rant, Thornburgh quietly asked if I could arrange a meeting with John McNichol. I told him I would try.

Just like Faith, at first, McNichol refused. When I assured him that it would be private, at my house, Kenmore Wood, he agreed.

When McNichol arrived on Wednesday at three p.m., Thornburgh was already there. I ushered them into my book-lined study. A fire burned brightly in the fireplace. I excused myself. They talked for an hour, which surprised me, because I thought McNichol would blow off Thornburgh tout de suite.

When McNichol left, I asked Dick how it went.

"He wants everything-the right to name Judges, special legislation for Delaware County, the whole nine yards. Bob, I never understood how monolithic this organization is. They refuse to recognize or deal with doing something just because it's right. Right and wrong are relative terms in this county. It boggles my mind."

"I tried to tell you, but until you see it in action, you can't comprehend the power they wield. They control every municipality, every government job, everything."

Thornburgh was on the May Primary ballot. I introduced him and Waldman to all the people I knew who might contribute and lend support. Thornburgh campaigned hard in western Pennsylvania and largely ignored Delaware County as hopeless, except for the annual Primary rally.

At that rally, twenty-five hundred of the faithful crowded the main ballroom at the Alpine Inn in Springfield, Charlie Sexton's Springfield. The bar was going full blast and a band was playing upbeat music like *The Pennsylvania Polka.* I was standing along the wall in the rear of the room with Terri Lazin. Terri was married to Malcolm Lazin, a Philadelphia lawyer who had lots of family money and big political ambitions.

Terri and I watched as the grand march started. The emcee would announce the name of each local dignitary or politico. As the flags were waved and the band played, the local pol would walk the length of the room down the wide center aisle and take his or her chair on the stage. It reminded me, in a small way, of the vivid descriptions of Hitler's rallies at the Sportsplast in 1933, which my old Maryland professor Gordon Prange had attended and related to his students in great detail.

As Charlie Sexton started down the aisle, with his massive body, bullet head, and beady eyes, Terri asked me who he was. I answered:

"That's Charlie Sexton, leader of Springfield, and if it was 1930, and we were in Munich, he would be in uniform wearing a brown belt, and everyone would be giving the party salute."

Terry jolted. She understood me perfectly.

On the afternoon of the Primary, I flew to Pittsburgh and booked into the Penn Harris Hotel. Thornburgh, Waldman, Murray Dickman and the rest of his staff were taking election returns in the penthouse. At eleven-thirty p.m., bedlam erupted when the Associated Press reported Thornburgh had beaten Arlen Specter for the Republican nomination for governor. The halls were filled with cheering supporters. Terri Lazin, who had run the campaign in the Scranton, Wilkes-Barre, Allentown area, ran down the corridor and jumped into my arms. She threw her arms around me. My exuberance, after the long campaign, matched hers as we hugged. Her earring somehow found its way into my shirt pocket. Luckily, I found it before Jean did.

The next day, I flew back to Media for a two o'clock hearing before Judge Joseph Labrum. It went well. Joe Labrum and I had tried many cases together and there was mutual respect. While he had to pay his dues to become a Judge, he seemed to try and maintain an attitude of independence.

As I left the courthouse, Tommy Judge was standing on the steps talking to Matt Ryan, my long-time friend who later became Speaker of the General Assembly. Tommy was the figurehead chair of the Republican Party. Tommy stopped me, and we talked for a minute about the Primary and Thornburgh's win. Tommy fixed me with a steady gaze and said:

"Bob, you know you are done in Delaware County."

"Come on Tom, it's still a free country isn't it?"

"Bob, you crossed the line supporting Thornburgh. McNichol, Sexton, Catania, Nacrelli — all want a piece of you. My advice is to sit with your back to the wall from now on."

Just then Nacrelli, "King Jack," walked up.

I said, "Jack, I understand you're pissed at me. Is that so? Why? You creamed Thornburgh in Chester."

"Bob, in one ward, Thornburgh got thirty-four votes out of six hundred and twenty. You know something? Before nightfall, I will know the names of all thirty-four who crossed me, just like I know what you did for Thornburgh. They'll find strange things happening to them. Do you get my drift?"

My client, who had been standing to the side, pulled my coat sleeve and said he had to get back to his job. I left knowing a war had started.

Several days later, I telephoned Thornburgh and indicated I would be willing to run his campaign in Delaware County. I saw it as good for me in several ways: my practice, my presence in the county, and perhaps, a future in politics should that interest me.

"I can't do that, Bob. I just told John McNichol that he could name the chair and he picked Charlie Sexton."

I almost dropped the phone. He had just thrown me to the wolves without a second thought!

Nothing personal — just politics.

LOSING YOUR VIRGINITY, DELAWARE COUNTY STYLE

Summer 1979

I had become Arthur Levy's partner when our brothers, Melvin and Barclay, became Common Pleas Judges in Delaware County in 1977.

Earl Haydt had just retained me to form a Pennsylvania corporation that would build and market a cable television system in Delaware County. In addition to a substantial monthly retainer and a heavy hourly rate, I had negotiated a ten percent interest in the cable company to be formed. Earl told me that Senator John Heinz had told him that I was the lawyer to go to in Delaware County. Cable television was in its infancy. No one knew what cable television was, other than a method in upstate Pennsylvania to get television signals, otherwise blocked by the mountains, to the homes in the valleys. Earl was a visionary who believed data and voice, in addition to television, would one day speed through the coaxial cable.

"Arthur, meet Earl Haydt. Earl, this is my partner Arthur Levy." I had walked Earl into Arthur's office after a two-hour meeting with Earl. I wanted Arthur to know I had just landed a major client.

I formed the corporation and provided Earl with political information about each of the forty-seven municipalities in Delaware County where he would have to obtain franchises to operate. It turned out that a rival company, Delaware County Cable Company, represented and partly owned by Robert E.J. (Bobby) Curran was doing the same thing. Bobby had been the U.S. Attorney for the Eastern District of Pennsylvania, until fired by Dick Thornburgh, when Dick was Deputy Assistant Attorney General of the United States. It seems that Bobby had connections that were unacceptable to the Attorney General. Nevertheless, Bobby was a political force in Delaware County and my implacable enemy. His father had seen me as a threat, or rival of Bobby. Every trial before Judge Curran was a battle because of his poisonous attitude toward me, and I was always fearful for my client's rights under the circumstances. Bobby hated me for embarrassing his father in the Profitt case.

The cable television franchise wars began in Delaware County with each company battling it out in each municipality. Earl soon realized that it was more than he could handle and asked me to make the presentations to each township and borough. Bobby had the political clout, but I had the vision and a better company. We fought tooth and nail, and I was winning all over the county. However, there were municipalities where I had trouble despite offering a better package. This caused me to suspect that some political heavyweights, including Judges, might have an interest in Bobby's company. That's the way Bobby did business.

I started a lawsuit against Bobby's company for building a system in Ridley Township without a township-approved franchise. The Township Commissioners, owned by the Catania faction, sat by passively while the illegal construction was taking place. I filed a Motion to require Bobby's company to produce its shareholder list, the sharebook. The lawsuit was assigned to Judge Joseph T. Labrum. Bobby wasn't heavy enough for this so he sent his partner, Bill Cherry. Bill had become part of the new breed of lawyer. He would misrepresent precedent to the court, shade the truth, distort the facts, and get away with it more often than not. Sadly, it was a dying axiom among Delaware County lawyers that "Your word was your bond." Bill Cherry and lawyers like him were changing that. Better get it in writing.

Ridley Township became the cable television battleground in Delaware County. While the Catania ancestral home is Sicily, their power base is Ridley Township. The sharebook, revealing the stockholders, would be the key to winning the battle in Ridley Township. I wanted that sharebook. It could cause a real scandal if my guesses were even half right about who owned stock in Delaware County Cable. I strongly suspected the President Judge, Franny Catania, or his straw, was a shareholder. Franny had a history of using straws in his business dealings.

Judge Labrum heard the Motion which I filed seeking production of the sharebook and decided that I had a legal right to see it. At that point, Bill Cherry, on behalf of Curran's company, asked Judge Labrum to recuse on the flimsy basis that his chambers were next to my brother's. It is unethical in the extreme to ask a Judge to recuse after the Judge decides the issue. If you think a Judge, for whatever reason, cannot fairly decide a case, you seek recusal before the issue is heard and decided. Labrum refused to recuse.

Cherry then asked to put his recusal application on the record. Judge Labrum suggested he go find a court reporter. Instead of looking for a court reporter, Cherry went to Judge Catania's Chambers, ex-parte, that is, without opposing counsel being present. That, in and of itself, is a serious ethical violation. Instead of throwing Cherry out, as he should have done, Judge Catania sent Judge DeFuria, the Administrative Judge, to intervene with Judge Labrum.

They didn't dare overrule Labrum. That would have been too obvious. Instead, without legal authority, Judge Catania, through Judge DeFuria, recused every Judge in Delaware County, including Judge Labrum. Judge Catania ordered the case sent to Judge James Cavanaugh, a politically connected Judge in Philadelphia County. The law is clear. The right to recuse is a personal right that belongs only to the Judge involved. One Judge can never recuse another Judge. What I had won fairly in a hearing before Judge Labrum was now, without benefit of any sort of legal process, being taken from my client and me!

Badly shaken, I went back to my office. I told Arthur Levy what had happened. He was appalled. I went into my office and closed my door and lay down on the couch. I was numb all over. Everything I believed in was a shambles. I lay there for hours reviewing every word, every detail, in my head. No matter how I looked at it, a case had been "fixed" right in front of me. Blatantly! This was not supposed to happen. What about the "majesty of the law"? What about, "for every wrong there is a remedy"? What about all my Law Day speeches where I had praised the outstanding Delaware County bench? I had overseen the Law Day ceremonies at the courthouse for years and spoken to hundreds, maybe thousands of high school students about the sanctity of the law. I thought about the Bar Association meetings where lawyer after lawyer spoke in glowing terms about the "outstanding Delaware County Bench and Bar".

Was it all chimera?

• • •

Because the recusal of the entire Delaware County bench was so outrageous, President Judge Catania had to rescind his Order to send the case to Judge Cavanaugh in Philadelphia. However, he had accomplished his purpose. He had put a screwdriver in the gears to gain time. He then assigned the case to Delaware County Judge Dominic Jerome, who would do what he was told and was smart enough to cover up what he was doing.

Before this happened, I had believed Judge Labrum was a shade different than the other Judges in Delaware County. He certainly promoted that image. I was puzzled by his passivity in this case. Cherry's unethical tactics and the intervention of Judges Catania and Defuria should have outraged him. It would take me many years to learn that one or more Judges or Justices will turn their heads while another Judge or Justice fixes a case in front of them. As you will soon see, this is a recurring theme.

I never saw the sharebook, and the identity of the stockholders of Delaware County Cable Company remained secret. But what I did know was that Judge Catania's bizarre intervention pointed to his overriding need to protect something important to himself. With what happened in this case, it began to dawn on me that what I had believed in for so long, what I had accepted as Gospel, was a very shaky foundation on which to advance my professional career.

I didn't know it but a long nightmare lay ahead.

ONWARD AND UPWARD?

May 28, 1979

"Do you want to be a Judge?" Dick Thornburgh asked, as he toweled himself after taking a quick shower in my bathroom while the guests mingled on the lawn. Standing naked with his round, dark-rimmed glasses, balding head and soft body, he seemed far less imposing than when I first met him. I was surprised at the soft appearance of a man who, in a matter of months, would be Governor of Pennsylvania and later Attorney General of the United States.

"Dick, you and I both know that the pay is lousy, the hours long, and the company not so hot. It costs a lot of money to run this place, and college for Bart, Laura and Craig isn't that far off. Thanks, but no thanks. But I do want to help in any effort to clean up the judicial system. Why don't you finish dressing and I'll run down to warm up the crowd?"

When Dick arrived at my home, it had been quite a sight. The state police, with sirens wailing, roared up the curving driveway through the massive rhododendrons, looked around, and radioed that all was clear. Thornburgh's car then rolled up to the Palladian front of this stately three-story, twenty-nine-room stone house with caretaker's quarters, stables, and a tack room as big as my first house. I had been fortunate to acquire this ten-acre property in 1970. This was where I very privately raised my Brady Bunch children.

My close friends, who had come early to this fundraiser, played the role, pretending this happened every day. They went about the business of making small talk and getting drinks from the white-coated black bartender at the starched white linen-covered bar set up on the manicured lawn.

Upon arrival, Thornburgh asked me, "Can I get a quick shower? It's been a long day and I'm beginning to smell."

"Follow me, my friend. Jean, is the coast clear on the second floor?"

"Jean, how are you? Good to see you again!"

"Dick, we are so proud of you. You are going to win this thing going away," Jean responded, always the perfect hostess. With all the bad that was between us, I had to say that Jean was the consummate society wife, always knowing what to say and when to say it. Lancaster County Day School and Lancaster Country Club helps with that sort of thing.

I led Dick into the house with its semi-antique Kerman, Bokhara and Hamadam rugs on polished oak floors, and up the circular staircase to the master bedroom

"Dick, I don't know if you know this, but this house is known as Kenmore Wood."

"Yes, I saw that engraved on the pillars at the beginning of your beautiful drive up through the woods to the house."

"Well, it gets the name from the man who built it, Fielding O. Lewis. Fielding Lewis was the great-great grandson of the Fielding Lewis who married Betty Washington, George Washington's only sister. They built Kenmore in Fredericksburg that is now an historic register home in Virginia. Many of the architectural features of Kenmore are incorporated into this house. Here's the master bedroom, and the shower is here, and the towels are on the towel bars."

"Bob, I can't tell you how grateful I am to you for holding this fundraiser. We need to talk about what you want to do in my administration."

"Dick, all I want is for you to win. I don't want a job."

"I'll find the right thing for you, you have my word on that."

In the years to come, I would learn how insincere and hollow these words were. But for now, it was time to get everybody ready to open their checkbooks and make campaign contributions to this former

U.S. attorney who had come out of nowhere to beat the favored Arlen Specter in the Primary.

As I came down the staircase and opened the screen door to go outside, Bart Cavanagh came up and asked if he could go upstairs and say "hello" to Dick.

"Go ahead, he's getting dressed."

Bart had been my close friend and confidant for many years. Bart and Toni's house overlooked the Springton Reservoir and was filled with hunting memorabilia and outdoor art. Bart was a very ambitious guy. During the Primary I had arranged for Bart to have Thornburgh over for dinner to meet a few of the local movers and shakers.

I went outside and surveyed the crowd. The women were dressed with impeccable taste, and the lawyers, doctors, legislators, and high muckety-mucks sipping my fine whiskey and wine and eating hors d'oeuvres were making the small talk that dominates social events. I was reminded of one of my frequent literature binges in college where, in two weeks, I read everything F. Scott Fitzgerald had ever written. I remembered being totally taken with *The Great Gatsby*. Had I re-created *Gatsby* in my own life? Would all this come to a tragic end?

Spying Toni Cavanagh on the lawn, standing next to the bar with Jean and Richard and Shirl Glanton, I walked over to them. Richard was the darkest-skinned man I had ever met. He had become one of the top people on the Thornburgh team. A graduate of the University of Virginia Law School, he would go on to become Counsel to the Governor. He would place me in the forefront of the judicial reform movement — a place that would radically change my life and contribute to my loss of Kenmore Wood with its manicured lawns, society parties, and the respect that the shallow give to money.

Turning to the Glantons, I said, "Richard and Shirl, I want you to come to Aronimink with me for dinner when this little tea party is over."

Aronimink is a very old-line club on Philadelphia's upscale and inbred Main Line. Jean and Toni blanched. No one had ever seen a black couple at Aronimink, except in the kitchen.

"Toni, tell Bart that's where we're having din-din."

"Whatever you say, Bob."

"All right. Let's get this show on the road."

I grabbed a big scotch and soda that my bartender "Jumbo" Johnson had waiting for me at the bar and started for the porch. Jumbo was my undersized fullback in high school. He had been tending bar at parties for me for years. Black, respectful and discreet, he saw everything and said nothing.

As Thornburgh signaled from the front door that he was ready, I stood on the porch and said, "May I have your attention?" several times before I actually got everyone's attention:

"My friends, last year I met a man who stands head-and-shoulders above the crowd. He has just won a smashing victory in a hotly contested Primary. You all know that for some time I have been deeply concerned about the quality, or lack of quality, in our judicial system. Today, I am proud to introduce to you, and ask you to support, a man who has committed to cleaning up the judiciary, and making Pennsylvania a shining example of how one man can make a difference. I give you our next Governor, Dick Thornburgh".

Dick bounded out the front door to the applause of everyone present and began:

"I want everyone here to share my thanks to Bob and Jean for this marvelous day, at beautiful Kenmore Wood, with you, their friends."

He then went on with his now standard laundry list of problems in Pennsylvania. He, of course, blamed former two-term Democratic Governor Milton Shapp. Shapp's corrupt cabinet set a record for jail sentences for high public officials in Pennsylvania that was no small feat.

As everyone listened with rapt attention, I slipped back to the bar and handed Jumbo my glass for a refill.

I looked over to the garage and saw sons Bart and Craig talking to the state police. They were great kids and I loved them dearly. I looked around for daughter Laura. Standing near Jean, at fifteen, Laura was beautiful. My heart filled with love. I thought about when she was seven, and we put her on a plane to Nicaragua to visit our friends June and Sam. She had worn her granny-gown and stood so tall and confident. She was fiercely independent.

Dick was reaching the end of his speech. I edged back to the porch to perform the perfunctory task of bringing the formal presentation to an end.

Thornburgh's mind was already on the next stop of his schedule. Mine was on Aronimink, so we parted quickly as the state police gathered up the candidate and moved out the driveway with Bart and Craig waving goodbye to their new buddies.

I told Bart Cavanagh, his wife Toni, and Richard and Shirl Glanton that it was time to move on and go to Aronimink. Bart and I poured our drinks into plastic cups, "walkers" we called them, and climbed behind the wheels of our respective Mercedes.

At the front door of Aronimink, the valets opened the car doors and chorused, "Good evening Mr. Surrick — good evening Mrs. Surrick." As President of Aronimink, I was treated with a deference that bordered on the obsequious. Aronimink was one of the most prestigious clubs on Philadelphia's Main Line. Bill Hagarty, President of Drexel University, and I had run against and beaten the establishment years before, and taken control. We spent our way into prosperity and the staff knew that their well being had been materially affected by what Bill and I had done. Kay Gallagher, our hostess for the last twenty-two years, had been alerted that I was on my way in, and she greeted our party as we entered. She did a double take at the Glantons, but never missed a beat.

"Do you want the Dining Room or the Mixed Grill, Mr. Surrick?" she asked.

"The Mixed Grill will be fine, thank you, Kay."

Heads turned as we entered the Mixed Grill, but everyone quickly went back to their drinks and the topic du jour, whatever that was — most likely some juicy gossip!

Spying Jay Sigel having a drink at the oak-paneled bar with his wife, Betty, I left my group and went over to talk to a man who would become two-time U.S. Amateur Champion, Walker Cup Captain, and one of the really great Senior Tour players of his era. For the moment, he was selling life insurance and playing the local and state amateur circuit.

"Jay, are the arrangements for Pinehurst okay?"

"I have the Number 2 course for three of the seven days."

Playing Pinehurst with Jay had become an annual event.

"I'll call you tomorrow for the details. Good to see you, Betty."

After everyone was seated, a round of drinks was ordered. I turned to Richard and asked, "What do the polls show?"

"Dick is strong in Western Pennsylvania, but we have problems in the Philadelphia and the Scranton/Wilkes-Barre area. It's a name-recognition problem. Those Polack coal-crackers don't know Dick."

The next morning, I picked up my suit, with suspenders attached, and my shirt and underwear that were strewn about the bedroom and took a cold shower. Due in court at ten, I dressed quickly in a three-piece summer suit, rep tie and polished shoes. A final look in the mirror told me that I was ready for battle. "Show time", I said to my reflection and drove to my office.

As the writer Jim Harrison noted years later, *"The danger of civilization, of course, is that you will piss away your life on nonsense."*

"I WOULD BE CHIEF JUSTICE BUT FOR THAT NIGGER"

February 1980

"Bob, Richard Glanton here."

"Richard, how the hell are you? Long time no see. What's going on in the Office of Counsel to the Governor?"

"We're swamped. Everywhere I turn, I find another crook in the executive branch."

"I know that, and I also know that I wouldn't want you and Jay Waldman on my case. What can I do for you?"

"What you can do for Dick is serve on the Judicial Inquiry and Review Board and help us get rid of some bad Judges. There's no pay and no glory, but Dick thinks you are just the man to stop the downward slide of our judicial system. From the Supreme Court on down, it's beginning to smell to high heaven."

"Tell me about it. I'm in court almost every day and know for sure that we are sliding into the judicial Dark Ages."

I barely knew anything about the Judicial Inquiry and Review Board. Few lawyers did. I knew the Board was supposed to monitor the conduct of all Judges in the state, at every level, including the Supreme Court. When necessary, it would recommend discipline for unethical behavior to the Supreme Court, our state's highest court. It operated in secrecy and not many lawyers knew what went on there. The Board was created by the new Constitution in 1968. I never personally knew of a

Judge who had been brought before the Board. I just assumed there wasn't much judicial misconduct. Now, in my busy practice I was beginning to see and hear of judicial misconduct in many forms. Maybe I could make a difference. Maybe serving on the Board would be a good idea.

"Sure I'll do it," I told him.

"Dick told me that you would come on board. I'll get the paperwork out this week."

"Good to talk to you, Richard. I'll stick my head in next time I'm in Harrisburg. Tell Jay I said hello."

"Good luck, my friend. Give 'em hell!"

"Bye."

And so it began.

When the paperwork came through, I was sworn in by Judge Melvin Levy as a member of the Board. It would meet either in Philadelphia, Harrisburg, or Pittsburgh once every month. The Board consisted of three Common Pleas Judges, two Superior Court Judges, two lawyers, and two lay people. The Executive Director was Richard McDevitt. He acted as sort of a prosecutor. He would take complaints, investigate them, and, when appropriate, bring a matter to the Board.

At first, I thought everything was on the up and up. The Judges seemed to take the matters brought before the Board very seriously. The Chairman, President Judge of the Superior Court, Bill Cercone, seemed to provide firm leadership. After the first half dozen or so meetings, it dawned on me that I was a participant in a charade. The Board didn't root out bad Judges. It protected them, operating under a cloak of secrecy with its five-Judge majority. The Board made its numbers by beating up on the minor judiciary, such as neighborhood Justices of the peace, and would give a pass to the politically powerful. It was insiders protecting insiders.

I came to see that Cercone wasn't providing firm leadership; he was keeping control of a perverse process while other Board members allowed themselves to be used. The minority, two lawyers and two lay members, were passive, while the Judges worked their will.

Seven months into my service on the Board, I received an engraved invitation from the Governor requesting the presence of "my lady" and me at a formal dinner at the Governor's Mansion to honor the Supreme Court. It would be my first trip to the Governor's Mansion. It promised to be interesting. I dressed in the custom-made tux that Jean had given me for Christmas and she wore a very stylish long dress.

The two-hour drive from Media to Harrisburg was mostly in silence. Whatever we had in the beginning was gone. I had become a very driven person who did not share my wins and losses with my wife. She had become the dutiful wife who arranged social events and took care of the house and children. There was no mutual joy, tenderness or warmth. We functioned in our respective roles.

As we pulled into the Governor's Mansion, uniformed state police opened our doors. After presenting our invitations, we were escorted by the police to the double doors forming the entrance to the mansion. The doors were opened, revealing Dick and Ginny Thornburgh in the vestibule.

"Bob and Jean, we are so glad you could make it," Ginny exclaimed in her usual enthusiastic manner. I saw her as a genuinely nice person.

Dick gave Jean the usual obligatory kiss on the cheek then turned to me. "Good to see you." Then he whispered. "You'll bring a little class to this party" as he looked around the room and rolled his eyes.

I followed his gaze. I saw the seven Justices of the Pennsylvania Supreme Court socializing with each other and the assembled important, and self-important, guests. Chief Justice Francis F.X. O'Brien was talking with Justice Robert N.C. Nix, who would one day be the first black Chief Justice of any state. Justice Rolf Larsen, a classmate at Dickinson School of Law, and a loner, was, as usual, standing alone. Justice John Flaherty, who had been elected in 1979 because everyone thought he was Pete Flaherty, the very popular mayor of Pittsburgh, was talking to Jay Waldman and Henry "Merk" Hager, the President pro tem of the Pennsylvania Senate. Justice Flaherty had been heard to say to the lawyers during oral argument that he was mentally translating their arguments into Greek because, "I think better in Greek." Can you believe that! Believe it, it happened.

A waiter appeared with champagne. I took two flutes and handed one to Jean. Turning back to Dick and Ginny, I thanked them for including us. We moved into the reception area and I immediately spotted Matt Ryan, ranking Republican in the General Assembly who would one day be Speaker of the House. Ryan was a long-time friend and colleague at the Delaware County bar. Matt was talking to Justice

Michael Eagan, a political war-horse from Luzerne County and next in line to be Chief Justice. In Pennsylvania, the office of Chief Justice was determined simply by seniority.

Jean was now in her element. She could make cocktail party conversation with the best. As we approached Matt Ryan and Justice Eagan, she greeted Matt like a long lost favorite relative. She turned to Justice Eagan and said,

"I'm Jean Surrick."

Matt was quick to say, "Justice Eagan, this is Bob and Jean Surrick from my home county. We've been friends for years," signaling I was part of the establishment.

Justice Eagan responded, "I know who Bob Surrick is. He has argued many cases before us, and I was particularly interested in *Surrick v. Upper Providence,* which we decided in 1978. Mr. Surrick's brief made a compelling argument about zoning being used to limit housing opportunities for lower income families in the suburbs."

"As you know, Justice Eagan, Upper Providence is my township, and I can tell you that at the first zoning hearing on Bob's application in 1970, four hundred people showed up to protest," Matt said.

"One thing I learned out of that whole business, Justice Eagan, is that you can mess with a man's wife and cause less problems than messing with his zoning," I noted.

Jean looked horrified at this somewhat pungent remark and changing the subject quickly asked, "When will you become Chief Justice?"

Before he could answer, Dick and Ginny Thornburgh asked for quiet and both spoke briefly in welcome. Justice Eagan had drifted away and Jean went to the ladies room. As I was standing alone, I spotted Justice Larsen across the room and went over.

Larsen was a small man, no more than five-feet seven or eight inches tall, with a slight build. He had dark hair and darting eyes. His boyish looks belied a ruthless ambition and obsessive drive for power. There were swirling rumors around about his having made a deal with a fast growing group of lawyers who called themselves the Pennsylvania Trial Lawyers Association, PATLA.

Rolf Larsen and I were at opposite ends of the spectrum in law school. I was newly a civilian after two years in the army and Rolf was fresh out of college. I was serious about being in law school while Rolf seemed to be there to bait the professors. When he would begin to question something a professor would say, many of the veterans like me in the class would protest and tell him to sit down.

"Rolf — Mr. Justice Larsen — how are you?"

"Bob, good to see you. I see that the Governor has appointed you to the Judicial Inquiry and Review Board." The Supreme Court appointed the five Judges and the Governor appointed the two lawyers and two lay people to the nine-member Board.

We chatted a moment about law school days and our classmates.

Larsen then said something that jolted me; that caused me to question my hearing.

Rolf had turned and motioned toward Justice Nix and said, "That nigger is the only thing standing between me and Chief Justice."

"What?"

He continued:

"O'Brien goes off next year. Eagan only has months. Sam Roberts only has a year. If it weren't for that nigger, I could be Chief Justice after their limited terms. But Nix is senior to me and his term is longer than mine. He will get there first and block me."

I was dumbstruck. Fortunately, Jean walked up and said, "Rolf, I haven't seen you since Dickinson Law School days."

At this point, small talk took over until we were seated for dinner. Jean was seated between Merk Hager and Matt Ryan. I could see the conversation was lively. Hager was a little drunk and was making speeches while Jean kept Matt Ryan in the three-way conversation. Toasts were made by Thornburgh to the Supreme Court and returned by Chief Justice O'Brien on behalf of the Court.

After dessert and coffee, Dick and Ginny stood up to signal that the dinner was over and everyone quickly went to the cloakroom to get their coats and leave. At the door, I handed the state trooper my ticket, and our car was quickly brought to the entryway. Exiting onto Front Street, we started the two-hour ride home. I asked Jean what she and Ryan and Hager were talking about.

"Merk was a little drunk and was angry with Thornburgh. Apparently, Merk and Matt, or the politicians that control them, want control over the appointment of Judges. It didn't make any sense to me because we elect Judges."

"The governor appoints when there is a vacancy by reason of death, resignation, or removal," I said.

"Okay, I get it now. Anyway, Merk and Matt were saying that unless Thornburgh agreed, they would hold up his budget. They were saying that Thornburgh wanted to run for President after eight years of balanced budgets in Pennsylvania, and they would see that he didn't have that record to run on unless he agreed to listen to the politicians on judicial appointments. They were sure Thornburgh would cave on this."

"Holy shit! And Thornburgh says he wants me to help clean up the judiciary while he is selling it to the pols!"

It was becoming clear that things weren't what they appeared to be both in my profession and the political world.

It was getting rocky.

THE O'BRIEN LETTER

December 1980

Newspaper articles were beginning to appear detailing so-called "Nights on the Town" meetings between Supreme Court Justice Rolf Larsen and some of the state's key political figures. The apparent purpose was to discuss the election of Justices and Judges he and his supporters would find acceptable. Larsen was building a power base in league with The Pennsylvania Trial Lawyers Association. The Association consisted of plaintiffs' lawyers who were interested in obtaining and protecting large verdicts. It was lucrative because, traditionally, the lawyer received a hefty percentage of the verdict or settlement.

Just before Christmas, Chief Justice Henry F.X. O'Brien wrote a letter to the Judicial Inquiry and Review Board requesting an investigation into political activity by Justice Larsen. It was historic and unprecedented. The Chief Justice of Pennsylvania had filed a formal complaint with the Judicial Inquiry and Review Board against a colleague on the Court.

As a member of the Board, when I saw O'Brien's confidential letter, I knew something significant was going to happen. I was generally aware of rumors and newspaper articles about Larsen's activities. O'Brien noted in the letter that he had engaged well-known attorney Richard A. Sprague to head the investigation.

Dick Sprague, a former First Assistant District Attorney of Philadelphia, was a lawyer with a national reputation. He had achieved star status as the successful prosecutor of Tony Boyle, who murdered rival Jock Yablonsky, in order to become President of the United Mine Workers, the largest union in the United States at the time.

As instructed, Sprague conducted a meticulous investigation of Justice Larsen that lasted over two years. He developed solid evidence of the use of racial epithets, cronyism, political activity, improper use of his office, and a concerted effort with leaders of PATLA to elect Judges at every level who would be sympathetic to their goals.

This investigation and prosecution was sure to change the legal landscape in Pennsylvania. It would forever change my life.

STOP THE WORLD

August 1982 to April 1983

My law firm, Levy and Surrick, P.C. was making money, but there were disquieting signs. Arthur bought a condo in Atlantic City, where gambling had recently been initiated, and he was seen all too frequently around the tables. His mother, Ada, our bookkeeper, was caught shoplifting, and only through my contacts as a lifetime resident of Media, was I able to get the storeowner not to press charges. Then, in the spring of 1982, Ada tried to influence Arthur not to pay his former partner, brother, and now Judge, Melvin Levy, the agreed-upon buyout of his interest in the practice. Ada was telling one of her sons to cheat the other son. Melvin went to Bill Cherry for legal representation. It was interesting to me that Melvin engaged Cherry. Melvin had told me in the past that he and Arthur regarded Cherry as a totally dishonest and amoral man. Years before, I had caught Cherry and Walter ReDavid, the Register of Wills, paying personal expenses from an estate and reported them to the President Judge. To say there was bad blood between Cherry and me would be a massive understatement. Cherry threatened a very public lawsuit. Things were obviously getting out of hand. I called Dick Sprague and asked him, as a personal favor, to mediate. He met separately with Arthur and Melvin and the problem was resolved short of litigation, with Arthur agreeing to honor his agreement. I didn't know it at the time but Sprague was really speaking for President Judge Franny Catania.

On the last Friday in August I walked to the post office to get the mail. I saw a thirty-five hundred dollar retainer check from the Chester Water Authority in the mail. I had another check in my pocket from Dr. Steve Friedman for seventy-five hundred dollars. I thought to myself August would be a good month. After turning the mail over to Ada, I went about the day's business. At the end of the day, I checked the bank deposits and was surprised to note that the Chester Water Authority check had not been deposited. Over the weekend, in the closed office, I checked the books and, to my horror, discovered that the Chester Water Authority retainer checks had not been deposited for the last seven months!

On Monday morning, I went straightaway into Arthur's office. We had restored a Victorian house and had furnished it richly. Arthur's office was large and his teak desk set with the leather chairs was impressive.

"Arthur, I noticed that the Chester Water Authority retainer was not deposited on Friday. Was there any reason for this?"

To my alarm, I saw Arthur's hands begin to shake.

"I don't know why it wasn't deposited, but I'll check and let you know."

"O.K. but please let me know."

As I returned to my office, I saw Arthur summon Ada to his office. I waited. About a half an hour later, Arthur came into my office and said, "Ada made a mistake. The check will be deposited today."

"Thanks for checking," I said, stalling for time to think about the firestorm that soon would be raging.

Later, I went back to Arthur's office, summoned Ada, and asked where the checks for the last seven months were. Both professed ignorance.

"I want an explanation and I want it by tomorrow at nine a.m.", I demanded.

That night I sought the advice of Dick McDevitt, the Executive Director of the Judicial Inquiry and Review Board. He urged caution and referred me to his partner, Bob Greenfield, at Montgomery McCracken Walker and Rhoades. Greenfield also urged that I go slow and get all the facts.

"I have the facts. Arthur and his mother have been embezzling, stealing," I told Greenfield.

The next morning at nine, I again went to Arthur's office and asked for an explanation. He said he had hired a lawyer.

"Get your sorry ass out of my sight. Move to the second floor immediately. We are done as partners," I told him.

Arthur moved to the second floor and the lawyers, Greenfield for me and Ted Mann for Arthur, began to negotiate dissolution of Levy and Surrick. The sticking point was the stock in American Cablevision. The company had recently offered two hundred and fifty thousand dollars for the ten percent interest that I had put in the name of Surrick and Levy, a partnership. I wanted it separate and apart from the law practice. Finally, an agreement was reached that I would pay Arthur one hundred and sixty-five thousand dollars for his interest in the stock, and we would dissolve the firm, each keeping our separate clients. I was willing to pay Arthur more than one-half of the offer we had received from American Cablevision for the stock because I wanted to be rid of him, and thought the stock would be worth more in time. Where I was going to get the one hundred and sixty-five thousand dollars was beyond me.

Arthur then began to get his back up about the settlement. While I tried to avoid him, each time I saw him, he was more aggressive. Greenfield and Mann hadn't put the settlement agreement in writing, and I pressed Greenfield to get it done.

Then the other shoe dropped! I received a call from a secretary in Bill Cherry's office, who didn't like Cherry, and for whom I had done a favor in years past.

Bob, please watch yourself," she warned me.

"What do you mean?"

"Yesterday there was a meeting in Bill Cherry's office with Cherry and Marvin Comisky. You know that Comisky represents Rolf Larsen in the Judicial Inquiry and Review Board investigation. I didn't hear it all but what I heard was that they cut a deal. Larsen would protect Levy where possible, particularly if there are Disciplinary Board proceedings, in return for which Levy will dirty you up so that Larsen can get you off his back."

"You're kidding. Will you go public?"

"Bob, I can't. My mother is dying and Bill Cherry represents her in a malpractice action against the doctor who butchered her. Levy has fired Ted Mann and Cherry is representing him. There will be no settlement."

I started suit against Levy to enforce the settlement. Later, I would file a complaint with the Disciplinary Board against Arthur for embezzling.

Before long I would come to understand the warning from Bill Cherry's paralegal.

On December 16, 1982, my lawyer, Sam Klein, deposed Levy. The transcript showed:

Were you aware that an agreement had been reached regarding disposition of the American Cablevision stock?"

Levy began a tirade that had nothing to do with the question, during which he testified:

*"In retrospect, I now understand where he (*Surrick*) is coming from. He has the responsibility, as a member of the Judicial Inquiry and Review Board, to find facts with respect to either Justice Larsen or Tony Semeraro, who is a Common Pleas Judge in Delaware County. He tells me he is going to get these people. They are going to go! I am in a state of shock. What do you mean, they are going to go?" This is supposed to be a free country. He said, 'no way' – we've got the goods on them. They are both going to go."*

A week later, this deposition testimony, making me, as a member of the Judicial Inquiry and Review Board, to appear biased and prejudiced against Justice Larsen, found its way into the *Pittsburgh Post-Gazette,* Larsen's hometown newspaper. Over the next several months, Larsen attorney Marvin Comisky filed a barrage of Motions for my recusal from the Larsen case before the Board. I refused to recuse.

The power of Justice Rolf Larsen became clear a year later. In response to the Disciplinary Board complaint I initiated against Levy, he invented a cock-and-bull defense. He claimed that because he brought in more business than I did, we had a "tacit" agreement that he "could take as much money as he wanted from the partnership without accounting to me." The Supreme Court's Disciplinary Counsel and the Disciplinary Board did what they were told and dismissed the charges of embezzling brought against Arthur Levy. Never mind that investigation revealed embezzlements in addition to the Chester Water Authority. Disciplinary Counsel never asked Levy if he had declared this ill-gotten income on his tax return—he hadn't. Disciplinary counsel also failed to ask if the stolen money ever went through the Levy and Surrick books—it didn't.

When the firm of Levy and Surrick shattered, Murray Eckell, Franny Catania's friend and lawyer, who headed a prosperous Media firm, took in Levy. Eckell was a leader in the ascendancy of the Pennsylvania Trial Lawyers Association. He was later appointed to the Disciplinary Board by the Supreme Court and would become chair of that Board. Larsen and PATLA had both Surrick and Levy where they wanted them. One would be protected and the other would be prosecuted.

The Supreme Court subsequently appointed Arthur Levy a Hearing Officer for the Disciplinary Board, where he would sit in judgment on the honesty and ethics of other lawyers!

The Faustian bargain had been kept.

RICHARD A. SPRAGUE

December 1980 to April 1983

Dick Sprague was sitting on the bed across from me in his room at the Penn Harris Hotel in Pittsburgh. He was a short, slight man with bulging, unblinking eyes and a very soft handshake. Looks can deceive. Sprague was brilliant, tough-minded, and relentless.

The Judicial Inquiry and Review Board would meet in the morning. Several things would be discussed. Sprague planned to outline the progress of his investigation of Justice Larsen. Another pending matter involved me. Marvin Comisky, Larsen's lawyer, had subpoenaed me to appear at a deposition later in the day. A deposition is a question and answer session under oath. He was trying to intimidate the Board. The Board would decide whether or not I, as a member of the Board, would be subject to deposition by the attorney for a Judge or Justice under investigation. This all came about as a result of the Cherry/Comisky meeting when Levy and Larsen's attorneys agreed I was their common enemy.

"Let me explain this to you, Bob," Sprague started. "Rolf Larsen is the point man for the Pennsylvania Trial Lawyers Association. They want a fail-safe at every level to protect their verdicts. That's why Larsen backs certain judicial candidates. They then provide sufficient money to ensure election. These Justices and Judges are then beholden to Larsen and PATLA. PATLA is also taking over the Disciplinary Board to protect their own against charges of unethical conduct."

I reminded Dick of the hearing during the investigation when I told PATLA's Jim Mundy, one of the witnesses, that "I believed every witness had tried to tell the truth but I do not believe your testimony, Mr. Mundy, to be truthful." Sprague told me I had made not only Larsen but also the trial lawyers enemies for life.

I had been trying cases at every level since the mid-sixties and had watched the ascendancy of the Pennsylvania Trial Lawyers Association. Nevertheless, it was difficult for me to accept that someone or a group could set out to take over the entire judicial system.

As previously mentioned, Rolf Larsen had been a classmate at Dickinson School of Law in Carlisle. The older students who were there to learn looked on him with some contempt. Many of us had been in the military for two or more years and were serious students. Larsen was a wise guy.

After graduation, Larsen became involved in local politics in Pittsburgh and ultimately became a Common Pleas Judge. His first act was to jail the first hundred or so fathers who were brought before him who were in arrears on child support orders. This gained him national publicity. His second act was to cut a deal with Frank Rizzo, the powerful law-and-order mayor of Philadelphia, to double-cross Lisa Richette, the favorite for the Democratic nomination for the 1977 Supreme Court vacancy. After beating Richette in the Primary, largely due to Rizzo's help in Philadelphia, Larsen went on to win the General Election in November as a result of heavy contributions from the trial lawyers to whom he had pandered.

In his book *We All Fall Down,* outlining the Larsen saga in Pennsylvania, William Keisling wrote about Larsen following his election to the Supreme Court.

His legend has him returning to Pittsburgh to teach other lower court judges how it's done. The mugwumps they must talk to, what they must do to get elected to the high court. First he helps Common Pleas Judge John Flaherty (elected to the Supreme Court in 1979), then Common Pleas Judge Stephen Zappala (elected justice in 1981), and then Common Pleas Judge Nicholas Papadakos (who ascended to the high court in 1983)

These protégés followed Larsen's formula of taking populist or law-and-order stances to get attention," one lawyer told me. "Papadakos, for example, focused on mortgage foreclosures." The extent to which, once elected, his protégés would, like Larsen, resort to politics would be of increasing controversy.

The whole time Larsen is seen by his growing list of enemies as politicking to build a power base in hopes of becoming chief justice. In our state's high court the chief justice post is awarded by seniority. At the time, in the early 1980s, the next in line for the chief justice's job was Robert N.C. Nix Jr., having served on the Supreme Court since 1972. In our state the Nix family breaks ground. Nix's father, Robert Sr., in 1958 became the first black to win a seat in our congressional delegation. Justice Nix now was all that stood between Rolf Larsen and the chief justice's chair.

Sprague went on: "Larsen knows no limits. He will do what he has to. Look at the evidence of his manipulating Phyllis Kernick, mayor of Penn Hills, to try and get the solicitorship for his pal, August Damian; and these so-called 'Nights on the Town' where he and PATLA lawyers were lining up support for judicial vacancies. Bob, this is an evil man who will stop at nothing. He must be stopped!"

The next day, Bill Cercone, the Superior Court President Judge, serving as Chairman of the Board, and several of the other Judges on the Board, to my amazement, hectored Sprague unmercifully as he tried to painstakingly outline Larsen's misfeasance and malfeasance. It became clear that they were trying to belittle Sprague's presentation so they could vote to end the Larsen investigation!

It was a moment of truth for me. Should I sit there and let Sprague get hammered or step in on the side of Sprague to keep the Larsen investigation alive. From Sprague's recitation, it was clear to me that he had substantial evidence of wrongdoing by Larsen. The Judges on the Board, who were clearly trying to end the Larsen inquiry, were really abusing Sprague, the man who had so clearly painted the picture of good vs. evil just the night before.

"Wait a minute!" I heard myself say.

"Judge Watson, (who was a black Common Pleas Judge from Pittsburgh), you have heard Mr. Sprague put incontrovertible evidence before us that Justice Larsen, on numerous occasions, used the word 'nigger.' Can this be tolerated from a Justice of our highest court? You have heard evidence that he talked about hanging defendants in cages in the courtroom as blacks were treated in the Old South. Is this tolerable?" I asked.

I went on, "Judge Breene, (who was a Common Pleas judge from Venango County), you have heard clear evidence that Justice Larsen accepted an envelope containing money while sitting on the bench — money meant for the campaign of someone he was supporting for the Supreme Court. Taking money while sitting listening to argument at our highest court? Is this acceptable?"

There was dead silence and a palpable sense of unease around the table. Lawyer members of the board were supposed to defer to the five Judges in the majority.

I kept it up. Once committed, I had nowhere to go but to press on. At a deeper level, I knew I had sealed my fate. Judge Cercone wanted a vote that day to end the Larsen investigation. But Judge Cercone could count, and he knew I had shamed enough Judges to vote against his planned dismissal of the Larsen charges. That day there would be no vote. It would be a big defeat for Cercone. I had made sure that Sprague would go forward with his investigation of Justice Rolf Larsen. Larsen's plan to take control of the judicial system was temporarily sidetracked.

As for the subpoena for my testimony, in spite of my obstructionism, the Judges voted to deny Comisky's request for my deposition.

WHY DID HE DO IT?

September 1982

I was sitting in Harold Kohn's office telling him that I might need his help. Harold, a tall, slim, white-haired, courtly man, with a narrow face and piercing eyes, was talking on the phone to Ted Mann, Arthur Levy's lawyer. Mann, who was a "player" in the Jewish community, was apparently lamenting a fundraising shortfall by the Allied Jewish Appeal. Harold was telling him that, instead of worrying about the Jewish community, he should "worry about the Israeli he was representing!" Harold told Mann that he had advised me to begin a criminal prosecution and report Levy to the Disciplinary Board. Harold wanted to rescue the settlement previously reached between Ted Mann and my previous lawyer, Bob Greenfield, that Levy was now disavowing.

At Harold's instruction, I went to John Reilly, District Attorney of Delaware County. Reilly was formerly a partner of Judge Catania, before Catania went on the bench. I outlined the conclusive documentary evidence of Levy's embezzlement. Reilly refused to consider a criminal complaint against Arthur Levy because, he said, Arthur's brother, Melvin, was a Judge. That was quintessential Delaware County.

Bill Cherry's first act as Arthur's lawyer was to start eleven lawsuits against me. I needed weight and that's why I had left Bob Greenfield, who would ultimately have to be a witness, and asked Harold Kohn to get in the case. Harold was a giant in the legal profession. He had conceived the idea of multi-district litigation that made class-action lawsuits worth millions. In spite of his soft-spoken manner, he was a very talented and able litigator. He and I had an affinity for each other with roots back to the Judicial Inquiry and Review Board. Harold had been one of the first members of the Board when it was created in 1968. He had stuck his neck out to go after a politically powerful upstate Judge and had taken a few lumps as a result. He admired my willingness to urge the Board to enforce the Code of Judicial Conduct where Larsen was concerned, but always warned that I would pay for it. Being young and naïve, I paid no attention.

Now, a week (it seemed like a year) after having been served with eleven lawsuits by Levy, I was back in Kohn's office. He called in his junior partner, Sam Klein, and asked him to work with me. I was disappointed because I thought Harold would handle it himself. Based upon appearances, Klein was not impressive to me. He was short, somewhat overweight, with thick glasses. Not my idea of a trial lawyer. Harold assured me Sam would be up to the job. Years later I would realize how shallow I was in those days. Sam Klein was a giant of a man.

Klein filed a Declaratory Judgment action, seeking to have the court declare that the settlement that had been reached by Mann and Greenfield was a binding contract. Cherry filed an Answer denying that there had ever been a settlement. Sam pushed the case to trial. Allegedly because brother Barclay was a Judge in Delaware County the case was assigned by the Supreme Court, Larsen's court, to Judge Stively, a Judge from Chester County. In future years, the Barclay connection was ignored as I participated in many trials in Delaware County. This was indeed a "special" assignment.

The trial was in Judge Stively's courtroom in Chester County. I testified about the acquisition of the cable stock and the settlement that had been reached. Bob Greenfield, a man of impeccable integrity, testified as follows from the transcript:

"Mr. Mann called me back at my home after talking with Mr. Levy. He stated and told me that Mr. Levy caved in and that he would accept the one hundred sixty-five thousand figure. I considered that an agreement had been concluded."

Levy's lawyer, Ted Mann, testified under cross-examination:

"Did he authorize you to accept $165,000?"

"My recollection is that, at that point, Mr. Levy said to me something to the effect that they had — we've got to settle. And I was authorized to proceed toward reaching a settlement."

We left the courtroom confident that the overwhelming evidence showed that a settlement had been reached and the court would enforce it. Not only was there a strong case on the evidence, but also we had in our favor the legal principle that the law favors settlements.

To my amazement, on October 12, 1983, Judge Stively entered an Order dismissing our Petition for Declaratory Relief because there had never been "an agreement between the parties".

Sam Klein filed Exceptions to this order to preserve the right to appeal.

I was disappointed to say the least. The evidence was clear. Instead of obtaining a clean and efficient way out of this problem, Judge Stively had doomed me to years of litigation.

Sam was from Philadelphia and in those days, lawyers from Philadelphia, particularly Jewish lawyers, were suspect in the suburbs. I decided to change lawyers and hire a Chester County lawyer.

I went to Bill O'Donnell, a fellow sailor, who was recognized by all to be brilliant. Some years before, Bill had sailed James Michener around the Chesapeake in his one-off sailboat, *Prince of Donegal.* Michener was good enough to write a nice acknowledgment in the Forward of *Chesapeake.* Bill was an inveterate boozer and womanizer, but also a very competent lawyer and former Judge who knew the Chester County scene.

In 1977, Bill had been Chairman of the Democratic Party in Chester County. When Larsen campaigned in Chester County, he told the Democratic Committee that, if elected to the Court, he would ensure that in the 1980 reapportionment, Chester County would get its own Congressional seat. At the meeting where this promise was made, Bill, in front of Larsen, told the Committee not to endorse Larsen because the pledge was a violation of the Code of Judicial Conduct.

Larsen was elected and in due course Bill lost his license to practice for over two years for a very minor infraction of the Rules. His license had been restored just before I engaged him.

The Order of Judge Stively was not a final Order from which an appeal could be taken. O'Donnell set about to obtain a final Order. The final Order was finally filed on February 15, 1985. O'Donnell filed the required Motion for Post Trial Relief on February 25, within the required ten-day period. To understand what happened next, it's key to know that this Motion was timely filed and it was the only Motion required under the Rules and precedent.

Seven months later, on October 8, 1985, in a strange maneuver, Judge Stively filed Findings of Fact and Conclusions of Law. To my utter amazement, Judge Stively now concluded that there had been a settlement agreement between Greenfield and Mann, but that the attorneys did not have authority from their clients to make the agreement.

I was ecstatic! Not only did the record show that Levy had given Mann authority to settle, but the law was crystal clear that attorneys, negotiating a settlement with the knowledge of their clients, have apparent authority to settle a case and their clients are bound by the attorney's agreement. The testimony was clear that Levy instructed Mann to settle.

(W)e've got to settle, were the exact words Mann quoted Levy as saying. Mann added:

I was authorized to proceed toward reaching a settlement.

On December 23, 1985, Judge Stively again heard arguments from O'Donnell and Cherry on the Motion for Post Trial Relief. O'Donnell argued strongly that once there had been the finding of an agreement between the attorneys, the doctrine of apparent authority made the agreement enforceable. On March 6, 1986, Judge Stively, without addressing the apparent authority issue, entered Judgment in favor of Arthur Levy!

It was a bad decision, a wrong decision, a decision not supported by the facts or the law. It didn't make any sense to me. Why would Judge Stivley, on clear evidence and certain law, reach such a tortured result? I had trouble coming to grips with the idea that Larsen would protect Levy this way. Why? Because I was still a virgin! But reality was beginning to force me to take a more sanguine look at what was happening to me in the courts, the last bastion of honor and integrity, or so I had believed.

We had no choice. We filed an appeal to the Superior Court.

• • •

In due course, I discovered that Bill O'Donnell had filed another Motion for Post Trial Relief on October 25, 1985 after Judge Stively filed his Findings of Fact and Conclusions of Law on October 8, 1985. While O'Donnell's filing was more than ten days after the Findings of Fact and Conclusions of Law, the filing was, or should have been, irrelevant. Why did Bill, a meticulous lawyer who knew the Rules backward and forward, file this curious Motion out of time when he knew that he had previously filed a timely Motion that was all that was required? While the Motion was of no legal significance in a normal case, I would come to understand that this would not be a normal case.

What was this Motion all about?

CROSSING THE RIVER STYX

The Hoffman Appointment

February 1983

It took chutzpah to pick up the phone and call the chambers of Chief Justice Sam Roberts. I asked for an appointment and was told that Chief Justice Roberts would see me in a room behind the ornate Supreme Court Chamber on the fourth floor of City Hall in Philadelphia.

I appeared at the appointed time and knocked on the door. Chief Justice Roberts opened the door and invited me in. There were two rooms, and he was meeting in the second one with someone I didn't recognize. There were boxes piled up all over the room and several chairs were scattered around. I took a seat and waited with some trepidation. My mission was without precedent.

Chief Justice Roberts finished talking to whomever he was talking to, ushered him out, and then turned to me. He put his hand out and offered me a very small smile. He was slight of build with black hair which was becoming white on the sides. He had been the political leader of Erie County before he was elected to the Supreme Court. It was generally known that he was still the political leader of that county. I was sure he didn't want this meeting any more than I wanted to be there.

"All right, Mr. Surrick, what can I do for you," he asked

"Mr. Chief Justice, I wanted to talk to you about the two vacancies on the Judicial Inquiry and Review Board."

Roberts' eyes hardened. He wasn't used to this kind of meddling in the Court's business by someone so far down the pecking order. The office of Chief Justice in Pennsylvania was extraordinarily powerful. The Chief Justice had total control over all aspects of the Court's business. No one suggests to the Chief Justice what he ought to do.

"Mr. Chief Justice, forgive me if I trespass but I'm concerned about the Judicial Inquiry and Review Board. There are two vacancies on the Board. There are important matters before the Board and it is critical that the appointments to the vacancies be of the highest caliber. There has been in-fighting on the Board, and we need appointees who will bring calm and firmness to the tasks the board is facing."

It suddenly became clear to me that Roberts knew everything that was going on with the Board with the Larsen case and deeply resented this intrusion. It was my first lesson that in the power structure of Pennsylvania, people who have power never dilute their power by appearing to heed anything from lessers.

"Mr. Surrick, I am due back on the bench. You may be assured that this Court will appoint only top notch Judges to these vacancies."

He turned and went out through the other door. Roberts was offended. He was pissed.

According to the Constitution, the vacancies coming up on the Board were to be filled by appointment of the Supreme Court. The Constitution specifically required that the vacancies must be filled from "Judges of the Superior Court." I took Roberts at his word that the vacancies would be filled by "top notch" jurists. I still wanted to believe that the Supreme Court would do the right thing.

A few weeks later, the Supreme Court announced the "top notch" appointments. The first was Steve McEwen, a political hack and former District Attorney of Delaware County. I had unsuccessfully tried to block McEwen's appointment to fill a vacancy on the Superior Court, an appointment made by Dick Thornburgh at the request of John McNichol. The 1979 meeting at my house between Thornburgh and McNichol had produced at least one agreement. McEwen's most well recognized character trait was that he never had anything bad to say about a Judge or lawyer. Even lawyers on their way to prison could count on Steve. He had, in years past, testified as a character witness on behalf of convicted gambler "Skinny" Barrow and other unsavory denizens of the political underworld in Delaware County. McEwen had presented Delaware County Judge Tony Semeraro's commission to the Delaware County Court when Tony became a Judge. At that moment, Tony was under investigation by the Board, having been named an unindicted co-conspirator by the District Attorney of Delaware County in an election fraud case in which I was deeply involved on behalf of the Board. I remembered the day years ago when Steve and I were trying a case in Delaware County. As usual, after the jury had gone out, the lawyers were relieving the stress by making small talk in the hall behind the courtroom. We were talking politics, and Steve said with some pride, "Look Bob, I'm just a nickel rocket. I just do what I'm told."

The second appointment was even more brazen. It was none other than retired Superior Court Judge Sidney Hoffman, now sitting, by temporary appointment, as Senior Judge in the Superior Court. It was an incredible act of arrogance on the part of the Supreme Court to appoint Hoffman to the Board. A former President Judge of Superior Court and a long-time friend of Justice Sam Roberts, Sidney Hoffman, as a Senior Judge, was clearly not eligible for appointment to the Judicial Inquiry and Review Board. The Constitution required the appointee be a *"Judge of the Superior Court."* Hoffman was a retired Judge, serving, at the moment as a Senior Judge assigned to the Superior Court. He, like all Senior Judges, served wherever and whenever the Chief Justice designated. He was not a *"Judge of the Superior Court,"* as defined by the Constitution.

More importantly, the Constitution provided that a member of the Judicial Inquiry and Review Board could only be removed for cause. Hoffman, as a Senior Judge assigned to the Superior Court, could be removed from assignment to the Superior Court by a stroke of the pen of the Chief Justice, thereby removing him from the Board. The appointment of Hoffman by Justice Roberts was in direct violation of the Constitution and a clear betrayal of the trust reposed in his high office.

Following the appointments of McEwen and Hoffman, I went to see Dick Sprague. Sprague readily offered to secretly help. I reluctantly agreed with Sprague that the McEwen appointment, while unsavory, was legal. He was a *"Judge of the Superior Court"*. Hoffman, whose political tentacles reached deep into the Pennsylvania political system, was another story. Dick assigned the legal issue to one of his brightest assistants, Ed Rubenstone, who drafted a Complaint in Quo

Warranto challenging the appointment. It called for my signature and my filing. There would be no fingerprints left by Dick Sprague. The suit directly challenged the Supreme Court's constitutional power and authority to appoint Senior Judge Hoffman to the Board.

Sprague never mentioned, and I didn't remind him, that he had a conflict where Steve McEwen was concerned. Back in the sixties and early seventies, McEwen, then District Attorney of Delaware County had appointed Sprague to conduct an investigation into macing of county employees. Macing is the act of requiring political contributions from government employees. It is illegal. Sprague's report had whitewashed the widely known criminal conduct that had openly gone on for years. He had provided cover for McEwen. Behind his desk, Sprague prominently displayed a coffee cup from Steve McEwen that read "We Did It Our Way."

Rubenstone produced a superb Complaint in Quo Warranto challenging the Hoffman appointment. I filed it on February 16, 1983. The newspapers picked up the filing. Joe Daughn of the *Philadelphia Daily News* (Sprague put me on to him), captured not only this story, but fit it into all the other controversies involving me which were now swirling. Daughn wrote on February 17, 1983:

A member of the Pennsylvania Judicial Inquiry and Review Board, which is investigating the conduct of Supreme Court Justice Rolf Larsen, yesterday asked the high court to remove retired Superior Court Judge J. Sydney Hoffman from the panel.

Delaware County lawyer Robert B. Surrick said the appointment is illegal under the state constitution and would create a precedent that could permit the Supreme Court to "effectively control" the board, which investigates wrongdoing against judges…

In an unprecedented suit filed with the Supreme Court, Surrick said Article 5, Section 18 of the constitution requires that the two positions on the panel reserved for Superior Court judges be filled by active, not senior judges.

At the time of the appointment of Hoffman and McEwen, Surrick wrote to Roberts attacking both appointments.

"The Judicial Inquiry and Review Board is controlled by judges who in my three years experience on the board almost without exception fail to find fault with other judges' conduct,"

He stated then that he believed Hoffman's appointment was illegal, and went on to denounce McEwen's appointment as "incomprehensible."

McEwen, said Surrick, had appeared as a character witness for defendants in two criminal cases and had hosted a cocktail party at the Republican State Convention "in apparent violation of the Code of Judicial Conduct."

Surrick did not take legal action to block McEwen's appointment, he indicated, because as an active Superior Court judge, McEwen — a former Delaware County district attorney — could legally sit on the JIRB.

I was stressed beyond belief because of the action I had taken. First, it made Hoffman, who took it personally, a mortal enemy for life. Second, to contest the right, legality, and authority of the Supreme Court to make an appointment to a constitutional Board was either an act of great courage and conviction — or sheer lunacy. At the time, I felt that I was taking a position that would preserve the integrity of the judicial system I so wanted to revere and to respect. I thought the mistake, when pointed out, would be rectified and the Board could then go about its business. It was clear to me that by this appointment, Justices of the Supreme Court were betraying their oath to uphold the Constitution, and I had a duty, as a member of the Board, to make them look at the facts.

The case was scheduled for argument on April 19th. I called Bob Cummins, a lawyer from Chicago and chair of the Illinois Judicial Conduct Board. I had first met Bob in New Orleans, and again in Denver, when I attended (the only Pennsylvania Board member who bothered) a National Conference on Judicial Accountability. Bob was a straight shooter. I asked him to come in and argue the case. He agreed if I would pay his expenses, which I quickly agreed to do. I paid his first-class air ticket out of my own pocket. Doing God's work can be expensive.

"Oyez, Oyez, Oyez," began the clerk, and the case was called.

Cummins barely began his argument when Justice Nicholas Papadakos laced into him. Papadakos was rude and arrogant and shot question after question, interrupting each answer Cummins tried to give to the previous question. When Papadakos began to flag, Justice Stephen Zappala took up the questioning, never giving Cummins a chance to answer. It was brutal! In contrast, Hoffman's lawyer, Stephen Feldman, was treated like a favorite uncle. It was over before it began.

On April 27, 1983, the Supreme Court handed down a per curiam (unsigned) Order dismissing the Complaint. The Court did not reveal who voted and gave no reason for the decision. The illegal appointment was merely ratified by judicial arrogance. The significance of the Justices hiding behind an unsigned Order cannot be overstated. It would soon be replicated.

The *Delaware County Daily Times* headlined:

Media lawyer loses bid to get judge off board

To his everlasting credit, Justice Nix filed a pungent seventeen-page dissent, decrying his colleagues' disregard of the Constitution. He wrote, in part, in unnuanced prose:

Thus, whenever a legitimate question is appropriately raised regarding the propriety of our discharge of this responsibility, ("supreme judicial power"), it is incumbent upon this Court to assess the complaint, without rancor, with reflective objectivity and to confess error where appropriate. The arrogant misuse of public trust is the precursor of tyranny. To obstinately refuse to admit error, and to perpetually seek justification, is to deny the fallibility of human nature and to assume a posture that is indefensible.

Years later, Bob Cummins told me he met Chief Justice Nix at an American Bar Association function where Nix apologized for the "unfair and rude" treatment Cummins had received at the oral argument.

This was not just the loss of a case. The Supreme Court had been caught making an illegal appointment, and I had the temerity to call it to their attention. In the beginning I was part of the establishment. I had made flowery speeches on Law Day using phrases like the "majesty of the law," "no man is above the law," and the "importance of the Rule of Law." All this now seemed a little hollow in light of events. I had launched my boat into the River Styx that carried this lawyer, who could no longer kiss the ring, to an uninhabited far shore.

I was proud of what I had done and the way I did it. It was lawyer-like, without heat or emotion, and legally sound. Did I receive any public support from the so-called leaders of the bar? The fact that I had to go to Chicago for a lawyer answers that question.

PROTECTING THE POLITICALLY POWERFUL

April 1983

The defining characteristic of Tony Semeraro was that he was dumb. A short, chubby man with an oversized nose, he always looked and acted like he was two steps behind everyone else. In fact, he was.

How he survived law school is not to be understood. He became Solicitor for the Nether Providence Zoning Hearing Board, an appointment which confirmed that the Peter Principle was alive and well in Delaware County. His written Opinions for that Board were convoluted and mystifying, in short, a joke. On the other hand, he was a loyal soldier in the monolithic Republican Party in Delaware County, where loyalty counts for everything.

Tony made his bones in Nether Providence doing what he was told and then for the bigger pols at the county level. It, therefore, was no surprise when the Delaware County Republican Party, led at the time by the Catanias, made Tony a Common Pleas Judge. He would always do whatever he was asked to do, which was the only real requirement for the office.

Tom Lynch was the Controller of Delaware County. A tall, overweight, smiling Irishman, he had run on the same 1977 ticket with my brother Barclay, and we had become friends. When he asked my advice about no-bid contracts being awarded by County Council in apparent violation of the County Charter, and probably the criminal

Code, I advised him that if he sat idly by and watched contracts which by law must be put out for bid, turned into no-bid contracts, he was as guilty as County Council. It was clear to me that people doing business with the county on no-bid contracts were an asset to their benefactors. Tom began to flag these contracts. The pols didn't take kindly to their gravy train being derailed. In 1981, they refused to endorse Tom for the usual second term allowed the political faithful.

I took Tom to Jon Aurett, the chairman of the barely functioning Democratic Party. I suggested that if Lynch, who was generally well known and popular, changed parties and was endorsed by the Dems, he would have a chance of winning, even if it was a slim chance. The deal was closed, and the fun began.

Charlie Sexton, the Republican leader of Springfield, is a certifiable Neanderthal. He always lets his emotions get the better of his limited judgment. Predictably, he went ballistic. Any normal person would know that there was little chance Tom could beat the Republican organization in the Fall election. But Charlie wasn't normal. He didn't want to just beat Tom, he wanted to destroy, to savage, to kill him. Tom was from Springfield and Charlie had brought him up through the ranks and made him Controller of Delaware County. Tom had embarrassed him. That was unforgivable!

Charlie Sexton went to Richard Burke, a registered Democrat and somewhat shady character from the Chester Pike area, and talked him into running in the Democratic Primary against Tom. He promised him undercover financing, undercover help, and the gratitude of the Republican Party, which for Burke probably meant freedom from arrest for the petty illegalities in which he was always involved. It wasn't the first time the Republican Party would try to control a Democratic Primary and wouldn't be the last.

Sexton then went to some of the trusted party faithful to raise money for Burke's campaign. One of his first calls was Tony Semeraro, who readily agreed to violate the Code of Judicial Conduct to funnel funds to Burke. As it turned out, he funneled cash. This was a felony, a felony independent and distinct from the felony of conspiring with Charlie Sexton to violate the Election Code. Tony had no reason for apprehension because it was the way things were done in Delaware County.

Burke jumped into the race and, as I expected, lost to Tom in the Primary.

During the spring, word of these political machinations got back to the feds, and the FBI opened an investigation. Burke, when interviewed, being a person of no courage, immediately cracked and told the FBI what was going down with Semeraro, Sexton, Nick Catania, the President Judge's brother and a couple of very overweight local Chester pols named Fratterola. The FBI talked Burke into wearing a body wire. After making the rounds with Semeraro, the Catanias and others, Burke had a goldmine. He was then subpoenaed to testify before a federal grand jury that was looking into corruption in Delaware County. The following wiretap telephone conversation was played for the Grand Jury:

Is Judge Semeraro in?
Yes he is. Who shall I say is calling?
Richard Burke.
Just a minute, please.
A pause and then.
Judge Semeraro here.
Tony, this is Richard. How's it going?
Ok. What's up?

I got this subpoena to go before the Grand Jury in Philadelphia about the money I got during the campaign.

You didn't report the money I gave you, did you?

No, that's why I'm calling. I want to make sure we are saying the same thing.

Look Richard, I didn't give you any money. You got that clear? It came from your Aunt Matilda or someone else but not from me. Ok.

Ok, got it.
We are on the same page. Take care and good luck with the Grand Jury.
Thanks Tony. Talk to you later.

The gang that couldn't shoot straight had nothing on these guys. With that little discourse, recorded for posterity, Judge Tony Semeraro added subornation of perjury to the crimes of election fraud and conspiracy to commit election fraud.

The United States Attorney for the Eastern District of Pennsylvania decided to indict Judge Tony Semeraro and the other miscreants. It was getting serious.

He went to Washington to have the Attorney General of the United States sign off on the proposed prosecution. He felt this was prudent in light of the high profiles of the prospective indictees, such as Judge Tony Semeraro, Nick Catania, brother of the powerful President Judge Francis Catania, Mayor Jack Nacrelli of Chester, Charlie Sexton, leader of Springfield Township, and other, lesser pols. At this juncture, Delaware County's formidable Republican juggernaut went into action using Drew Lewis, the Secretary of Transportation, from neighboring Montgomery County. Under pressure from Lewis, Reagan's Attorney General, William French Smith, mirrored Pontius Pilate, by washing his hands of the matter. He directed that the evidence be turned over to the District Attorney of Delaware County for further proceedings.

The Philadelphia Inquirer December 8, 1981, editorial page blasted the Attorney General's obvious bow to political pressure as follows:

It's a federal fix in Delaware County

The Inquirer wrote:

President Reagan's Justice Department, in its 11th-hour refusal to prosecute corruption charges involving politically powerful figures in Delaware County, has sent an appalling message far beyond that county and the state of Pennsylvania.

The message is that all the talk by the President and Attorney General William French Smith about getting tough on criminals does not apply when the alleged crimes involve political corruption and the suspects are important Republicans in a state crucial in a re-election campaign.

That began a four-year campaign by the Inquirer for judicial reform, which produced a number of Pulitzers for Executive Editor Gene Roberts' newspaper. Led by editorial page writer Mike Pakenham and staff writer Dan Biddle, the *Inquirer* put unwavering and constant criticism on Supreme Court Justices Larsen and McDermott, both of whom sued the *Inquirer* in their own court systems.

These were heady days. It was possible for people like me, who wanted to end the "good-old-boy" system, to speak and be heard. Unfortunately, the Larsen and McDermott libel lawsuits, as well as lawsuits from other judges, such as Delaware County's Steve McEwen on the Superior Court, largely silenced the *Inquirer* in the late 1980s and 90s. They were getting hit in the cashbox, where it hurt them the most. Something had to go, and investigative journalism about corrupt public officials became expendable. The *Inquirer*, the largest daily newspaper in

Pennsylvania, and fourth largest in the United States, would be intimidated into silence.

The United States Attorney turned the evidence, including the wiretaps, over to Frank Hazel, the District Attorney of Delaware County. Frank had a problem. He finally figured out how to contain the scandal and indicted all involved, Nick Catania, Charlie Sexton, etc., except for Judge Tony Semeraro, who was listed on the indictments as an unindicted co-conspirator. That designation on a criminal indictment is usually reserved for someone who is going to testify against his co-conspirators. Hazel's motive was different. If he had indicted Judge Semeraro, the Judicial Inquiry and Review Board, on which I was sitting, would immediately have asked the Supreme Court to suspend him. That would put Tony at risk, and as Tony was not known to be a man of courage, it would have put the Republican poo-bahs at risk. It also meant that before a suspended Semeraro could be re-instated, there would have to be a hearing. That could cause the whole house of cards to fall.

On behalf of the Board, I arranged to depose D.A. Frank Hazel. Under oath, Frank wanted to appear cooperative but was nervous as a cat on a hot tin roof. I went around and around with him before a court reporter. I probed directly on the lack of an indictment of Semeraro. His Assistant District Attorney, Roy DeCaro had written a report stating that Semeraro was clearly indictable. Semeraro's subornation of perjury, by a Judge no less, was the most serious criminal charge of all the malefactors. Hazel kept saying he didn't want to ruin a man's career just because he was "stupid." Here is a Judge, a man sworn to uphold the law, committing at least three felonies, and the District Attorney is concerned about his career. Gimme a break! It's called the fix is in.

At the meeting following this deposition on July 19th, 1982, I reported to the Board that the Investigating Committee of the Board had concluded, as had the District Attorney of Delaware County, that there was sufficient evidence to indict Judge Semeraro. I moved that Judge Semeraro be suspended pending investigation and hearing. The motion failed on a four-to-four vote, the four Judges voting in lockstep to protect their colleague.

The Supreme Court then appointed Judge Cherry (no relation to Bill) of Blair County to hear the criminal cases against the Delaware County defendants. It was part of the long-standing method of operation of the Supreme Court to assign an out-of-county Judge to a politically sensitive case. The assigned out-of-county Judge would then fix the case and return unscathed to his home county. Cherry, a good-old-boy Judge if there ever was one, dutifully traveled to Delaware County. He held a so-called "in-camera" hearing. None other than Dick Sprague represented Nick Catania, the President Judge's brother. The press and public were excluded. He then announced that he had dismissed all of the indictments.

At the meeting following Judge Cherry's issuing passes to the Delco pols, McDevitt told the Board that the dismissal of the indictments was the end of the matter. Before I could say anything, new Board member Judge Steve McEwen moved to dismiss the charges pending against Semeraro. The motion was seconded, and passed with the five Judges on the nine-member board voting in lockstep.

I started to protest and was told I was out of order. I left the room and found Peggy, the board secretary, and asked her if either Hoffman or McEwen had asked to see the file on Semeraro. She said she had the only key to the file cabinet and neither had asked to see the charges or the evidence. They voted to dismiss <u>without ever having seen the charges or evidence.</u>

I decided to go public. When testifying before the Senate Judiciary Committee on judicial reform, I told them that the public would be appalled if the facts of the Semeraro case were known. The state press picked up the story. *The Delaware County Daily Times* on August 17, 1983, headlined:

Lawyer on Semeraro case 'Public would be appalled'

Among other things they wrote:

Surrick made the statement while testifying under subpoena at a Senate Judiciary hearing. ...Surrick cited Semeraro's case among many recent board probes as proof the board's confidentiality provision must be abolished. That provision keeps the board's proceedings — and its evidence against judges — behind closed doors. "If the public ever saw the material before the board (regarding Semeraro), it would be appalled that nothing has happened," Surrick told the committee.

Reality in this case was the clear and conscious corruption, a betrayal of public trust now permeating the judicial system. I looked it in the eye and knew that I would face life-changing decisions before long.

The River Styx wasn't all that wide. The shore was in view.

THE VOTE AND THE XYZ PETITION

April 1983

Eleven of us sat around a conference table in the offices of the Judicial Inquiry and Review Board. There was Dick McDevitt, the Executive Director, and the nine-member board, plus Senior Judge Sidney Hoffman.

"Judge Hoffman, I object to your participating in this proceeding," I said. My challenge to Hoffman's appointment to the Board was still pending before the Supreme Court.

I went on, "The Constitution provides for only nine members on the Judicial Inquiry and Review Board. Now, we have ten people here in this room considering the charges against Justice Larsen. I have previously objected to Judge Cercone sitting because his term expired January first, but he insists on sitting. If he sits, you can't."

Hoffman had been appointed to fill Cercone's seat on the Board. But Cercone insisted on sitting. These Judges did what they pleased, despite the Constitution. The situation was surreal. I looked around to the other Judges for help. They sat impassively. The tension in the room was overwhelming.

"Mr. Surrick, I have been appointed by the Supreme Court," Judge Hoffman said aggressively. "I have been elected Chairman of this board, and I will sit."

For four years, I had been complaining about the fact that a five-Judge majority dominated the nine-member board. That majority heard no evil and saw no evil. Now, there were six Judges.

I had previously objected to Judge Mirarchi being named chairman of the panel that heard the evidence in the two (plus) years of the Larsen hearings. Marvin Comisky, Larsen's lawyer had been honorary chair of Mirarchi's recent Retention election campaign. He had also represented Mirarchi in a lawsuit in 1980. I couldn't believe the five Judge majority turned their heads to this blatant conflict-of-interest. It was mind-boggling. It was absurd.

"I call for a vote," Judge Hoffman said.

"Judge Hoffman, you can't do this," I said with some heat in my voice. "We haven't even discussed the charges, the evidence, and the findings of fact filed by Judge Mirarchi, Mr. Rackoff, Ms. Marston, Judge McClosky, and me."

"Mr. Surrick, this case has been going on for twenty-nine months, and we are going to put an end to it right now," a clear signal that he had in his pocket the votes to dismiss.

"Judge Hoffman, I move the charges against Justice Larsen be dismissed," said Judge McEwen.

"Judge McEwen has moved for dismissal of the charges. Is there a second? Judge Mirarchi has seconded the motion. All in favor raise their hand."

"Judge Hoffman, can we at least have a secret ballot?", I asked

The other Judges sat impassively. I would receive no help from them. It was taking thirty seconds to dismiss twenty-eight months of investigation. It was all happening very fast.

"All in favor of dismissal raise their hand. The motion carries and the charges are dismissed. What's next on the agenda, Mr. McDevitt?"

"Judge Hoffman, for the record, I vote to remove Justice Larsen from the Supreme Court."

"I agree with Mr. Surrick," said Linda Marston, one of the lay members.

"So do I," echoed Ray Rackoff, the other lay member.

The Judges, a majority, had voted in lockstep to dismiss the charges. The two lay members of the Board had voted with me to remove Justice Larsen from the Supreme Court.

I glanced around the table. The Judges avoided my gaze. I felt as if I had just been run over by a speeding freight train.

Thus ended the Sprague investigation of Justice Larsen that produced seventy-five hundred pages of testimony. The testimony came from many witnesses who had much to lose in crossing a powerful Justice and his allies in the system. It had been the most important investigation into judicial misconduct in the two hundred years the Commonwealth had been in existence. My sense of outrage at these willful and corrupt Judges, whose arrogance knew no limits, was smoldering. I feared it would burst into flame. I had to be careful and measured in what I said and did.

I now anticipated the destruction of the record. Even though it had been Board policy to make public the record of a proceeding at the conclusion of the case, I had no doubt that these Judges were not about to let the public see the overwhelming evidence developed by Sprague.

I went back to my office in Media and dictated a "Petition for Extraordinary Relief" to try and block what I saw coming. The Petition would attempt to prevent destruction of the record and seek to have the Supreme Court remove the proceedings from a Judicial Inquiry and Review Board. There had been accusations of conflict-of-interest involving several Board members, numerous Petitions filed by Larsen's attorney to recuse Board members, and the just-concluded, irregular meeting with ten participants.

On my desk was a copy of *The Philadelphia Inquirer* article titled:

A Media Lawyer's Lonely Quest For Justice

Ed Guthman, former press secretary for Bobby Kennedy, wrote it. He was now Editorial Page Editor for the *Inquirer.* I had met with Guthman the week before in the hope that the *Inquirer* would share my outrage at what I saw as the coming blowout of the Larsen case. He wrote:

The law is not a game to Surrick. He has a passion for justice.

I called Dave Bruton, a partner at Drinker, Biddle and Reath and told him what had happened and asked for his help. He agreed to help and asked me to bring my draft Petition to Philadelphia and meet with him.

The problem of how to proceed was difficult due to the pernicious constitutional requirement that all proceedings before the Board must be secret. That meant I couldn't have Larsen's name in the caption. We decided to overcome this obstacle by putting the Petition in proper form for filing and sealing it in an envelope. Let the Prothonotory of the Supreme Court figure out how to docket it. When we attempted to file it, Marlene Lachman, Prothonotary of the Supreme Court, refused to take it on instruction of Chief Justice Roberts. To the everlasting credit of Dave Bruton, he refused to take no for an answer and marched over to the chambers of Justice James McDermott, who was the duty Justice that day, and told him what had happened.

Justice McDermott didn't like the sealed envelope because there was no way to docket the document without a caption. Bruton suggested to Justice McDermott that the solution would be to delete Justice Larsen's name from the caption and file the body of the Petition under seal. McDermott agreed. We went back to Bruton's office to change the caption.

We talked with Jim Eiseman, one of Bruton's associates, who suggested we caption the Petition, "In The Matter of XYZ." This was a reference to the infamous case of three French agents who attempted to negotiate a ten million dollar loan from the U.S. for France. At the time, France was at war with England, and President John Adams wanted to help end the war. When it became known that the French agents had earmarked two hundred and fifty thousand dollars of the loan as a payoff to French Minister Talleyrand, public outrage in the United States killed the loan, which was labeled in the newspapers as the "XYZ Affair." The names of the three French agents were never revealed.

The next day, I filed our so-called "XYZ Petition." The Petition was more than twenty-three pages in length, detailing the dismissal of the charges against Larsen and the serious legal problems with the procedure.

Prior to the meeting where the Larsen charges were dismissed, I had taken several days off and went to my sailboat, Maverick, to read the seventy-five hundred and fifty pages of testimony. It was all there. There was absolute proof of an amoral man with unbridled ambition sitting on our highest court. Justice Larsen clearly was unable to tell right from wrong.

I decided to try and focus the issues by preparing proposed Findings of Fact. I circulated my Findings to the other Board members. This prompted lay members Linda Marston and Ray Rackoff to separately follow suit with their own Findings. Most curiously, Judges Mirarchi and McCloskey also filed proposed Findings of Fact. I brought all these Findings together in the "XYZ Petition" and they form a devastating portrait by five members of the board-a majority-who together painted a picture of racism, cronyism, misuse of office, potential felonies and unethical political activity, all in violation of the Code of Judicial Conduct.

Each area may be summarized as follows:

- Racism — Five members, a majority, found that Justice Larsen used the word "nigger" on numerous occasions. He told Pittsburgh coroner Cyril Wecht that he planned to make voters aware that Justice Nix "was a nigger," thereby seeking to racially influence Nix's pending Retention Election. He told Arlene Bell, a Supreme Court law clerk at the time of the racially contentious MOVE trial in Philadelphia, "They ought to hang those niggers in cages from the ceiling and try them like that."
- Misuse of office — Five members, a majority, found as fact that Justice Larsen attempted to intimidate Phyllis Kernick, mayor-elect of Penn Hills, a Pittsburgh suburb, into appointing his friend, August Damian to the seventy thousand dollar a year solicitorship of that municipality. Interestingly Justice Larsen denied to the news media that he ever contacted Kernick.
- Anti-Nix activity — Five members, a majority of the Board, found that Justice Larsen wanted to derail Justice Nix's ten-year retention election in 1981. Justice Larsen wanted to be Chief Justice but Justice Nix had seniority. Justice Larsen met on a number of occasions with Justice Nix and attempted to intimidate Nix into not running, offering him instead support for a United States Senate run or a high-paying job in a prestigious Philadelphia law firm.
- Political activity — Five members, a majority of the Board, found that, beginning in 1980, Justice Larsen initiated a series of dinners throughout the state convening trial lawyers, elected officials, politicians, businessmen, educators, potential contributors, and others to advance the candidacy of Robert

Colville, District Attorney of Allegheny County for a seat on the Supreme Court. These were euphemistically called "Nights on the Town". A year before (all five agreed) Justice Larsen had successfully promoted the candidacy of Allegheny County Common Pleas Judge John Flaherty for the Supreme Court. All five agreed that Justice Larsen called upon then Philadelphia District Attorney Ed Rendell for help, and Rendell directed Justice Larsen to Howard Gittis, at Wolf, Block, Schorr and Solis-Cohen. At the direction of Justice Larsen, Nathan Fishback, his law clerk, met Howard Gittis, where he was given an envelope containing cash and checks. Fishback then delivered the envelope to Justice Larsen, who was on the bench at the time, hearing cases before the full Supreme Court. Accepting cash contributions in amounts greater than one hundred dollars is a felony violation of the Election Code. Also, all five members found that Justice Larsen attempted to advance the candidacy of Bruce Kauffman to the Supreme Court by calling Jay Waldman, General Counsel to Governor Thornburgh, as well as Senators Zemprelli and O'Pake. Also, each found that Justice Larsen telephoned members of congress and wrote a letter to President Jimmy Carter advancing the candidacy of Leonard Mendelson for a federal court judgeship.

Thus, five members of the nine-member Board, a majority, found facts that were clear violations of the Code of Judicial Conduct, and perhaps felonies, which normally would require the imposition of discipline, probably removal. Three of the five, who were not Judges, voted to remove Justice Larsen from the Supreme Court. Incredibly, two of the five, Judges Mirarchi and McCloskey, in spite of finding substantial judicial misconduct, had voted with the other Judges to dismiss the charges.

The XYZ Petition containing the above findings by a majority of the Judicial Inquiry and Review Board was now before the Supreme Court.

The Pennsylvania Supreme Court had before it a chance to change the course of judicial history in the Commonwealth. It was a momentous opportunity.

The opportunity to restore respect for the Court, battered by three years of public revelations about the seamy and sordid way it operated, was at hand. Would ward-leader politics or probity prevail?

LARSEN CASTS A CRUCIAL VOTE

The Turning Point

May 1983

On May 6th, 1983, the Supreme Court entered an Order, without explanation, not to accept the "XYZ Petition." The Petition was under seal, and, although every Justice well knew what was in the sealed envelope, it was only captioned "In the Matter of XYZ." In essence, they were voting on whether they should open the envelope. It became a matter of contention whether Justice Larsen would admit that he was the subject of the sealed Petition. If he conceded what he knew, that he was the subject of the Petition, he would, under constitutional mandate, have to recuse and not vote. However, since the Petition's caption did not mention Larsen by name, he insisted he would vote, because, he said, he had "no way of knowing" that the sealed Petition concerned him.

So Larsen voted, with the other Justices on whether or not the sealed Petition should be opened and considered. His "no" vote was the deciding vote.

The unalterable fact was, and is, that Larsen knew he was the subject of the "XYZ Petition," and the other Justices knew it, and knew he knew it, when they and he voted. They denied the obvious. This was made clear several years later, on October 1, 1986. It came to light in a deposition of Justice McDermott in a libel lawsuit he had filed against *The Philadelphia Inquirer.*

Sam Klein, the *Inquirer* attorney, went fishing about the vote on the "XYZ Petition." Remember, it was Justice McDermott who authorized the filing of the "XYZ Petition." And remember, it was Dave Bruton who told McDermott that Larsen was the subject of the Petition. The transcript of the deposition reveals:

BY MR. KLEIN: Justice McDermott, can you tell us what Justice Nix said during the conference on the XYZ Petition?

I can't tell you that because I don't remember, but I think that Justice Nix wrote an opinion in that matter and I think there was an opinion by Justice Zappala.

Q. Do you recall what you said during the conference?
A. Yes.
Q. Can you tell me what you said during the conference?
A. I said that I thought Justice Larsen should not vote in the case.
Q. Did you say why?
A. Well, because I thought he was involved.
Q. Did you tell him he was involved in the case?
A. I said that I thought — I said, I think that is a case involving you and if it is, you ought to recuse yourself.
Q. And what did Justice Larsen say?
A. He said…

*Mr. Beasley (*McDermott's attorney*): Wait a minute. I don't understand what relevance it has to this lawsuit. I am going to instruct him not to answer. I don't know whether you are on a fishing expedition…."*

The most outrageous aspect of this whole charade was not that the Supreme Court refused to look at Petition that was properly before the Court. What is most revealing is how the vote went, that is, how each Justice voted. While the public record shows the vote to be five to two not to open the envelope, Justice Larsen's vote to dismiss the Petition was, in fact, the deciding vote. The vote really was four to three.

In a chance conversation with Chief Justice Roberts before he died, he told me that the Chief Justice always votes last. When it was time for him to vote, Larsen and his cronies, Zappala, Papadakos and William Hutchinson, a majority of the seven Justices, had already voted against opening the envelope.

Roberts saw that if he voted to accept the Petition, Larsen's vote to dismiss would be the swing vote on a four to three decision. He couldn't let that happen, so he voted to dismiss, making the vote of record five to two. He sought to avoid the criticism that would surely flow from a case being decided by the vote of a Justice who was the subject of the case. Of a certainty, all of the Justices knew that Larsen voted to dismiss a matter in which he was a party, the party. That, in and of itself, is a very serious violation of the Constitution and the Code of Judicial Conduct not only for Larsen but also for all the Justices.

Justice Zappala filed a separate Opinion concurring with, but not explaining, the Order. He excoriated me for filing the "XYZ Petition." He gave like treatment to Justice Nix for filing a Dissenting Opinion. Once again, a majority of the Justices of the Supreme Court of Pennsylvania, in a serious matter involving the integrity of the judicial system, entered an unsigned Order betraying the trust reposed in their high office.

To his everlasting credit, Justice Nix dissented. The language of the Dissent, which follows, sheds light on the magnitude of the judicial corruption in Pennsylvania:

I must strongly dissent to this Court's denial of the application of Robert B. *Surrick for leave to file a petition relating to a matter pending before the Judicial Inquiry and Review Board. Initially, it must be emphasized that the request being considered merely seeks the right to file a Removal Petition with this Court either under seal or in the alternative without placing the matter under seal. Without any information before us upon which to assess the merits supporting the petition for Removal, a majority of this Court by its ruling has flagrantly disregarded the constitutional mandate of Article 1 Section 11, of the Pennsylvania Constitution which provides access to all courts of the Commonwealth and thereby abrogated Mr. Surrick's right to due process of law afforded him under the Fourteenth Amendment of the Constitution of the United States. Moreover, the participation of Mr. Justice Larsen in the deliberations and decision in this matter, over objection, represents a deliberate and callous disregard of constitutional mandate.*

The circumstances surrounding this decision were that Robert B. *Surrick, through his counsel, James Eiseman and* Robert *Hoelscher for the firm of Drinker, Biddle and Reath, obtained an order from Justice McDermott that allowed him to file the removal petition under seal. The parties apparently thought it necessary in view of the rule of confidentiality required by Article 5, Section 18 (h) and Section 3334 of the Judicial Code, to file the petition under seal apparently because certain of the allegations and exhibits were protected by the confidentiality rule relating to a pending matter before the Judicial Inquiry and Review Board.*

The filing was refused at the direction of the Chief Justice and a telephone conference was scheduled and held with all Justices participating. The majority concluded, without any information as to the substance or nature of the complaint, that the petitioner would be foreclosed from any consideration.

At the outset of the Court's deliberation on this subject, objection was made to the participation of Mr. Justice Larsen. The basis of that objection is Article 5, Section 18(i) of the Pennsylvania Constitution that prohibits, without qualification, a justice from participating in any proceeding involving his suspension, removal, discipline or compulsory retirement. It was argued in support of the refusal of Mr. Justice Larsen to recuse himself, because it was not apparent the matter under consideration was related to the charges currently pending before the Judicial Inquiry and Review Board against Justice Larsen. In view of all of the information that has been made public through the media and through prior applications to this Court, it is ludicrous to suggest that it was not absolutely obvious that the Petition for Removal was a request in connection with the Larsen inquiry.

Moreover, as to the decision of the majority, we merely need to cite this Court's recent decision in Boyle v. O'Bannon, wherein in an opinion authored by Justice Larsen, a majority of the Court agreed with the language quoted at page 4 in the Slip Opinion.

For more than a century the central meaning of procedural due process has been clear: "parties whose rights are to be affected are entitled to be heard."

Although at that time I did not believe those principles were applicable to the case then before the Court, its applicability here is unquestioned. In Boyle, the petitioner's papers were allowed to be filed and were considered by the Court. The question there was the right of this Court to summarily dispose of the matter prior to service and responsive pleading. Here Mr. Surrick is being prevented at the door of the courthouse from even articulating the basis of his complaint. Such constraint by a judicial body is frightening.

For both of the above stated reasons I must again express my strenuous disagreement.

Mr. Justice McDermott joins in this dissenting opinion.

By his tie-breaking vote in his own favor, Justice Larsen escaped, leaving himself free to begin prosecuting me before the Disciplinary Board of the Supreme Court. It would be his appointees, his prosecutors, and his PATLA cohorts.

But the larger picture, the far more important picture, was of the entire Pennsylvania Supreme Court, in the *Hoffman* and *XYZ* cases, irreversibly crossing to the Dark Side from which there would be no return. The Court's cowardly disposition of these cases, without written Opinion or explanation, was dishonorable, dishonest and disillusioning on the extreme. Over the years, Sam Klein frequently warned me that with the *Hoffman* and *XYZ* Orders, the Court placed itself in an indefensible position, and the seeds of those two contrived Orders would bear bitter fruit. He believed that stung by the exposure of wrongdoing, the Justices would become ruthless in their quest to destroy the exposer.

My take was that the Justices had abdicated their responsibility for moral leadership and the Judges and lawyers would follow this lead. It would become every man for himself.

The slouch to Gomorrah was underway.

STONEWALLING AT ITS FINEST

July 1983

Following the Larsen whitewashing by the Judicial Inquiry and Review Board and my unsuccessful effort to open the record of that investigation to public scrutiny, the Pennsylvania Crime Commission served a subpoena on the Board for the Larsen transcripts and records.

The Crime Commission was an independent agency created by the legislature to investigate white-collar crime and government corruption. It had broad investigative powers, including the power to subpoena witnesses and records. It was not under the direct control of the Pennsylvania Attorney General, Governor or legislature and, as such, was seen as an independent body, often the last resort to fight corruption in Pennsylvania.

In all prior cases going back to the inception if the Judicial Inquiry and Review Board, if charges against a Judge were dismissed, the record was <u>always</u> made public. But the Larsen record was hot — too hot. The Judges who ran the Board told Executive Director McDevitt to stonewall the subpoena, which he dutifully did.

A June 18, 1983 *Philadelphia Inquirer* article said it all:

Board fights Subpoena of Larsen file

The state Judicial Inquiry and Review Board has voted to fight a Pennsylvania Crime Commission subpoena for records of a confidential 28-month investigation of state Supreme Court Justice Rolf R. Larsen.

The decision was made Thursday during a closed-door meeting in which the board also declined to undertake a further investigation into a new conflict-of-interest complaint against Larsen, according to sources on the board.

The inquiry board's decision Thursday not to open a new case against Larsen concerned a complaint made by one of its members, Media lawyer Robert B. *Surrick.*

Surrick, a dissenter in the decision to exonerate Larsen, had contended Larsen should not have participated in a state Supreme Court vote May 6 in which the court refused to take over the probe from the board.

I called Don Johnson, a lawyer working with the Crime Commission, and told him I wanted to talk to the staff but would need a subpoena to protect myself. He agreed, and we met for about six hours during which I provided the staff with documents and anecdotal evidence about the Board's refusal to fulfill its constitutional mandate of investigating allegations of misconduct and prosecuting where appropriate. To say they were shocked with what I gave them would be an understatement. They vowed to redouble their efforts to enforce the subpoena that was scheduled for hearing before President Judge James Crumlish of the Commonwealth Court.

At the court hearing, Dick Sprague testified on behalf of the Crime Commission and urged the court to make the record public. At this time Sprague saw his power with the anti-Larsen forces. How he came to represent Larsen before the Supreme Court in 1991 is another story for another chapter. Dick Sprague always will be where the power is — he backs away from making moral or value judgments when self-interest is at stake.

Judge Crumlish was an old Philadelphia political war-horse, and there was no way he was going to let the Larsen records see the light of day. As I expected, he quashed the subpoena of the Pennsylvania Crime Commission for the Judicial Inquiry and Review Board's records on Larsen.

The Larsen matter, as in Charles Dickens' speech, was like Jacob Marley, "Dead as a doornail."

My term on the Board ended in December 1983. For four years, I had watched the Board operating under a cloak of secrecy; dismiss cases of egregious judicial misconduct such as allegations of misconduct against Judges Joseph O'Kicki, Semeraro, Cirillo, Avellino, Sweet, Lipschitz and Bernie Snyder. In fact, the Board's ineffectiveness was made even more obvious when the electorate voted "No" on Judge Bernie Snyder in his Retention Election. The Board had refused to pursue charges against Snyder. The electorate did what should have been done by the Board and took him off the bench. I was angry, disappointed, and frustrated over the hypocrisy of the Board, indeed, the whole judicial mess in Pennsylvania. For example, the O'Kicki case, which included allegations, among other things, that he sat in his underwear in his chambers, ended not with Board action but finally in criminal prosecution in Cambria County, from whence he fled to Slovenia and died a fugitive from justice.

I talked to Don Johnson about the Semeraro case, and he agreed that it offered the Crime Commission the cleanest and clearest path to establish the corruption of the Board. While the facts were a little complicated, given all the players involved, what happened was clear. The Crime Commission issued a subpoena and served it on the Board, calling for production of the Semeraro records.

Again, President Judge Crumlish assigned the matter to himself. And once again, he blocked the Crime Commission from obtaining the records it needed.

The Crime Commission appealed to the Supreme Court.

Finally, on September 26, 1986, the Supreme Court affirmed President Judge Crumlish's Order quashing the Crime Commission's subpoena to the Board for the Semeraro records. The relevant part of the Opinion, written by the increasingly powerful Justice Zappala, said:

As best as can be determined from the oblique testimony of Crime Commission investigation director Frank E. Booth, the only witness to appear at the enforcement hearing, the Commission was investigating the Judicial Inquiry and Review Board's practices in regard to cases where disciplinary action was not pursued after preliminary investigation. In the case of Anthony Semeraro, the Federal Bureau of Investigation and the United States Attorney for the Eastern District of Pennsylvania have investigated allegations of election law violations arising out of his judicial campaign. No prosecution was deemed to be warranted. And the matter was referred to the District Attorney for Delaware County, who also decided that there was no basis for prosecution. These same allegations were brought to the attention of the Judicial Inquiry and Review Board that apparently decided after preliminary investigation not to conduct formal hearings or pursue disciplinary action. The Commission's investigation of possible public corruption was based solely on an unnamed informant's 'tip' that there was a connection between the Board's vote, said to be 4-3, and an unfulfilled informal agreement allegedly struck between Judge Semeraro and the Delaware County District Attorney to have Semeraro testify in an unrelated criminal case, and the supposed belief of the amorphous 'political structure' of Delaware County that they could influence the Board's decision.

This last sentence is classic "fix" language in an Opinion. Distort the allegation beyond reasonable understanding and then knock down the unintelligible charge. The allegation I made was that there was a conspiracy between the Delaware County District Attorney, the Delaware County politicians, (notably the Catanias) and the leaders of the Board that there would be no criminal indictment of Semeraro, who was clearly guilty of criminal conduct. Everyone involved knew that Semeraro was weak and would break under the pressure of a criminal prosecution. His conduct was therefore referred to the Judicial Inquiry and Review Board where confidentiality would remove the matter from public view and give Semeraro an excuse not to talk.

The District Attorney could then, with the help of an out-of-county Judge appointed by the Supreme Court, cause the criminal charges against Semeraro's co-conspirators in the underlying election fraud case to be dismissed. Then, the Board would dismiss the charges against Semeraro. This is exactly what happened. It shows how the board's confidentiality mandate can actually become part of a criminal conspiracy.

Zappala then thrust his judicial sword deep into the Crime Commission and me as follows:

A detached overview of the testimony fails to dispel the impression that the Commission's claim of relevance between the testimony sought and the purpose of the investigation of the Board's decision-making practices was manufactured out of whole cloth.

. . .

Footnote 1. In assessing the evidence produced in support of enforcing the subpoena, it must not be overlooked that the information relied on by the Commission was apparently obtained in violation of the Board's confidentiality requirements, requirements imposed by the rule, statute, and the state constitution. The nature of the information received indicates its source must of necessity have been an employee of the Board involved in the investigation, or worse, a member of the Board. We cannot express strongly enough our disapproval of this indiscriminate breach of trust, an illegal act undertaken on an individual assessment of what the rules should be, in callous disregard of law as it had been ordained by the citizens of the Commonwealth, promulgated by their democratically elected representatives, and interpreted by the judiciary.

This Opinion, clearly not detached, didn't require a rocket scientist to understand what it said. It said three things:

1. The Semeraro inquiry, like the Larsen case, was "Dead as a doornail."
2. The Crime Commission better give up its attempts to investigate the Pennsylvania judicial system.
3. Footnote 1 made it abundantly clear that citizen Surrick had angered very powerful people in the power structure of Pennsylvania.

Zappala would never forgive the Crime Commission's attempt to investigate the judiciary. A few years later, when things quieted down, Zappala, using his friend and political compadre Senator Vince Fumo, whose influence in the legislature was awesome, caused the legislature to abolish the Crime Commission, leaving the politicians free to rape and pillage at will.

Zappala and Fumo would go on to have many more high (or low, depending upon your point of view) adventures. They would influence cases, look after each other in their respective spheres of influence, and pack the Supreme Court with their minions. These powerful elected officials were far more interested in beating the law than upholding it.

We had entered the Judicial Dark Ages.

LARSEN STRIKES BACK

1983 to 1987

The summer following the Larsen hearings was busy. There was my second Merion-to-Bermuda sailboat race. Maverick acquitted herself well. Brother Barclay and my college roommate, Stu Jones, a world-class sailor, were crew. My practice was in a shambles due to the time spent challenging the appointment of Judge Hoffman to the Judicial Inquiry and Review Board, my appeal to the Supreme Court of the Larsen case, the "XYZ Petition, and working with the Crime Commission on the Semeraro matter. As I had anticipated, on May 6 the Judicial Inquiry and Review Board voted to seal the record of the Larsen case, forever removing it from public scrutiny.

In July, I hosted a party at Kenmore Wood that was spectacular. Guests were murmuring under the huge oaks in the circle. Dinner was catered by Aronimink at tables of eight on the manicured lawn as the sun went down. There was a disco in front of the three-car garage until the early hours. Bart had his Bowdoin College pals, while Laura and Craig invited their local friends. It was straight out of *Gatsby*. It was to be my last bash before I moved out.

In August, I was shocked to receive a letter from the Disciplinary Board of the Supreme Court stating that an investigation was being opened into my conduct as a member of the Judicial Inquiry and Review Board. I was mortified. I couldn't believe it! I believed with all my heart that I had done the right thing for the right reasons. A constitutional Board had been corrupted and they were coming after me for pointing it out? The incongruity was obscene.

I went to see John Rogers Carroll, one of the top trial lawyers in the country. John was horror-stricken when he learned that Justice Larsen had filed a seventeen-page complaint with the Disciplinary Board of the Supreme Court, a Board over which he and his fellow Justices exercised oversight responsibility and budget control. The Disciplinary Board oversees conduct of attorneys, and is itself appointed by the Supreme Court. Through appointed Disciplinary Counsel, it investigates complaints about lawyers and recommends discipline (which can include disbarment) to the Supreme Court.

To make matters worse, Larsen had filed his complaint on his Supreme Court stationery and copies of the complaint were sent to each member of the Board, the jury, if you will. I am sure that they all understood clearly what Justice Larsen wanted. On top of this, Larsen filed a libel suit in the Court of Common Pleas of Allegheny County against *The Philadelphia Inquirer,* the *Pittsburgh Post-Gazette*, various reporters, editors, and me! He contended that I controlled the editorial policy of the *Inquirer.*

John Carroll agreed to help. When I pointed out that Larsen was controlling the power structure, John suggested that maybe I was being a little paranoid. He then laughed and opined that as far as he knew, "Paranoids were the only realists."

Arguably, Larsen was the most powerful man in Pennsylvania. A man who knew no limits on the use of power was now my mortal enemy. Larsen was striking back!

The disciplinary proceedings dragged on. Finally, I filed a Petition for Extraordinary Relief in the Supreme Court asking the Court to end the Disciplinary Board proceedings. I argued that the Disciplinary Board had no jurisdiction over a lawyer serving on the Judicial Inquiry and Review Board. I urged that as matter of public policy, a lawyer member of the Board had to be insulated from intimidation by the Disciplinary Board when a vindictive Judge, whom the lawyer had voted against, files a complaint against the lawyer. More importantly, the Constitution provided the only remedy for Board member misconduct: Removal from the Board.

On December 9, 1985, the Supreme Court entered an unsigned Order dismissing my Petition.

The charges against me were three fold:

First, I had prejudged the Larsen case by supposedly telling my then-partner, Arthur Levy that we "had the goods on Larsen."

Second, the First Amendment Coalition, represented by Sam Klein, had filed a lawsuit in the United States District Court seeking to have the Larsen record made public. Perry Bechtle, the lawyer for the Judicial Inquiry and Review Board, had given Judge Pollak and opposing counsel a memo he had written to the Board advising that the record should be sealed. I was in possession of another memo from Pennsylvania Law School professor Paul Bender, who had also been advising the Board. He urged that the record should be made public. I attached a copy of this memo to the Motion I filed seeking to intervene and be a party to the proceedings. I was charged with making public confidential papers of the Board. My answer was that I didn't do anything different than the Board's attorney.

Lastly, I was charged with making public confidential material in a letter to the Speaker of the House and in a newspaper article I authored. My response was that everything I said was already in the public domain by virtue of investigative reporting by Dan Biddle of *The Philadelphia Inquirer.*

The newspapers became deeply disturbed at Larsen's use of the Disciplinary Board to seek revenge. *The Delaware County Daily Times,* on July 27, 1986, wrote an extraordinarily long editorial under the headline:

The silent crucifixion

In part, it wrote:

If the politicians on and off the bench can corrupt the judicial system and then use that same system to punish honest dissent or public complaint, will they stop there? Will justice be openly sold to the highest bidder over the bench? If any attorney dare complain then, who will he complain to? The judicial board, the Supreme Court? The public? It will be too late.

The attorneys have learned to keep their mouths shut, but they haven't learned what follows. Tyranny punishes the silent too.

The *Times* followed up, on October 12, 1986, with another long editorial titled,

The engines of tyranny

where they wrote, in part:

The proceeding is plainly vindictive, and for that reason alone void. The facts themselves are too feeble to support prosecution. Did Surrick discuss a case with his partner? How many members of that board, or of (the) judiciary, have never done the same? In any case, that is not a public communication. The public itself was aware of Larsen's predicament long before Surrick filed an appeal and confirmed it. The spectacular transgression in this case would appear to be that of Larsen, who voted on his own case in violation of court rules. In any case, the judicial board itself admitted in court documents that under its own policy Larsen's case was going to be made public.

The Philadelphia Inquirer weighed in on December 22, 1986, in an editorial entitled,

The Larsen-Surrick case must be resolved publicly

demanding that the closed-door Disciplinary Board hearings be conducted openly.

The News of Delaware County headlined:

It's time to drop probe of Surrick

The pages flew off the calendar as my traducement dragged on. Even the out-of-state *Trenton Times* condemned what was happening in an editorial entitled:

Surrick's Kafka-esque nightmare

Prior to the Disciplinary Board hearing on Larsen's charges, I put in a call to Dick Thornburgh to ask him to testify on my behalf. I couldn't get through to Dick. One of his aides, Henry Barr, took the call. I explained to Barr what I wanted and the importance of Thornburgh testifying on my behalf. Barr told me that, as a matter of policy, Thornburgh would not appear. I was angry. Thornburgh had asked me to put myself at risk on his behalf, and now, he was letting me twist slowly in the wind. Henry Adams once observed when Roosevelt turned on Elihu Root in the Northern Securities Trust case that "Theodore betrays his friends for his own ambition". I guess the more things change, the more things stay the same. Several years later, this Thornburgh aide, Henry Barr, would go to jail for lying about cocaine use while an attorney in the Attorney General's office.

During this period of time, I noticed that Orders in my case from the Disciplinary Board were signed by Robert Daniels, Larsen's advisor during the Board hearings and one of the leaders of PATLA. Daniels was Chairman of the Disciplinary Board in 1984 and 1985. Later, John Elliott, a prominent trial lawyer, signed Orders. While not a PATLA member, he had significant ties to the establishment. He caused quite a stir when he hosted a trip for Justice McDermott and Judge McEwen to tour the coal region prisons where the Mollie McGuires were hanged. At the time, he and his firm had cases pending before their courts. Elliott was Chairman in 1985 and 1986. PATLA leader Jim Mundy was Chairman in 1989 and 1990. PATLA had gained firm control of the Board.

Hearings were finally held on October 8, and November 12, 1987. Arthur Levy, my former partner, was the only live witness called by Disciplinary Counsel. His testimony was feeble and contrived. No one believed him and with good reason. When called, I readily agreed that I had attached the Bender memo to the Motion to Intervene in the First Amendment Coalition case. I pointed out that I had done nothing different than Board attorney Perry Bechtle in releasing this other internal memo. I also identified the letter I had sent to then Speaker of the House, K. Leroy Irvis, and a magazine article I had authored. I pointed out, using newspaper clippings, that all the information in the letter and the article was already in the public domain.

I called as witnesses on my behalf Ed Rendell, former District Attorney of Philadelphia, later Philadelphia's mayor, and later Governor, Dick Sprague, Sam Klein, Charlie Rogovin, former chair of the Pennsylvania Crime Commission and law professor at Temple Law School, Harry Dunn, president of the Delaware County Bar Association, and Dave Franklin, noted bond lawyer. All testified that I was a lawyer of outstanding integrity and professional standing.

On August 20, 1987, the three-member Hearing Committee filed its Report. In a split two-to-one vote, they found that I had breached confidentiality by making public the Bender memo and by my letter to the Speaker of the House. The two-person majority recommended that I receive a private reprimand. Private reprimand is the least sanction the Board can recommend. The recommendation amounted to a slap-on-the-wrist for what should have been a very serious offense of violating the Constitution. It reflected the true state of mind of the two who voted against me—Surrick didn't do anything wrong, but we have to do something.

Jean Green, a Montgomery County lawyer on the panel dissented, writing:

Respondent's present difficulty appears to stem from the manner in which he sought to accomplish those goals. However, he was frustrated at every turn when he tried to act in accordance with the law. The Supreme Court of Pennsylvania would not accept his Petition to remove the inquiry as to Justice Larsen's conduct from the JIRB to the Supreme Court itself. Justice Larsen himself voted for that prohibition. The JIRB, after receiving Surrick's complaint of Justice Larsen's action in voting to refuse to remove the matter of his own alleged misconduct to the Supreme Court, dismissed it without an investigation. There appeared to be no other avenue left open to Respondent other than to join the suit in the federal district court and bring to that court's attention the memorandum authored by one of the two counsel of the JIRB. In addition, Respondent wrote to an important official of the state legislature as well as to presidents of the various county bar associations. He also made information available to the media as well as writing his own articles that were published in various newspapers and other journals. There was very little information, if any at all, which was made public by Respondent that was not already in the public domain by various leaks from the JIRB proceedings. None of the leaks that made information available to the press, which therefore became public, has been attributed to Respondent.

It seems to the undersigned that in the midst of the celebration of the 200th anniversary of the Constitution of the United States of America, and especially the veneration of the trial of John Peter Zenger, that it is exquisitely inappropriate that a lawyer should be subjected to disciplinary action for attempting to bring to the public's attention the very serious and important manner in which our Commonwealth's system of disciplining Judges had broken down.

I had heard that Jean Green was a man of honor and principle, and he proved it with his eloquent dissent.

The Report of the Hearing Committee was only a recommendation. The Disciplinary Board would make the final decision. The Board would appoint a panel to hear argument on the

Recommendation. The arrogance demonstrated by the make-up of the panel offended *The Philadelphia Inquirer* that asked in a November 11th editorial:

Is deck stacked on Surrick?

The editorial noted:

You'd think that a panel considering the ticklish question of whether to discipline a lawyer who called Pennsylvania Supreme Court Justice Rolf Larsen to account would be as above reproach as Caesar's wife. Think again. The chairman of the panel that will report to the Disciplinary Board of the Supreme Court has a troubling conflict: He chipped in $1,000 to a campaign fund for Justice Larsen...The Chairman's name is William L. Keller, a past president of the Philadelphia Trial Lawyers Association...

Keller, a PATLA stalwart, went on to become Chairman of the Disciplinary Board in 1991 and 1992.

As expected, this panel recommended that the Board recommend the discipline recommended by the Hearing Committee to the Supreme Court. The Board, now controlled by PATLA, in league with Larsen, was only too happy to recommend discipline for Larsen's foremost critic.

I could have accepted the private reprimand, and that would have been the end of it. On the other hand, an appeal to the Supreme Court could have cleared me while running the risk of major penalty or sanction such as disbarment.

No way was I going to take this. Not only was I convinced I was right, I believed that what I had done was within the constitutional mandate of confidentiality.

The way I counted it, I had three votes on an appeal to the Supreme Court: Nix, Flaherty and newly appointed Juanita Kidd Stout, a black jurist long associated with the Nix family in Philadelphia. I assumed that not even Larsen would have the chutzpah to vote, having filed the complaint against me. Justice McDermott, through his attorney, Jim Beasley, was threatening me with a libel lawsuit so I assumed he would recuse himself. I had written an article published in *The Philadelphia Inquirer* critical of the *"rot and decay"* in the judiciary, citing Supreme Court Justices Larsen and McDermott suing their critics in their own court system. That left only Larsen's protégés, Zappala and Papadakos, to vote against me. Joe Lawless, a lawyer in Dick Sprague's office, also had told me that Justice Nix had said more than once that he would "protect Surrick." Lawless was Sprague's intermediary with Nix. Sprague never, ever, left fingerprints.

I appealed to the Supreme Court. Sometimes, the line between courageous and foolhardy is indistinct.

"NEPOTISM WILL NEVER DIE"

October 1, 1986

Justice McDermott was suing *The Philadelphia Inquirer* for libel arising out of a series written by Dan Biddle entitled **Above the Law.** Biddle earned a Pulitzer for a later series entitled **Disorder in the Courts.** Biddle and I had many conversations about the mentality of the Justices of the Supreme Court, whose corruption was permeating the entire court system. I was being deposed as a witness because of the articles I had written. The McDermott lawsuit was part of what was becoming an organized and concerted effort to silence any potential media criticism of Judges and Justices.

During an interview by Biddle, Justice McDermott had been asked about all of his relatives, including his children, who were on the Supreme Court payroll. In his usual flippant and arrogant manner, McDermott had said, "Nepotism will never die," which, of course, Biddle reported. I was reminded of the time McDermott, as a Common Pleas judge in Philadelphia, had told the jury several times in a loud, forceful voice, "I am the law!" He was one of the arrogant and willful men who populated the Supreme Court.

Justice McDermott sat across the table glowering at me. What the hell was a Supreme Court Justice doing attending a deposition, I thought, if it wasn't to intimidate the lawyer being deposed? Sam Klein, attorney for the *Inquirer,* sat several chairs away, next to the court reporter. I was not represented. I didn't think a lawyer was necessary.

"Mr. Surrick, what did you mean when you wrote that the judicial system was rife with 'rot and decay' in the article that was published in the *Inquirer*?" asked Ellen Suria, Justice McDermott's attorney. She was a partner with Jim Beasley, a nationally known libel attorney. Beasley and Sprague were on their way to enrich themselves and acquire awesome power and influence by bringing libel lawsuits on behalf of Judges and politicians against the print media.

I replied: "I meant that with the Larsen shenanigans out in the open and not dealt with, with Judges like O'Kicki in Cambria County sitting in their chambers in their underwear not dealt with, with Judges and Justices suing their critics in their own court systems, with a dozen Judges in Philadelphia caught taking bribes from the Roofers Union, and I could go on and on, the public perceives that the system is full of rot and decay."

"Do you believe that Justice McDermott is part of the rot and decay?"

Okay, Bobby boy, I thought, here we go and where it will end nobody knows. I was already a defendant in a libel suit brought by Justice Larsen in Allegheny County. Still, I thought, if I dance a little, maybe she'll get tired and go in another direction.

"To the extent Justice McDermott is part of the system, my answer would be yes."

"But were you referring directly to Justice McDermott? In the article you refer to Justice McDermott suing his critics in a court system over which he has oversight responsibility."

"My feelings on that subject have appeared in numerous articles which I have published around the state."

"You are not answering the question, Mr. Surrick. The question is, did you intend in this article to say that my client is part of what you see as rot and decay?"

The moment of truth. Do I weasel or stand and fight?

"Ms. Suria, let me ask you — who is paying you and Mr. Beasley for representing Justice McDermott? What coin of the realm is being exchanged for this legal service? Is he paying money? Are you and Mr. Beasley getting something of value from him for your representation? Let me be more specific. Tomorrow you and I have an argument in the Supreme Court. You represent the other side. My client knows you represent Justice McDermott. My client is not a fool. He knows that even if Justice McDermott recuses, he still has influence with other Justices."

I thought McDermott was going to explode. His normally ruddy Irish complexion transfused beet red. His hands clenched and unclenched, and his face appeared apoplectic. Despite this show of anger, I thought I might as well keep going.

"Let me ask this? Are you the only attorneys Justice McDermott could hire? Couldn't he go out of state and get lawyers to represent him who don't practice before his Supreme Court? New Jersey and Delaware, with lots of good lawyers, are almost within walking distance. Why is Mr. Beasley representing Justice McDermott? Mr. Beasley probably has more cases before the Supreme Court than any other lawyer in Pennsylvania. It looks bad — no, it looks terrible — no, awful — that's what I mean by rot and decay."

McDermott nearly knocked over the table as he leaped to his feet. He pointed his finger at me and started to speak, but before he could utter a word, he wheeled and stormed from the room.

"Perhaps we should take a break," Ellen said as she followed her client out the door.

I looked at *Inquirer* attorney, Sam Klein, who seemed about to burst with laughter and said, "Shit happens." I turned to the court reporter and said, "That's off the record."

• • •

As noted above, in 1983, *Inquirer* reporter Dan Biddle wrote a hard-hitting series about corruption in the Supreme Court. Justice McDermott was the subject of some of the articles. Jim Beasley started a libel suit against the *Inquirer* in the Court of Common Pleas of Philadelphia County. For years, McDermott had been a Judge on that bench which he now supervised as a Supreme Court Justice. The suit resulted in a six million dollar jury verdict against the *Inquirer* in 1990. McDermott died in 1992, but his estate insisted on continuing the suit for alleged damage to his reputation. The trial Judge recognized that the verdict was fatally flawed and ordered a new trial in 1993. In 1994, the Superior Court agreed with the trial Judge that a new trial was necessary if the estate persisted with the lawsuit. On appeal to the Supreme Court in 1996, that Court predictably ruled in favor of their dead colleague. They reversed the Superior Court as well as the Court of Common Pleas and remanded the case to that Court for a further hearing. The lower Court then entered rulings on the original verdict, again against McDermott, which rulings were once again appealed. As of 2003, the appeal has been pending before the Supreme Court for more than two years.

During this period, Richard Sprague, represented by Jim Beasley, won a thirty-four million dollar libel verdict against *The Philadelphia Inquirer*. Following appeal after appeal, it was finally settled. The *Inquirer*, it is said, paid twenty-four million dollars. I remember seeing *Inquirer* Executive Editor Gene Roberts in the hall outside the courtroom during the trial talking to Stu Ditzen, one of his reporters. Gene was lamenting the fact that it was his seventeenth day as a witness under cross-examination by Beasley. I told Gene he had to be able to take a joke. Prior to the trial, I had written Gene and told him that he was about to "get his ass handed to him." I knew the trial Judge, Charlie Mirarchi, from Judicial Inquiry and Review Board days. Mirarchi hated the print media for exposing that while he was Chairman of the Hearing Committee of the Board on the Larsen case, he was negotiating with Ed Mezvinsky, State Democratic Party Chairman, a partner of Larsen's attorney, Marvin Comisky, for backing for a vacant Supreme Court seat. Mirarchi's permitting Beasley to cross-examine Roberts for an unheard of seventeen days proves my point.

The Larsen libel suit against the Inquirer paved the way for numerous libel lawsuits by Judges against the print media. Such lawsuits by Judges in their own court systems would have, in the past, been considered unseemly, if not unethical. Larsen showed the way and others followed.

This eighteen-year saga of lawsuits cost the *Inquirer* millions of dollars in legal fees not to speak of verdicts and settlements paid. Years later, in a 1996 *Inquirer* article, Editor Max King was quoted as saying the *Inquirer* would not settle the McDermott case.

King said:

> *"This is the strongest imaginable public official case. If we can't publish these stories, we can't cover City Hall, Harrisburg, Washington or the local dogcatcher."*

As the new millennium turned, it was clear to everyone that the corporate overseers of the *Inquirer* had made the decision not to cover City Hall, Harrisburg or Washington. The dogcatcher was still fair game.

The *Inquirer* was not the only newspaper intimidated by the libel suits. The smaller dailies got the message. The publisher of *The Bedford Gazette* said it best when he told me, "Bob, one libel suit would put us out of business."

There was a tragic human side to these libel suits. At the McDermott trial, Dan Biddle was called as a witness. Lanky, bearded and brilliant, Biddle was an idealist. He believed in our system of government and thought his journalism would end the misfeasance and malfeasance that was becoming so apparent in the courts. When he was writing the series **Above the Law**, we shared many cups of coffee and many hours talking about the Supreme Court Justices slouching toward Gomorrah. His favorite expression was from the movie *Chinatown* that, "It is hard to tell what is going on." He was brutalized on the witness stand. More devastating to his psyche, he couldn't believe Justice McDermott, a Supreme Court Justice, would commit perjury on the witness stand. At the end of the trial, Sam Klein told me that Dan was a broken man. He could not cope with the mendacity permeating the judiciary. He had finally come face to face with overwhelming evil and his faith was shattered.

A $750,000 FIX

January 28, 1987

Life was becoming unbearably hectic. I would finish one problem only to have to address another. Or, most of the time, I'd address two or three problems at the same time while trying to maintain a law practice. The appeal with Levy over the cable stock, now in the Superior Court, had been briefed and argued. My lawyer, Bill O'Donnell, had asked me not to attend the argument in Superior Court, and I acceded to his request. Why he asked was a mystery.

After the argument, he reported that he was sure we would win. The law was clear that both attorneys had apparent authority to reach a settlement and bind their clients.

The three-Judge panel of the Superior Court filed an unsigned Opinion on January 28, 1987. I just couldn't believe it! They did not deal with the merits. On their own, without the issue being raised, briefed or argued, the Panel found that the (unnecessary) Motion for Post Trial Relief filed by Bill O'Donnell on October 25th was not timely filed and for this reason alone, dismissed my appeal. The law is clear. The Rules are clear. A case can only be decided on the issues raised by the parties in the lower court. All lawyers know: Raise it or waive it.

This same Superior Court had recently ruled that once a timely Motion for Post Trial Relief has been filed, no further Motion is necessary no matter what subsequent filings in the lower court.

In *Surrick v. Surrick,* I had appealed an outlandish support order for Jean, who was living at Kenmore Wood, a twenty-nine-room house, by herself. I dug it out and found that in part of that Opinion, the panel of the Superior Court held:

"As part of this argument, Appellant also contends that the lower court erred in ordering appellant to maintain the marital residence of the parties in which appellee resides. We note, however, that appellant has failed to raise this issue in the lower court; therefore, we must conclude that appellant has waived his right to address this issue on appeal."

Bill O'Donnell was my lawyer in *Surrick v. Surrick.*

Bill Cherry, who would use every opening he had, never raised the issue. Why? Perhaps he knew something. Maybe he knew that raising that argument in public would kill it. It would not stand scrutiny of a public courtroom full of lawyers waiting their turn. If he had raised it, O'Donnell would have been forced to demolish it.

There was a common Judge on both Surrick cases — Judge Olszewski. My anger and frustration knew no limits. I remembered that Sam Klein had told me that by chance he was sitting next to Olszewski on a plane, and Olszewski expressed his dislike of me because of my criticism of Justice Larsen. Like a thunderclap, it struck me. Olszewski was about to turn seventy, the mandatory retirement age. Larsen controlled the appointments to the coveted slots of Senior Judge on the Superior Court!

It was a stealth attack. Larsen's fingerprints were all over the decision. His deal with Levy, sealed by Cherry and Comisky back in 1983, was very much alive.

Meanwhile, one of the numerous lawsuits involving the Levy/Surrick breakup was called for trial. It involved a claim for the unpaid lease on a copier used by Levy and Surrick. Levy testified that "all claims arising out the breakup had been settled." The Judge appointed specially by the Supreme Court to hear the case accepted this and found against me for some six thousand dollars. I was ecstatic. In his greed to avoid this claim, Levy had forgotten my claim that there was an agreement to settle the stock ownership issue. I then engaged Dick Sprague who required a twenty thousand dollar non-refundable retainer. After I paid him, he told me that he had settled all claims with Bill Cherry. I would pay Levy one-half of the proceeds of the sale of the stock and Levy would retain my interest in our pension fund. I was livid. When I told Sprague that federal pension law prohibited this, he backed off on the pension but insisted the stock claim had been settled.

I now knew, for sure, that I was never going to get justice so long as Larsen and his minions on the Supreme Court could reach any case involving me in the Pennsylvania court system.

Shortly thereafter, I began to negotiate with Jerry Lenfest, who was buying out American Television and Communications in Delaware County. He wanted to buy out the Surrick and Levy interest in American Cablevision of Pennsylvania, a subsidiary of American Television. We had a number of negotiating sessions, and finally reached an agreement that they would pay one million five hundred thousand dollars for the interest. Because of the Superior Court decision, Levy received almost eight hundred thousand dollars.

In the mid-80s, Tom Spano introduced me to Vatahn Gregorian, a lawyer from Philadelphia, with whom Spano was doing business. At the time, I was representing Spano in a divorce from his first wife. At one of the meetings where the three of us were together, Gregorian revealed that he had been with Comisky at the meeting with Cherry. He had been a young lawyer, carrying Comisky's brief case. He told me that Comisky, on behalf of Larsen, agreed to protect Levy and help him wherever possible with his Surrick problems, if Levy would, in return, "dirty up" Surrick wherever possible. Levy had been exonerated by the Disciplinary Board on the charges that I had filed for embezzling from our professional corporation. He'd now received this extraordinary payday.

I felt like I was the rabbit in a shooting gallery.

SOMEONE HAS IT ALL WRONG

July 1987

"Mr. Surrick, it's Mark Lichty on line three."

"Do I know him?"

"I don't think so. He says he's with something called Common Cause."

"Okay, I'll take him."

"This is Bob Surrick, Mark, do I know you?"

"No, we haven't met but I know a great deal about you. I am the chair of Common Cause/Pennsylvania."

"Is that good or bad?"

"Actually, it's good."

I later learned that Common Cause was a national government reform group started after the Watergate scandals of the 1970s. Lichty was chairman of the Pennsylvania chapter.

He told me, "I'm calling to see if you will accept our nomination for our 1987 Public Service Achievement Award. We give the award annually to the person in Pennsylvania who has done the most to bring about reform in government. We think your efforts to bring about judicial reform have shown great courage and you have made a difference."

"Mark, I'm flattered beyond words. What do I have to do?"

"Our annual meeting is on July 18 at Dickinson College in Carlisle. We'll make the presentation at about four p.m. Just bring yourself, and anyone else you'd like."

"Mark, I'm honored, and I will be there. I look forward to meeting you."

On July 17, second wife Bobbie, my Craig, her Craig and her elder son, Eric, drove with me to Carlisle. We stayed with her parents at their home in Plainfield, several miles west of Carlisle. The next day, at four p.m., we arrived at Dickinson College.

Mark Lichty introduced me to the forty or so people in attendance, made the presentation of the award, and asked me to speak.

I looked over the group and began:

"Ladies and gentlemen, in May of 1983, the Judicial Inquiry and Review Board, the constitutional body having oversight responsibility with regard to the conduct of Justices and Judges in the Commonwealth of Pennsylvania, voted to dismiss formal charges against Supreme Court Justice Rolf Larsen. The Board's five-Judge majority, voting in lock-step, did so in spite of the fact that Justice Larsen was clearly guilty of racial slurs, engaging in political activity to unseat Justice Nix in order to increase his opportunity — based upon seniority — to become Chief Justice of Pennsylvania, and seeking political favors for his cronies from people in public office.

At that time, I stated publicly that this failure of the judicial accountability process signaled Pennsylvania's entry into the judicial dark ages. I stand here today to tell you, with regret, that my prophecy was accurate. We have entered into an era where Judges are wielding the power of judicial office as a weapon to silence their critics. Worse yet. Judges, through the Disciplinary Board, now have a potent political weapon to intimidate lawyers.

Let me explain. It was in 1983, as a member of the Judicial Inquiry and Review Board, I voted for Justice Larsen's removal from the Supreme Court. Because of that vote, two months later, Justice Larsen filed a complaint against me with the Disciplinary Board of the Supreme Court of Pennsylvania. The complaint has been hanging over me for four long years. The charges are spurious and without basis in fact or law. Although the charges against me arise out of my service on the Judicial Inquiry and Review Board, that Board has never registered a complaint about anything I did during the four years I served.

Based solely on Justice Larsen's complaint, I am charged with revealing matters about the Larsen hearings, which were already in the public arena. In a Kafka-esque atmosphere, I have had to defend myself while being denied access to the records of the Larsen hearing, which officially never existed, and which would prove the charges false. I have had to defend myself before the Disciplinary Board's panel of lawyers, all of whom practice in the Supreme Court of Pennsylvania, which many believe to be controlled by Justice Larsen, in league with his three Allegheny County colleagues on that court.

Lastly, I have to defend my license to practice law when the matters I am charged with have nothing to do with the way I practice law, but in fact, arise out of my unpaid service on a statewide Board at the request of the Governor of Pennsylvania. The only problem I had in voting for Justice Larsen's removal was being a lawyer. Fortunately for them, the other two members of the Judicial Inquiry and Review Board who voted for Justice Larsen's removal are outside his reach since one works for the federal government and the other is a Pittsburgh industrialist, both non-lawyers.

However, I did not come here today just to talk about Bob Surrick, or Justice Larsen. What happens to me, or to him, is not important to the over-all. The principles are bigger than either of us.

After observing first-hand the failure of the Judicial Inquiry and Review Board to investigate and recommend discipline where judicial misconduct was obvious, I felt my first priority was to educate the public about the Board, its functions, and, most of all, the pernicious effect of the cloak of secrecy under which it operates. I began to write extensively, and newspapers began to regularly publish my commentary. Twice, I have testified before the Senate Judiciary Committee and once before the House Judiciary Committee, urging reform of the judicial accountability system.

There is legislation presently pending in both the Senate and the House, which would at least partially open the Board to public scrutiny. Senate Bill One modifies the secrecy requirements and changes the composition of the Board to end domination of the board by Judges who, sadly, have adopted a 'circle-the-wagons' mentality and refuse to find fault with their brethren.

I need not tell you what it was like, as a practicing lawyer, and as a member of the Board, to sit across the table from five Judges in whose courts I have to practice, and tell them I disagree with their policies.

Unfortunately, Senate Bill One has structural flaws. While the stated intent of the Senate and House Judiciary Committees is laudable, and I can testify that while these legislators are now aware of the problems in the judiciary and are committed to correcting them, the passage of Senate Bill One will only make matters worse.

I have proposed to the House and Senate Judiciary Committees the Surrick Plan for the creation of a strong and independent Chief Disciplinary Counsel in Pennsylvania, with oversight responsibility for both lawyers and judges. Senator Jubilier, chairman of the Senate Judiciary Committee, has indicated interest in this proposal and has referred it to his committee's legal staff for review. It therefore appears that while progress is slow, progress is being made and that judicial and attorney accountability systems may ultimately be reformed.

That brings me to what I really want to talk about. Following the Judge-dominated Board's vote, dismissing the charges against Justice Larsen, he initiated a lawsuit in the Court of Common Pleas of Allegheny County, his home county, against *The Philadelphia Inquirer,* the *Pittsburgh Post-Gazette,* various editors, reporters, and me. This litigation has been dragging on since 1983. When Justice Larsen didn't like what Senior Judge Williams did in dismissing most of his libel lawsuit, he petitioned for his removal, claiming that Judge Williams was biased and prejudiced. Bear in mind that Judge Williams is a respected Senior Judge whose paycheck, and future assignments are controlled by the State Court Administrator and the Chief Justice, a colleague on the Court upon which Justice Larsen sits.

In point of fact, Justice Larsen is using the court system over which he has the responsibility for oversight, to silence his critics in the news media and to intimidate the Judge hearing the case. If this were an isolated case, I would say that we have the misfortune of putting up with a Justice who has no regard for the appearance of impropriety, and that there is no general over-riding public concern to be addressed. However, this lawsuit is not an isolated case.

Supreme Court Justice McDermott is presently suing *The Philadelphia Inquirer.* Judge McEwen of the Superior Court is presently suing *The Philadelphia Inquirer.* Judge DeSalle of the Superior Court is suing *The Pittsburgh Post-Gazette.* Judges Prattis and Durham are suing the *Philadelphia Daily News.* Judge Avellino is suing the *Inquirer.* Justice Larsen has set the example and many have followed.

These lawsuits have had a chilling effect upon not only the newspapers that are being sued, but on other newspapers that have now become reluctant to print criticism of Judges. I have seen threatening letters from Justice Larsen to the *Delaware County Daily Times* and *The Harrisburg Patriot-News.* I can tell you that the op-ed page editor of *The Philadelphia Inquirer* has rejected material, which I have recently submitted, even though he admits that the material is appropriate for publication, and is timely. He said that my articles were not being published 'because of the lawsuits.' If that is not chilling the press, I don't know what chilling is!

Worse yet, actual news is not being reported. There was an historic first in Pennsylvania that has gone essentially unreported. At least three bar associations, the Bucks County Bar, Schuylkill County Bar, and Delaware County Bar Associations overwhelmingly voted Justice Larsen not qualified for Retention Election this fall. *The Philadelphia Inquirer* reported not a single account of these very newsworthy events. These are earth-shattering events that have never happened before in the history of this Commonwealth — and they go unreported in Pennsylvania's largest metropolitan daily.

There can only be one explanation and that is, that the Inquirer has been intimidated.

What reporter or editor wants to run the risk of being sued in a court system presided over by the person suing? Does the Inquirer dare assign Dan Biddle, who won a Pulitzer Prize for his series, **Disorder in the Courts,** who is presently being sued by Justice Larsen, to cover this story? With knowledge that Larsen will sue at the drop of a hat, does the Inquirer ask Pulitzer Prize-winning reporter Ric Tulsky to take the risk of reporting this story? The point is that the very fact of these lawsuits causes the media to alter its normal practices in covering stories thereby depriving the public of full coverage of what it pledges to report.

I asked Common Cause to consider, as a project in 1988, the education of Pennsylvania legislators about this problem. The solution to the problem is legislation amending the Constitution of Pennsylvania along with the coming reform of the judicial accountability system to provide in Article 5, the Judiciary Article, a new subsection 17 which would reiterate the common law rule of judicial immunity and make it part of our constitutional framework and, at the same time, prohibit Judges from bringing libel suits in the Pennsylvania judicial system for defamation, invasion of privacy, etc., based upon criticism of the Judge's conduct while holding office. The trade-off seems fair enough and I urge you to consider this project.

Mark Lichty's letter confirming this recognition, which has been given today, made reference to the 'loneliness of the ethical quest.' I don't have the eloquence necessary to properly convey the gratitude that I feel having been noticed by an organization whose very name is synonymous with public morality, high principles and integrity. Words really fail me. You have given me the strength to renew my efforts to bring reform to the Pennsylvania judicial system so that scandals such as the Roofers Union, buying Judges by the dozen in Philadelphia, will not happen again. Perhaps if Common Cause adopts, as a project in 1988, the issue that I have talked about today, we can march together and make common cause for a better Pennsylvania.

Thank you very much."

To my complete surprise, the group stood and applauded for a full three minutes. While the applause rolled through the room, I pondered the incongruity of the Disciplinary Board trying to disbar me while Common Cause was praising me for what I had done.

Someone has it all wrong!

. . .

Following this meeting, The Governing Board of Common Cause unanimously voted to press the Disciplinary Board to dismiss all charges against me. It wrote that the charges were: *spurious* and *legal harassment of a former public servant. . .Surrick worked. . .in an attempt to achieve a judicial system marked by honesty, integrity and justice. His reward for his efforts has been unconscionable legal harassment which has nearly ruined his law practice, has placed undue stress in his family and cost him much of his personal assets.*

A SHAMEFUL DEAL

Summer 1987

The Disciplinary Board prosecution dragged on—and on—and-on.

Over the summer and into the fall of 1987, I received editorial support and favorable publicity as a result of the Common Cause Public Service Achievement Award.

That summer, the Pennsylvania Bar Association's Judiciary Committee voted to endorse Justice Larsen for Retention Election in November. I had started out believing in the integrity of our legal institutions such as the courts and the bar associations. But no independent group of lawyers could endorse Larsen after what had been revealed about him. Here were lawyers with high responsibility trying to get ahead by turning a blind eye to the obvious. They were in denial about Larsen's numerous betrayals of his oath of office by his cronyism, his racism, his political activity and his overriding ambition. Ambition makes for strange bedfellows.

I called on the Pennsylvania Bar Association to poll all Pennsylvania lawyers rather than to accept a sixteen-member committee's vote as representative of the entire association of thirty thousand plus lawyers. The Bar Association didn't even answer my letter, but the news media began to pick up on the controversy.

Using contacts with county bar associations and invitations to speak at luncheons, I began to build support for an "unqualified" vote for Larsen from the counties. It worked. The Philadelphia Bar Association polled their members and voted Larsen unqualified.

The Philadelphia Inquirer, in a September 23, 1987, article titled,

Bar poll, Larsen unqualified

reported:

Members of the Philadelphia Bar Association have voted overwhelmingly that Justice Rolf R. Larsen is not qualified to remain on the state Supreme Court.... In the results of a plebiscite released yesterday, sixty-one percent of the Philadelphia lawyers voting said Larsen was not qualified to serve, sixty-three percent said they did not have confidence in his integrity, and fifty-nine percent said Larsen failed to demonstrate "proper judicial temperament."

I was really stirring it up. The Union County Bar Association, the Bucks County Bar Association, the Chester County Bar Association and the Schuylkill County Bar Association also cast overwhelming votes against Larsen's Retention Election bid.

Despite the rising groundswell against Larsen, on September 26, 1987, the Pennsylvania Republican Leadership Committee voted to endorse him, a Pittsburgh Democrat! Larsen had made a deal with the Republican Leadership. In return for Republican support for his retention, Larsen would deliver the Allegheny County Bar Association to none other than former Delaware County District Attorney Steve McEwen. McEwen, now a Superior Court Judge, was backed by the powerful Delaware County Republican party, who now had their eyes on a vacant seat on the Supreme Court. Allegheny County, of course, is traditionally a blue-collar, Democratic Party stronghold. McEwen was the Board member who had moved for the dismissal of charges against Larsen and had also voted to dismiss the Semeraro charges without having read the file. If elected to the Supreme Court, he would fit right in.

Larsen's deal with the state GOP leadership outraged the rank and file. Some walked out of the Republican State Committee meeting. One Cumberland County lawyer complained bitterly to the press, *"It's not as if we have Oliver Wendell Holmes here. This is Rolf Larsen."*

The Philadelphia Inquirer headlined:
A divided GOP backs Rolf Larsen

It noted that Mark Phenicie, lobbyist for the Pennsylvania Trial Lawyers Association, managed the floor fight to block the rank and file from overruling the leadership's endorsement. Although not a member of the state GOP committee, Phenicie was all over the floor, demanding quorum calls and delaying the vote until enough time elapsed for the trial lawyers and Larsen supporters to scurry from the room. When a quorum call failed to identify a quorum, the motion to override the leadership died, and the meeting ended with Phenicie yelling out: "Let's go party." Larsen and his PATLA allies had controlled a Republican State Committee meeting.

PATLA would go on to exercise control over legislation and the judiciary on behalf of their agenda which was big verdicts, lots of them, and a fail–safe at every level as Dick Sprague had predicted back in 1983. The genie was out of the bottle.

Larsen's power was on full display in April 1988, when he delivered the Allegheny County Bar Association, in Pittsburgh, to McEwen. McEwen had several years earlier been voted "not qualified" by the same bar association.

I published a long article headlined:

A shameful deal

in *The Delaware County Daily Times,* wherein, in part, I observed:

"Pennsylvania Republicans understand that politics makes strange bedfellows, but most of us never expected to be sharing the sheets with the likes of Rolf Larsen."

The Delaware County Republican Party, in spite of its county bar association having voted Larsen unqualified, stuck with its deal and endorsed Larsen.

He carried heavily Republican Delaware County and won Retention.

RICHARD SPRAGUE REDUX

Spring 1988

In 1988, Allen Ertel, a lawyer and former member of congress from Williamsport, came out of the northern tier of counties to win the Democratic Party nomination for the Supreme Court. Ertel would not play the game; he didn't know how. Several years before, Larsen had cemented a majority on the court and stripped Chief Justice Nix of his power. The victors divided the spoils amongst themselves, creating centers of power to reward, or punish, their friends and enemies. Larsen was firmly in control and used his power openly and with telling effect. It wasn't by chance that Larsen and the Pennsylvania Trial Lawyers Association grew powerful together. For Larsen and the trial lawyers to keep their power, the likes of Allen Ertel had to be stopped.

Under the Pennsylvania Constitution, Judges are to be elected in odd-numbered years. The Ertel primary victory was an election held in an even-numbered year due to a vacancy.

This variance from the state constitutional mandate was brought about by an earlier Supreme Court decision. In 1982, there was a vacancy on the Supreme Court. Philadelphia Common Pleas Judge James Cavanaugh wanted to run. He brought a Declaratory Judgment action asking the Supreme Court if the Constitution meant what it said. The Supreme Court ordered the election to proceed, holding that judicial elections could be held in even-numbered years if the election was to fill a vacancy. Cavanaugh ran, but didn't win. A Common Pleas Judge from Pittsburgh, a Larsen crony, Nicholas Papadakos did.

So in 1988, another vacancy arose, and Allen Ertel had won the Primary on the Democratic side. On the Republican side, Steve McEwen, in spite of all the effort by the Delaware County pols, lost. Larsen was about to lose control of this seat.

Richard Sprague knew where the power was and, as always, drifted toward it. Sprague, the citizen taxpayer, brought suit to void the election as being unconstitutional.

Sprague should have been whistling-in-the-wind being faced with the Cavanaugh case. But this was Pennsylvania. Banana Republic style, just weeks before the General Election, the Supreme Court, interpreting the same constitution, ruled that a Primary Election could not be held in an even numbered year despite its prior ruling six years before, and voided the May Primary result. It was another stunning victory for the legendary Mr. Sprague.

In the election the following year, the Larsen forces got their act together and defeated Ertel in the Primary. They put Ralph Cappy on the Court. Cappy was a Pittsburgh Common Pleas Judge and ally of Justices Larsen and Zappala. He would do what he was told by Zappala whose family money made Cappy's election possible.

We now move to 1989. Charges against Justice Larsen have again been brought before the Judicial Inquiry and Review Board. The Board found that Larsen had improperly intervened in lower court matters to help his friends. The Board ruling was now before the Supreme Court. Larsen needed help. Larsen hired none other than Richard Sprague to represent him. Never mind that Sprague previously had prosecuted him before the Board. The role that Larsen played in having Sprague bring the lawsuit to void the Primary Election in 1988 is unclear, but their relationship was now a matter of public record.

What was clear was that the Sprague thirty-four million-dollar verdict against *The Philadelphia Inquirer* would ultimately be decided by the Larsen-controlled Supreme Court.

Bob Keuch, Executive Director of the Judicial Inquiry and Review Board, filed a Motion in the Supreme Court objecting to Sprague's representation of Larsen. In a secret vote the Supreme Court ignored the obvious conflict-of-interest and ruled that Sprague could represent Larsen. I filed a Petition asking the Court to reveal who voted and how they voted. The Petition was dismissed by another unsigned

Order. The Supreme Court, reflecting entrenched arrogance, had decided that even though Justices are elected in Pennsylvania, the public doesn't have a right to know how they vote on matters of public importance.

In 1991, a constitutional Amendment emerged from the legislature to restructure the Judicial Inquiry and Review Board. The new structure would strip away the secrecy behind which the Board operated and take Judges out of the majority. These were two of the reforms I had been writing and speaking about for ten years.

Larsen and the other insiders were not about to give up their power to protect their cronies from judicial accountability. Citizen and taxpayer Dick Sprague again brought suit, this time to block the public from voting on this reform Amendment. The Supreme Court decided that the Amendment had not been properly advertised and ordered it stricken from the spring Primary ballot.

There would be little dispute in the legal community with the assertion that Dick Sprague approaches representation of a client with righteous fervor. It is good versus evil and he is always on the side of good. But self-interest is always at the core. Take for example, when he was First Assistant to Philadelphia District Attorney Emmitt Fitzpatrick. Fitzpatrick had at one time argued a Federal case before the Supreme Court of the United States on behalf of a Mafia hoodlum named Nardello. Subsequently, Nardello was convicted of a state criminal infraction pushed by First Assistant Sprague who wanted to jail Nardello. Emmitt Fitzpatrick had now become the District Attorney of Philadelphia. Without informing Sprague or Judy Dean, the Assistant DA who had handled the trial, Fitzpatrick appeared before the Judge who was about to sentence Nardello and told the Judge that his office recommended probation. This representation to the Court was directly contrary to the Sprague recommendation in the file for a sentence of three to five years in prison. Sprague became righteously indignant and was the chief witness against Fitzpatrick in the Disciplinary Board proceedings charging Fitzpatrick with conflict-of-interest. But he had no problem prosecuting Larsen before the Judicial Inquiry and Review Board and subsequently undertaking representation of him.

The Supreme Court upheld Sprague's libel verdict, leading to a twenty plus million dollar settlement against *The Philadelphia Inquirer.*

Sprague had come a long way since that night at the Penn Harris Hotel in Pittsburgh.

I WON THE GAMBLE — OR DID I?

October 1988

I had appealed the Disciplinary Board's Recommendation that I receive a private reprimand. Argument was held before the Supreme Court on October 25, 1988 in Philadelphia. Another case held that morning concerned Ernie Preate, Attorney General of Pennsylvania, who had been charged with attorney misconduct by the Disciplinary Board. After that argument, I went to the men's room, and I swear I saw the state's chief law enforcement officer sniffing something. When I walked into the men's room he appeared startled. Within the decade, Preate would be jailed for taking bribes from gamblers while District Attorney of Lackawanna County.

The courtroom was packed. My attorney, Tom Rutter, ably argued my position that the facts did not warrant discipline. Most importantly, he urged that a member of the Judicial Inquiry and Review Board was not subject to Disciplinary Board jurisdiction. That argument was given significant weight when the American Civil Liberties Union and the Judicial Inquiry and Review Board filed friend-of-the-court briefs protesting my prosecution by the Disciplinary Board.

The Delaware County Daily Times offered an editorial titled:

A man's plea for justice

It wrote:

Robert B. Surrick is seeking justice today at the Pennsylvania Supreme Court, of all places.

It was Mr. Surrick's insistence that the Supreme Court itself is not above the law that led to a six-year campaign of charges against him, a campaign that would have destroyed a lesser man.

The Philadelphia Inquirer editorial page also found prosecution unjust. An October 27, 1988 editorial was titled:

Two kinds of justice: A cash-taking judge, a whistle-blowing lawyer

The *Inquirer* pointed out the irony that my court hearing happened to be on the same morning as a hearing involving one of the Philadelphia Judges who had taken a three hundred dollar cash bribe from the Philadelphia Roofer's Union.

The Roofer's Union scandal had erupted in 1986 after the F.B.I. wiretapped the union's Philadelphia office looking for evidence of union racketeering. It turned out the racketeers were Judges. While the feds listened, one Judge after another came into the office to pick up envelopes stuffed with cash. The Business Manager, Steve Traitz, had hit upon a sure-fire plan to keep his union boys safe from jail. Before the investigation had ended, seventeen Judges had visited the office and received cash. How many Judges were slipped cash outside the office is unknown. While this seems unbelievable, even perversely funny, this sad episode sheds light on how the system in Pennsylvania works.

The Philadelphia Inquirer October 27, 1988 editorial contrasted the two cases:

Spectators crowded the ornate City Hall chambers of the Pennsylvania Supreme Court Tuesday morning to hear the first two cases on the court's daily docket. One involved a judge who is accused of taking Roofers Union cash, the other an attorney who is accused of challenging the actions of a Supreme Court justice.

Both cases speak volumes on the status of the state's judicial system and obstacles confronting those who seek to clean it up.

In the first case, attorney James E. Beasley made an impassioned defense of his client, suspended Philadelphia Common Pleas Judge Joseph P. Braig. Mr. Braig, he said, "did nothing wrong" in accepting money from Roofers' Union business manager Stephen J. Traitz Jr. Traitz wasn't trying to influence the judge's actions with an envelope of cash; it was merely a Christmas gift between friends, according to Mr. Beasley. Therefore, the judge should be returned to the bench, though the state's Judicial Inquiry and Review Board is asking the justices to remove the judge permanently.

The second matter on the court's docket Tuesday involved Robert B. Surrick, a West Chester lawyer who for the past five years has been waging an almost single-handed battle against the secrecy that permeates the state's judiciary and its disciplinary apparatus.

Mr. Surrick, a former member of the Judicial Inquiry and Review Board, contends that Supreme Court Justice Rolf Larsen improperly voted in 1983 on an issue in which Mr. Larsen was directly involved — a petition was filed by Mr. Surrick asking the high court to reopen an investigation into misconduct by said Justice Larsen.

Justice Larsen then filed disciplinary charges against Mr. Surrick, accusing him of breaking the inquiry board's rule on confidentiality. That action, according to Mr. Surrick, was a blatant effort to punish him for speaking out and to silence others who might also raise questions about judicial actions.

Despite the rule of confidentiality, Mr. Surrick had not only a right but a duty to "make known a miscarriage of justice," argued his lawyer Thomas B. Rutter. "If the rule of confidentiality is used to punish Surrick, any wrongdoing is hidden in the darkness of the night."

In an ironic twist to the Surrick case, the supposedly injured Judicial Inquiry and Review Board on Monday filed a brief with the court on behalf of Mr. Surrick, noting that disciplining him would have "a chilling effect" on whistle-blowers who challenge the secret actions of the board.

There's a common thread in the cases of Judge Braig and Mr. Surrick.

Mr. Surrick has risked his professional career to take on a system that has fostered a belief among some judges that their office can be used for their personal benefit.

The fact that Judge Braig stands charged with doing precisely that — and defends his actions as entirely proper — starkly demonstrates how pervasive that attitude has become.

The Supreme Court has a chance to send two strong messages in these cases — messages that will encourage those who hope to give Pennsylvania a court system it can be proud of. Mr. Surrick must be exonerated, and Judge Braig must be permanently barred from the bench.

This editorial, written during the tenure of Executive Editor Gene Roberts, marked the sad end of the *Inquirer* drive to bring to public light the problems of Pennsylvania's judiciary. The lawsuits brought by Larsen, McDermott and other Judges would intimidate the *Inquirer* into silence once Roberts departed to go on and become Editor of *The New York Times.* It wasn't only the state's whistle-blowers and lawyers who were "chilled," but also a once-great newspaper.

On March 7, 1989, I was ecstatic when the Supreme Court, in a three to two vote, handed down its decision dismissing all charges against me. Justice Flaherty, for the majority, opined that to allow the Disciplinary Board to prosecute a member of the Judicial Inquiry and Review Board for actions taken as a member of the Board would violate the Board's integrity. This was the exact principle I had argued in the Petition for Extraordinary Relief that the Supreme Court rejected four years before. As I hoped, Justices Nix and Stout agreed with Justice Flaherty.

Justices Zappala and Papadakos dissented, calling me, under the protection of judicial immunity, the moral equivalent of a murderer or cocaine smuggler. Justices Larsen and McDermott recused.

The state's judiciary was not the only thing going to hell; so was my personal life. Even the press was beginning to pick up on the turn my life was taking. In a lengthy, March 12, 1989 feature article entitled:

For a long-embattled lawyer, vindication

Inquirer reporter Katherine Seelye wrote:

Larsen's complaint triggered a series of legal maneuverings that would play out in secret over six years and would nearly result in Surrick's being disbarred from the practice of law.

Over the years, as he fought Larsen, Surrick lost clients, his marriage broke up, and he split with his law partner.

"There's a certain reluctance on the part of people to go to a lawyer who appears to have a problem," Surrick said last week in recalling those days. "They worry that if their cases go to the appellate courts, they wouldn't stand a chance with me."

The good news is that I had been successful in getting legislation proposed to reform the Judicial Inquiry and Review Board. My case, at least, put reform of the system into the public arena, even if the reform would go nowhere.

The bad news is that Larsen protégé, Justice Stephen Zappala, had become a mortal enemy. In his Dissent to the Courts dismissal of the charges against me, he wrote:

*The evidence clearly supports the allegation that the respondent (*Surrick*) breached his duty of confidentiality. What circumstance distinguishes this character flaw from that of Casety, Simon and Stern, all of whom we had no problem disbarring? I can find none.*

Casety was a murderer, Simon a cocaine dealer, and Stern facilitated a bribe. To equate me with these felons clearly demonstrates, at a minimum, an absence of balance and lack of rational judgment on the part of a Justice of the Supreme Court. Zappala hid behind the immunity of his high office to utter bizarre comparisons aimed at destroying a critic. At the same time, a plethora of lawsuits against Pennsylvania's major newspapers was ending investigative journalism of the judiciary. Simply stated, the seeds of tyranny were taking root. If the lawyers and press are silenced, who will tell the people?

Several months later, Judge Albert Acker, of Mercer County, sitting specially on the Larsen libel suit, had the courage to grant my Motion for Summary Judgment, ending, I thought at the time, my legal problems arising out of the Larsen complaints against me. Judge Acker, diminutive in size, and soft-spoken in manner, became a giant in my eyes when he had the courage to tell a Supreme Court Justice he had no case against Surrick. Of course, Larsen appealed this decision to his own Court. But that is another story for another day.

What I thought might be the end was not the end. It was only the beginning.

A SECONDARY MOTIVE?

January 1990

Following the Supreme Court dismissal of Larsen's charges against me and the dismissal of the Larsen libel lawsuit, I decided in 1989 to try and shake up the system by running for the Supreme Court. I sent two separate letters to the lawyers in Pennsylvania, decrying the corruption in the system and asking for their support. These letters brought the Disciplinary Board back to my front doorstep. Once more, I called my friend and lawyer, Sam Klein.

"Is Mr. Klein in?"

"Yes he is, Mr. Surrick, I'll put him on, please hold."

"Bob, how are you? Happy New Year."

"I was doing fine until I received a letter from the Disciplinary Board. They are starting another investigation of me. The letter is dated December 31."

"What for?"

"Do you remember last year I sent a letter, no, two letters, to thirty-thousand Pennsylvania lawyers criticizing the Supreme Court for disregarding the Judicial Inquiry and Review Board's recommendation for discipline for Judges Sylvester and Braig?"

"So, what's wrong with that?"

"They say I violated the Code of Judicial Conduct because I asked for money to run for the Supreme Court. They also claim that it was a violation to speak out on disputed legal issues or cases before the courts."

"Bob, that's bullshit about speaking out on disputed legal issues. Those cases were finished and over with. You had a perfect right to comment on Supreme Court decisions. On the asking for money thing, you remember I warned you about that at the time."

"You did and, after I mailed the letters, I called Bob Keuch, who is the new Executive Director of the Judicial Inquiry and Review Board, and asked him about it. He said it was a violation but it happens all the time. They warn a judicial candidate and if he or she stops doing it, it's over. Only if the candidate does it after warning do they take action. I told Bob I wouldn't do it again, and he was satisfied."

"I remember that. But why is this coming up now when it happened over eighteen months ago?"

"Sam, you remember what John Rogers Carroll always said, that 'Paranoids are the only realists!' Look, Judge Acker threw out the Larsen libel action against me a couple months ago. The Supreme Court stuffed the Disciplinary Board. Larsen lost whatever hold he had on me, so he starts it up again. Can we go to the District Court and stop this?"

"Bob, you know we can't. We've been over this time and again. A Federal Judge is not going to hear a case where there is a state proceeding in progress."

"Goddamnit Sam, this involves speech, the First Amendment, that's Federal Court stuff."

"Bob, it won't fly."

"If I figure out how to get Federal Court jurisdiction, will you take it in for me?"

"Sure I will, but I don't think you're going to be able to manufacture federal court jurisdiction."

"Okay Sam, let me think about it."

Well, I thought, and I thought. Starting with the Nixon appointees, federal jurisdiction was being narrowed with every new decision. I had believed in states rights but there has to be a forum to obtain relief when government begins leaning on people. Hell, there would not have been a civil rights movement under today's standards. Okay, the case can't involve me. Maybe somebody else I thought, and then it hit me. Sam Stretton is a Chester County lawyer who ran and lost every two years. He was running for Judge again that year. He could test the constitutionality of the Code of Judicial Conduct's limit on speech by candidates for judicial office. I called Sam.

"Sam, you're running for Judge again, aren't you?"

"Yes."

"You know you can't make it as a Dem in Chester County."

"It's hard. There hasn't been a Democrat elected in the county for over one-hundred years."

"Sam, the only way you can win is to speak out on judicial issues, raise hell, go after the Republican Judges, raise money directly."

"Bob, you know I can't do that. It would violate the Code of Judicial Conduct. They'd be all over me."

"I think the Code provisions limiting speech are unconstitutional."

"So do I, Bob, but I don't have the resources to fight it."

"How about if I got you a lawyer, a free lawyer?"

"Yes, in that case I would love to go into Federal Court and test the Code."

"Let me get back to you."

Now back to Sam Klein, who agreed that if we could overturn the Code sections in an action brought by Stretton, the same sections the Disciplinary Board was using against me, the Board would have to quit its harassment of me, at least for the present. Sam Klein started suit on behalf of Stretton.

On April 1, 1991, the case was called before Federal Judge Clarence Newcomer. I testified about the Disciplinary Board's letter and how it came about. I explained that, in Pennsylvania, a candidate for judicial office could be prosecuted for speaking out on judicial matters and raising money. I suggested the prohibition was a violation of core First Amendment rights of free speech.

Sam Stretton testified. He made the case that he couldn't risk speaking out about problems on the Chester County bench because of the Disciplinary Board's position. Sam Klein then savaged Robert Davis, Chief Disciplinary Counsel, to the point that Davis had to admit that my letters did not violate the Code of Judicial Conduct.

Judge Newcomer decided that the speech restrictions in the Code of Judicial Conduct were unconstitutional and Stretton could speak out. Following this decision from the bench, Judge Newcomer laced David Donaldson, the attorney representing the Disciplinary Board, about the Board having waited a year and a half from the time of my letters until opening an investigation. He said it "suggested the possibility of a secondary motive." Here a Federal Judge was raising the issue of serious prosecutorial misconduct. It struck me that Newcomer had figured out what was really going on in the case before him.

One week later, I received a letter from the Disciplinary Board saying the investigation would be dropped.

It's a hell of a way to have to defend yourself.

• • •

The Disciplinary Board filed an appeal from Judge Newcomer's decision to the Court of Appeals for the Third Circuit. I was only marginally interested because I had accomplished my purpose with the Stretton case of getting the Disciplinary Board off my back. Newcomer had awarded Sam Klein forty thousand dollars in counsel fees, so Sam had a real incentive in having the Third Circuit uphold Newcomer.

Ultimately, the Third Circuit reversed Newcomer and upheld the constitutionality of the prohibition on speech by judicial candidates in the Code of Judicial Conduct. As a result of the Third Circuit decision, it was not only the right of free speech found by Newcomer that was struck down, Sam's forty thousand dollar counsel fee also disappeared.

Fast forward with me twelve years to June 27th, 2002. On that date, in *Republican Party of Minn. v. Kelly,* the Supreme Court of the United States decided a case challenging the speech prohibition for judicial candidates in the Code of Judicial Conduct, exactly the same as the challenge to the Code by Stretton. The Supreme Court struck down the prohibition as an unconstitutional deprivation of the right of free speech.

Sam's reaction — he had no reaction.

THE POLS LOSE ONE

March 17, 1990

State Representative Matt Ryan had pushed a curious Bill through the House of Representatives that was quickly approved by the Senate. It now required only the signature of the Governor to become law. The Bill provided that a Judge or Justice would not be seventy, the mandatory retirement age, until December 31 of the year in which he or she becomes seventy. What the hell was this all about?

The mystery soon became clear. It didn't take me long to find out that the Bill was really special legislation for Franny Catania, the President Judge of Delaware County, and Jim Crumlish, the President Judge of the Commonwealth Court. Catania and Crumlish were unquestioned powers in the judicial system, and they loved their power and perks. Catania's seventieth birthday was in March and Crumlish's in May. The Constitution of Pennsylvania provided:

Judges...shall be retired upon attaining the age of seventy years.

Catania and Crumlish wanted to hang on as long as possible and used their political clout to get this Special Legislation passed. It was necessary because the issue of mandatory retirement had been litigated before the Supreme Court only a year previously in the case of the retirement of Justice Juanita Kidd Stout. Stout had outraged Justices Zappala and Papadakos by voting in my favor in my disciplinary case before the Supreme Court, on March 6th, 1989, which coincidentally was her seventieth birthday.

Justice Stout wanted to finish her appointive term that ran through December 1990. Murray Dickman, a top aide of Dick Thornburgh, told me that the Petition for Quo Warranto, challenging Stout's right to sit after her seventieth birthday was prepared in Justice Papadakos chambers and delivered to Attorney General Ernie Preate for filing and prosecution. Sam Klein represented Justice Stout before the Supreme Court. He argued that because she was appointed for a specific term until December 31, 1990, the mandatory age seventy requirements did not apply. "Oh yes it did", said Justice Papadakos in an Opinion removing the first black female Supreme Court Justice in the United States from the Supreme Court. Writing for the Court in the Stout case, Papadakos declared that the Constitution said:

in the simplest language possible...that jurists must retire upon reaching their seventieth birthday.

I decided to attend a Common Cause Board meeting to whip up opposition to this ridiculous legislation that clearly violated the Constitution. Son Bart and his wife Tracy happened to be in town. Bart, by this time, was in the MBA program at the University of Texas at Austin. I invited them to tag along to see the old man try and put a screwdriver in the political gears. They agreed and off we went.

I was warmly welcomed to the meeting by Morris Slater, State Chair, and at the appropriate time asked for the floor. As Common Cause is really dedicated to government process issues, I received strong support from the Board when I described the legislative high jinks in progress. I had prepared a letter the day before and passed it out. It proposed a resolution calling upon the governor to veto the legislation.

The Board approved this unanimously. After the meeting, Morris Slater wrote to Governor Robert P. Casey as follows:

On behalf of the Governing Board of Common Cause/Pennsylvania, I respectfully request that you veto Senate Bill 1046.

Article V, Section 16 (b) of the Pennsylvania constitution clearly states, "Justices, judges, and justices of the peace shall be retired upon attaining the age of seventy years." Therefore, SB-1046 is unconstitutional.

The General Assembly does not have the ability to change a person's birth date, and it should not make a practice of enacting laws that violate the commonwealth's constitution. If the General Assembly wishes to alter retirement requirements for members of the Pennsylvania judiciary it must do so by amending the constitution.

After the meeting, I wrote to the major newspapers around the state, enclosing the Common Cause resolution, and was rewarded with supportive editorials.

The Harrisburg Patriot-News on March 17, 1990, asked wryly:
When do you become 70 years of age?
A. On your birthday.
B. On some other day.
C. On December 31 of the year that you turn 70.
Greater minds than our modest collective one are regularly boggled by the doings of the Legislature and the judiciary, so we won't belabor the point further, except to observe that if it has become necessary for the judges to go to the Legislature to learn how old they are, perhaps it is time to entertain earlier retirement for both groups.

The Philadelphia Inquirer asked on March 21, 1990:

What's this bill for? It's unconstitutional and unneeded

It wrote:

The law is clear. Only last year, the 70-and-out retirement age for judges was upheld by the state Supreme Court. State Attorney General Ernest D. Preate Jr. is convinced the legislature's proposal to fiddle judges' retirement is unconstitutional. And within the last week the public-interest group Pennsylvania Common Cause has urged a gubernatorial veto.

On Wednesday, March 28, 1990, Governor Bob Casey did the honorable thing and vetoed this special legislation.

I really had to marvel at the audacity of the pols in trying to pull this one off, which they would have done without a citizen activist who was willing to take on political and judicial heavyweights.

Why did I do it? Why did I get involved? It really wasn't my fight. What difference did it make to me whether or not some Judges got a few extra months to which they were clearly not entitled under the Constitution? Why did I drag my kids along?

There are stock and obvious answers to these questions. First, as a lawyer, I took an oath to uphold the law. Secondly, the Constitution was being abrogated to benefit a few powerful Judges and this offended me. Third, if I didn't do it, who would?

I know that when Governor Casey vetoed the legislation, I felt good, and I didn't bother to examine why. Maybe I should have.

Bart and Tracy left the meeting disquieted by the fervor of my commitment to what to them was an obscure cause.

In the final analysis, what did I win?

• • •

Ten years later, in May 2001, Pennsylvania politicians, through their minions in the legislature, put a Constitutional Amendment question on the ballot that asked:

Shall the Constitution of Pennsylvania be amended to provide that the justices of the Supreme Court, judges and justices of the peace shall be retired on the last day of the calendar year in which they attain the age of 70 years, rather than on the day they attain the age of 70?

The Amendment passed. I discovered that Justice Zappala, who was next in line to be Chief Justice, would face mandatory retirement shortly after assuming that office. He wanted the extra months as Chief Justice that this Amendment would give him, so the Fumo/Ryan led legislature obliged. It was submitted to an uninformed electorate who would not be warned by a thoroughly chilled media. As best I can tell, there was virtually no press coverage of the pending Amendment and no editorial comment.

There is a systemic evil in this Amendment, which the press failed to point out and consequently the voters didn't understand. Now, on each January 1, there will always be twenty or so vacancies from the almost four hundred Justices and Judges in the commonwealth who have become seventy during the prior year.

Under the Constitution, the vacancies are filled by appointment of the governor and require confirmation by a two-thirds vote in the Senate.

As long as anyone can remember, neither political party has ever held a two-thirds majority in the Senate. Over the years, the two parties developed the practice of dividing up the judicial vacancies, giving the names of their chosen to the Governor who would then send them, two-by-two, one from each party, to the Senate, where hearings on qualifications would become an irrelevant sham.

Now, every January 1, the twenty or so vacancies will be packaged and qualifications will become even more irrelevant. Two at a time is bad enough, but twenty becomes a bonanza for the political leaders to negotiate with each other to reward the loyal and the pliable and slip the corruptible into judicial office.

I first came to comprehend the intense need of the politicians, through their toadies in the legislature, to control judicial appointments at a dinner party at the Governor's Mansion in 1981.

They had now moved the process to a new level.

HERE WE GO

Spring 1992

When the Bill to reform the Judicial Inquiry and Review Board was removed from the ballot in 1991, I closed my moribund law office and sailed Maverick to the Exumas. I had married Bobbie in 1987, following the divorce from Jean, and it was not working out. There was no point in staying around. I anchored off Stocking Island, grew a beard, and became part of the local scene.

"You know who I am," I said to the attractive women I was talking to at the bar of the Blue Hole. The Blue Hole is a tikki bar several miles from Georgetown. It was in the middle of nowhere. With a couple of other yachties, I had found my way there and had put myself near two couples who seemed to be interesting. I finally asked the usual to one of the women, "Where are you from?" She answered "Philadelphia." I asked her what she did. She told me she and her husband, who she then introduced, were living aboard in Hurricane Hole Number One at Stocking Island. She was on Sabbatical as a reporter for *The Philadelphia Inquirer*. When I told her that she knew who I was and then told her my name, she said, "Bob Surrick, what in the world are you doing here?"

"Same thing you are. Who are you?"

"Sandy Bauers — and this is my husband Bo. You've been all over the *Inquirer* for years with your fight with Justice Larsen."

It turned out Bo was a journalist also. "I did a story about you a few years back when I was working for *The Bucks County Courier-Times*—about you as a whistleblower getting the Common Cause award for something or other." We then started on the "do you knows." It was amazing how many people we knew in common.

The winter passed too quickly. I left one of the most beautiful places in the world to return to Pennsylvania to answer a lawsuit brought against me. I single-handed north.

The sail up the Bahama chain was uneventful and the crossing of the Gulf Stream was calm. I made landfall at Fort Pierce and started up the Inter-Coastal Waterway.

As usual in the spring, the Carolinas were spectacular. The leaves on the trees were new, and the flowers and water animals with their just-born offspring promised a new beginning. I stopped in Wrightsville Beach and spent a day with Carol Johnson, wife of longtime friend Hal, little knowing that I would become embroiled in their divorce as Hal's lawyer and friend. I was running behind as I reached Morehead City, North Carolina, so I found a marina, tied up, and rented a car to make court in Delaware County the following week.

The lawsuit came about because two years after I bought Kenmore Wood in 1970, I took the adjacent twelve acres under Agreement of Sale, contingent on rezoning for a higher density than the one-house-per-acre which was permitted under existing zoning. It was, in effect, an option. The tract was bounded by Providence Road, Sycamore Mills Road, and Rose Tree Road and was owned by Charlie and Verral Leedom. I wanted to control the development of this land next to the house and grounds I loved so much and hoped to make a dollar doing so. I filed a challenge to the zoning ordinance. I alleged that it was exclusionary in that it completely excluded apartments and townhouses. I hoped to ride the tide of Supreme Court decisions that dealt with exclusionary zoning that de facto kept the suburbs white and the cities black.

In 1979, the Pennsylvania Supreme Court, in an Opinion written by Justice Nix, decided that the Upper Providence Township zoning ordinance was unconstitutional and ordered that multi-family zoning be permitted on this site. I then sold the Agreement of Sale, which I had with the Leedoms, to local developers Tom and Vince Spano. The Spanos wanted the Leedoms to take back a mortgage for the full sale price. For tax reasons, the Leedoms agreed but only if Jean and I would guarantee the mortgage. I agreed. That was a very bad decision.

The Spanos started to build and the interest rate crunch of 1981 hit. They defaulted on the mortgage but continued to build and sell units under forged releases of liens. The Leedoms did nothing to stop this for eight years until they started suit in 1989. Jean and I were named defendants in the lawsuit because of the guarantee we had signed.

The case was called for trial before Judge Harry Bradley. My attorney was Tom Rutter, who had been representing me in the Disciplinary Board proceedings and the libel lawsuit brought by Justice Larsen. Rutter was recognized as one of the top trial lawyers in the United States. But he and I had been having problems. In preparing for trial, his assistant, Joe Cronin, had all but ignored the statute of limitations defense. I saw red and insisted that the thrust of the defense should be the six-year statute of limitations that had expired almost two years before the Leedom's lawsuit. I also told Rutter that Judge Bradley was owned, lock, stock and barrel by Charlie Sexton, the powerful Republican leader in Delaware County, who had put Bradley on the bench. Sexton thought I was responsible for his indictment in the early eighties for election fraud and had vowed that he "would not be happy until he saw me on a slab in Cavanagh's morgue." Bart Cavanagh, always looking for advantage, had become close to Sexton and related Sexton's remark to me. Rutter told me, "Don't worry, it is a jury case and he can't hurt you there."

When the case was called for trial, the Leedom attorney called me on cross-examination to try and make his case against the Spanos. After another witness, the Leedom attorney rested. Tom Rutter then moved for dismissal of the case against me. After back and forth with Judge Bradley in open court, the Judge said he thought the claim against me was barred by the statute of limitations but he would "think about it over the lunch hour." After lunch, the Judge asked to see the attorneys in his chambers. A discussion took place for about twenty minutes. When Rutter emerged, he picked up his papers and told me to leave the courtroom. "Bradley is going to decide in your favor, let's go."

"Not on your life. I have been an attorney too long to ever leave the courtroom without having the Judge put his decision on the record."

"I'm your attorney and I am telling you to leave. If you don't leave, I'm leaving without you."

What choice did I have? I left. We had a heated argument about leaving without anything being put on the record. Tom told me that the case was going to the jury without me, meaning that the jury could not find against me. This procedure was so irregular that I became very apprehensive, but what could I do? If you can't trust your lawyer, who can you trust?

The next day, I drove the rental car back to Morehead City. Aboard Maverick, I continued my northward journey across Pimlico Sound; up the Neusse and Alligator rivers past Oriental and Bellhaven; across the Albemarle Sound; up Currituck Sound; and finally through southern Virginia, and up the South Branch of the Elizabeth River to the Waterside at Norfolk. After tying up, I found a phone and called Tom Rutter just to check in.

"Bob, I have bad news."

"What could be bad?"

"I have an Order from Judge Bradley entering judgment against you for two hundred and twenty-five thousand dollars."

"What the fuck are you talking about," I screamed into the phone, drawing stares from a half dozen passersby.

"Bob, I can't explain it. It makes no sense. The Order says it is molding the verdict, but there is no verdict against you."

"The fucking case was fixed! You and I both know it! Bradley admitted to you that the statute of limitations had run out. I'm beside myself! Goddamit, Tom, file a Motion for Post Trial Relief."

"Don't worry, I'm going to take an appeal to the Superior Court today."

Hearing this, I really lost it.

"Jesus Christ, Tom, you can't appeal to the Superior Court. You have to first file a Motion for Post Trial Relief in the lower court and give the lower court a chance to correct the mistake."

"You're wrong, Bob."

"Don't fucking tell me I'm wrong. Read the fucking rules. Goddamnit, Tom, read the fucking rules. I can't talk any longer, or I'll say something I'll regret. I'll call back at five o'clock. Please be there."

As I hung up, I knew my worst fears had been realized. No one will ever know how hard it is for an attorney of my ability to have to sit and listen to my attorney try to tell me he's right when I know he is wrong, and my money is at stake. Why was this experienced trial lawyer seemingly unaware of the basic Rules of Civil Procedure? I thought about his not focusing on the statute of limitations defense. I also thought about his suggesting an appeal to the Superior Court that would be dismissed because the Rules require a Motion for Post Trial Relief to be decided before an appeal to the Superior Court can be filed. Why would he do that? He had to know that when the improper appeal was dismissed, the ten day period for filing a Motion for Post Trial Relief would long since have passed and the judgment against me would stand. What the hell was going on? I thought about his leaving the courtroom without having an Order entered in my favor that set this chain of events in motion. I thought about Tom being a Judge Pro Tem appointed by the Supreme Court — Larsen's Court, and I remembered John Rogers Carroll always telling me "paranoids were the only realists."

At five, I called back, and Tom conceded that I was right, that a Motion for Post Trial Relief had to be filed in the lower court before Judge Bradley. He read me the one sentence Motion he intended to file and I blew again.

"Jesus fucking Christ, Tom, Rule 223 requires you to put specific reasons in the Motion. That Motion will be summarily dismissed."

"No, the Rule doesn't," Tom replied.

"Tom, read the fucking Rule — right now — while I'm on the phone."

"Okay, I'm reading it. You're right, Bob. I'll prepare a new Motion and file it."

"You will not file it until I read it. I'll call tomorrow."

The next day, I called from Solomons Island in southern Maryland, a day's sail below Hartges Boatyard on the West River just south of Annapolis, where I intended to leave Maverick. The Motion contained the necessary allegations. I told Tom I would be in his office in two days.

When I went to Rutter's office, I was dumbstruck to find that Judge Bradley had already dismissed the Motion for Post Trial Relief without briefs or oral argument. His Order was clearly and specifically in violation of Rule 223 of the Pennsylvania Rules of Civil Procedure, which requires the filing of briefs and oral argument in the lower court before the Court makes a decision on the Motion. I had never been faced with a Judge just ignoring a clear and unambiguous Rule of Civil Procedure. This betrayal of the Rule of Law made me crazy.

"Tom, you and I both know that the fix is in."

"Bob, I can't disagree with you."

"File an appeal to the Superior Court. I am being forced to go where I don't want to go. The sons-a-bitches know no limits. Tom, it's a fucking war where the Rules mean nothing. File the goddamn appeal. I'll talk to you later," I hurled over my shoulder as I walked out of his office, forever distrusting him, the court system, and the Justices and Judges in it.

Rutter filed the appeal. At the same time, I filed a Motion to Recuse purportedly seeking to disqualify five Judges on the Superior Court. The real purpose of the Motion was to alert all fifteen Judges on the Superior Court that this was no ordinary case. My reasoning was that they all couldn't be crooked.

I wasn't going to let Judge Bradley off the hook. His betrayal of his oath of office had to be called to the attention of his brethren on the bench. I fired off a letter to Judge William Toal, now President Judge of Delaware County, with a copy to the other Judges. I wanted my brother Barclay, who hadn't spoken to me in years, to know what was going on. When Bradley filed his almost laughable Opinion, I again wrote to Toal. When Judge Toal responded, I hit him again with another letter calling into question the irregular procedures taking place in his Court. These letters accurately reflect Bradley's clumsy efforts to fix the case and my anger at what had happened.

The hell of it was that I was right about what would happen. The Superior Court did look at the case carefully. I later found out that because the entire court knew that this was no ordinary case, it forced the three-Judge panel to play it straight. Because there was no legal doubt about the statute of limitations defense, they had to reverse Bradley and enter judgment in my favor. I was off the hook on a two hundred and twenty-five thousand dollar verdict.

But the Motion to Recuse, which accused Judge Bradley of fixing this case and Olszewski of fixing the Levy case, resulted in more trouble than I have ever had in my life.

PREPARING FOR THE GOOD RUN

Fall 1992

Back from the Exumas, I sensed trouble on the horizon. The Motion to Recuse was bound to cause problems. Publicly accusing Judges of fixing cases is high-risk territory. Retaliation would surely come. Knowing I had to get to the high ground, and firmly believing I had a responsibility to follow through on my previous efforts for judicial reform, I approached Common Cause about the obvious problems with the Pennsylvania judiciary, particularly the Supreme Court. Common Cause welcomed me with open arms, elected me to the Board, and made me chair of the Judicial Reform Task Force. I had a forum!

Supreme Court Justice Larsen was again in the news. This time he had been charged by the Judicial Inquiry and Review Board with improper contacts with lower court Judges about matters in which either he or his allies had an interest. Back in 1986, Larsen had contacted Allegheny County Common Pleas Judge Eunice Ross. He sought to influence Judge Ross on behalf of attorney James Ashton, a crony. To motivate Ross about the case before her, he suggested there was talk on the street that she was guilty of judicial misconduct concerning another matter. If Larsen felt Ross, or any other Judge, was guilty of misconduct, he was obliged by law to report it to the Judicial Inquiry and Review Board. Instead, he tried to leverage Ross. An angered Ross filed a complaint against Larsen in September 1987, with the Judicial Inquiry and Review Board. Fortunately for Judge Ross, when she telephoned the

United States Attorney for the Western District of Pennsylvania, and told him of Larsen's intervention, he made notes of the conversation.

Another Judge, Emil Narick, then came forward and testified about four separate occasions when Larsen asked to meet Narick outside of Narick's chambers and improperly intervened in cases before Narick. Narick kept no notes and unfortunately, told no one about these contacts. The Board dismissed the Narick accusations because of lack of corroboration. The Ross charges were a different story. The U.S. Attorney came forward with his notes to corroborate Ross and her complaint stuck.

Realizing that my Motion to Recuse had accused Larsen of intervening (fixing, if you will) in the Spano/Leedom case with Judge Bradley, and in the Levy litigation with Judge Olszewski, I saw a significant defense to possible Disciplinary Board charges on my Motion to Recuse. I had accused Larsen of intervening in two cases involving me. JIRB had found that this is exactly what he did in another case independent of mine. Larsen's pattern was clear.

Unfortunately, *The Philadelphia Inquirer*, under siege from the lawsuits by Justices Larsen, McDermott and other lesser judicial luminaries, began to waffle on coverage of the judiciary. Veteran investigative reporters were jumping ship. Three of the best reporters who dealt with corruption issues, Bill Marimow and Ric Tulsky (both Pulitzer Prize winners), and Wally Roche, felt the chill and went to the Baltimore Sun. Emilie Lounsberry, who on her best days could only deal with press release hand-outs, was now attempting to cover the expanding judicial corruption story. On September 15, 1992, Lounsberry filed a story entitled:

Lawyer asks Pa. Court to reveal votes

She wrote:

In a move that would give the public a better view of the decision-making by the state's highest court, the Pennsylvania Supreme Court was asked to disclose how each justice votes in all public rulings.

Lounsberry, however, missed the point of my demand that the Court reveal its votes. A hard-hitting story would have focused on the incongruity of elected Justices refusing to reveal how they vote. Instead, she mushed around in defense of the Court, writing:

...frequently, the court rules 'per curium,' a legal term meaning simply, 'by the court.' Such rulings do not, as a matter of court policy, specify exactly how each justice votes.

The pot began to boil over in October 1992. The Supreme Court voted two votes to one (with four Justices recusing), to find Larsen guilty of improperly communicating with lower Court Judge Eunice Ross, and decided he should be censured. Justices Zappala and Cappy, former allies and protégés of Larsen, saw with his demise increased power in their hands, so they joined forces to plunge the dagger into Larsen's heart. Ironically, Zappala's and Cappy's votes had nothing to do with their concern about Larsen's interventions. Pennsylvania Supreme Court Justices improperly intervene all the time. It was a power play, pure and simple.

This same October, spurred by the legal profession's universal dislike of mandatory continuing legal education, I filed a Petition to the Supreme Court calling upon the continuing legal education program to apply to Judges as it did to lawyers. The Petition was subsequently denied, again, by unsigned Order, but I made my point.

Instead of giving serious treatment to the issue of mandatory continuing education for Judges, Lounsberry wrote a cutesy article on December 9, 1992, titled:

Court: Judges can cut lawyers' ethics classes

It began:

Judges in need of ethics classes?
Nah, the state Supreme Court has ruled.

In-depth coverage of the issues and the willingness to dig up and report misfeasance, malfeasance, and outright criminal conduct by public officials by the *Inquirer* under Gene Roberts was history.

LARSEN BEGINS HIS FALL

October 1992

To his everlasting regret, I'm quite sure, Justice Larsen responded to the censure by filing a Motion to Recuse Justices Zappala and Cappy. If he could cause Zappala and Cappy to recuse, the vote to censure him would be reversed. It would leave standing Justice Papadakos, the only vote in his favor. Six Justices would have been wiped out.

In a remarkable revelation into his inner psyche, Larsen alleged in his Motion to Recuse that Zappala and Cappy were trying to sabotage his right to one day become Chief Justice. It eerily echoed Larsen's 1981 statement to me at the Governor's Mansion that, "I would be Chief Justice but for that nigger."

In his Motion attempting to recuse Zappala and Cappy, Larsen, among other things, charged that they were "fix artists" who "specially steered" cases through the Supreme Court. It was an astounding charge from a Supreme Court Justice about fellow Justices.

He went on to allege, among other things, that Justice Zappala had been fixing cases to the benefit of Zappala's bond underwriter brother; that Justice Zappala had helped get bond work for this brother; and that Justice Zappala himself received what Larsen called "indirect kickbacks" from this misbehavior. Larsen alleged that, because he hadn't voted the way Zappala wanted on several decisions, he'd earned Zappala's wrath. For good measure, he alleged that Zappala was illegally recording conversations in his chambers. As for Justice Cappy, Larsen charged that he was no more than Zappala's pawn, that he similarly had it in for Larsen, and had fixed a case with the purpose of hurting Larsen.

Larsen charged that Zappala had reached down and fixed two cases, using extraordinary "King's Bench Powers," on behalf of the cities of Philadelphia and Pittsburgh. Zappala's brother's investment banking firm, Russell, Rea, Zappala, was underwriting municipal bonds for those cities. Specifically, Larsen detailed how Zappala crony, State Senator Vincent Fumo, chartered a politically-connected lawyer's private plane to fly to see Zappala at the latter's vacation home in Ohio. He would importune Zappala to intervene in litigation which threatened Philadelphia Mayor Ed Rendell's budget which would affect the bonds. Zappala, on fact, intervened.

Having been deeply involved with these characters over the years, I knew Larsen's charges were true. I knew for a fact that Larsen frequently intervened with lower court Judges and Justice Zappala had frequently similarly intervened to promote political allies and his brother's investment banking firm.

Larsen then filed a Supplemental Motion charging that Justice Zappala had tried to run him over in front of the expensive and elegant Four Seasons Hotel in Philadelphia. Justice Zappala was not driving but was instead a passenger in Senator Fumo's Mercedes at the time. Only those of us who understood what was going on knew that the Supplemental Motion was a warning to Zappala that Larsen could go public with information about the seamy relationship between Zappala and Fumo.

Who was Vince Fumo? Fumo had first been elected to the Senate to fill the un-expired term of his uncle and mentor, Senator Henry J. "Buddy" Cianfrani, who was removed from office and went to jail after being convicted of racketeering, mail fraud, and obstruction of justice. Funo's father had gone to jail for extortion. On October 25, 1980, Fumo was himself convicted of fraud by a Federal Court jury in Philadelphia. It seems Fumo had been padding the state payroll with "no-show" jobs for the party faithful. Several weeks later, even though a convicted felon, Fumo was re-elected to his seat in the Pennsylvania Senate. He escaped jail when Judge Clifford Scott Green entered an Order finding that the government had failed to prove its case, even though the jury had found otherwise. Fast forward to 2003 when it came to light that Fumo, using his enormous power as a state senator, extorted fifty-seven million dollars from the Philadelphia Electric Company and the Delaware River Port Authority to use for pet projects that he controlled. He also used seventy-three thousand dollars of taxpayer money to pay for meals at the high-end La Veranda Ristorante over a two year period. I never could understand why a Supreme Court Justice would hang out with a sleaze-bag like Fumo, but politics makes strange bedfellows. I also wondered why Judge Green gave Fumo a pass.

The press began to pick up on the long relationship between Zappala and Fumo. An *Associated Press* article of September 12, 1993, was titled:

Justice ruled in pal's cases

and reported:

State Supreme Court Justice Stephen A. Zappala did not disqualify himself from a 1990 ruling where the court declined to hear a child support case involving a close friend, state Sen. Vincent J. Fumo, it was reported yesterday.

The justice's decision came 17 months after Zappala presided at the senator's second wedding, according to the Philadelphia Inquirer.

The child support case regarding the cost of educating Fumo's elder daughter was one of three cases involving Fumo family interests in which Zappala played a role as a justice.

Three days later, on September 15, 1993, the *Inquirer* wrote about the Fumo plane trip to intervene with Zappala on behalf of the Rendell administration. The sub-headline writer obliquely hinted at the real story when he wrote:

It was July 1992. Mayor Rendell's chief of staff arranged an airplane ride for State Sen. Vincent J. Fumo. Soon the court was taking up the city's case

Unfortunately, reporter Lounsberry wrote a weak and somewhat confusing article that didn't dig deeply into what was really happening. The *Inquirer* downplayed what obviously was a major political scandal involving Zappala and Fumo and the fix of a case important to Fumo's Philadelphia interests. In point of fact, the *Inquirer,* still a defendant in the Larsen libel lawsuit, was openly denigrating Larsen's charges and protecting Zappala. It was, as they say in the Middle East, "the enemy of my enemy is my friend."

All of this atrocious behavior merely confirmed what I had been saying for years. What I couldn't understand was the absence of moral and ethical leadership from the legal profession. No one was looking at the betrayal of public trust by elected officials. No one was speaking out about a disgraceful and corrupt Supreme Court.

Using the turmoil as a springboard, I prepared a monograph entitled, **The Case for Abolishing the Supreme Court,** and hand-delivered it to the two hundred and fifty-three members of the Pennsylvania House and Senate. I was well known to many legislators, having testified about judicial reform seven times before the House and Senate Judiciary Committees, and many received me warmly. Others made it clear they couldn't stand me.

In early December 1992, Ernie Preate, Attorney General of Pennsylvania, convened a Grand Jury and appointed two Special Prosecutors, Ed Dennis, former U.S. Attorney for the Eastern District of Pennsylvania, and Jim Tierney, former Attorney General of Maine. They were charged with investigating Larsen's charges that Zappala and Cappy were "fix artists."

The *Inquirer* praised Preate's appointment of the Special Prosecutors. They were strong in their conviction that Dennis and Tierney would do the right thing. It characterized Larsen's accusations as "increasingly bizarre." The *Inquirer* had taken sides! Stuart Ditzen wrote a puff-piece about Justice Zappala that was embarrassing.

I met with Dennis and Tierney in Philadelphia and outlined what I knew. I gave them newspaper articles and documents concerning Supreme Court Justices intervening in lower court cases. I left the meeting convinced that these men would do what was right. Maybe the full sordid and shocking story of judicial corruption would finally come out.

On the way back to West Chester I stopped for a beer with *Inquirer* reporter Fred Cusick to keep him posted on what was happening. He scoffed at my naiveté in believing that Dennis and Tierney would do an honest job. He predicted that they would both go "in the tank" and do what their masters wanted, that is, get Larsen.

I found this hard to believe, but Fred's predictions seemed to have a way of coming true.

THE CANDIDATE

Spring 1993

In the 1992 presidential election, Ross Perot received nineteen percent of the vote both nationwide and in Pennsylvania. For the first time in memory, a third party had credibly challenged the two-party system.

In January 1993, I noticed that the Perot supporters in Pennsylvania formed the Patriot Party to continue the outsider challenges to insider politics. A lawyer named Nick Sabatine seemed to be the driving force behind the new party, so I called him and suggested a meeting.

We met at Sabatine's office in Wind Gap and had a pleasant chat. I pointed out that there was a vacancy on the Supreme Court that would be filled by election this year. I suggested that the Patriot Party might want a statewide candidate to keep its right to minor party status under Pennsylvania's Draconian ballot access laws. He was interested. Soon thereafter I met with other party leaders and quickly found that interest and support was there.

I announced as a candidate for the Supreme Court on the Patriot Party ticket. And so, this life-long Republican changed direction and accepted a nomination from a third party.

I lost no time grabbing headlines. First, I sent out a letter to the thirty-five thousand lawyers in the state asking for support. I outlined where I stood on the sorry state of the Supreme Court and the judicial system. I strongly criticized the twenty-five thousand dollar a year unvouchered expense accounts that the Supreme Court Justices had given themselves. It was, in effect, an unauthorized pay raise and an end run around the legislature.

Next, I sharply condemned Justice Papadakos. He was running for a ten-year term even though he was sixty-nine years old and the mandatory retirement age was seventy. I sent him a letter calling for him to withdraw and gave it to the press. *The Delaware County Daily Times* on March 4, 1993, published an article titled:

Surrick tells justice: Drop re-election bid

They picked up on the Papadakos retirement angle and went farther into my letter to him with the following:

- *Papadakos violated the Code of Judicial conduct when he voted in favor of a decision that will double his pension to $94,000 a year, Surrick wrote.*
- *Papadakos violated a judicial canon which requires justices to hire employees on the "basis of merit, avoiding favoritism," in 1983 when he hired his son, Peter, as a law clerk, Surrick said. Peter is now being paid $79,850.*
- *Papadakos improperly intervened in a 1990 libel suit by fellow Justice Rolf Larsen against the Philadelphia Inquirer and the Pittsburgh Post-Gazette and Robert Surrick.*

By this time, my son Craig, who had computer skills, came aboard full-time, and we were in instant touch with every newspaper in the state. Much like a broken record, on a daily basis, I protested the Supreme Court Justices having voted themselves the unvouchered expense accounts. It paid off when Senator Richard Tilghman and Justice Zappala publicly clashed on the issue at a Senate Appropriations Committee hearing. *The Philadelphia Daily News*, on March 3, 1993, reported:

Supreme Court Justice Stephen Zappala got an earful from a Republican state senator yesterday, but stood his ground and thumbed his nose at the notion of a high court justice accounting for his expenses.

In the last three paragraphs of this article, Zappala was caught in a lie when he defended the Justices' practice of staying at the very upscale and pricey Four Seasons Hotel in Philadelphia. He told reporters the Supreme Court Justices enjoyed a "special rate" of only one hundred dollars a night. The article reads:

After the hearing, Zappala was asked by reporters how to get a Four Seasons room for $100.

"It was a state rate," he said, "given through the court system. Ask them, don't ask me."

The Four Seasons says it offers no government vouchers or rates at all. Single rooms run from $215 to $255 per night; there's a corporate rate of $195.

In the past, we might have said "Liar, liar, pants on fire". By now, this kind of dissembling was routine from our highest judicial officers.

On March 28, 1993, the Patriot Party met in convention and formally endorsed me as its candidate for the Supreme Court. The *Inquirer*, on March 29, 1993, writing of my Patriot Party endorsement, noted that I told the convention:

"{T)he Supreme Court is out of control.... It is long on greed and short on scholarship."

The reform of the Judicial Inquiry and Review Board I had fought so hard for in the 80's had been removed from the ballot in 1991. Watered down and gutted, it was back on the ballot in 1993. Because the reform had been neutered, I opposed the Amendment and called for its defeat.

Ron Castille, former District Attorney of Philadelphia, was the Republican nominee, and Common Pleas Judge Russell Nigro, Vince Fumo's minion, was the Democrat nominee.

It had been a good spring except for the Disciplinary Board lurking in the background. Judges Bradley, Olszewski, and Cirillo had filed complaints against me with the Board over my Motion to Recuse in the Spano/Leedom case.

For the moment, I held the high ground and foolishly thought I might have the key to real judicial reform in Pennsylvania.

LASHING SURRICK TO THE RACK

The Complaints

March 1993

The Motion to Recuse, which I filed in the Superior Court in the Leedom/Spano case, contained language that I had never before used in a pleading. I used the word "fix" with regard to Judge Bradley. I alleged that Olszewski's decision in the cable television stock case with my former partner Arthur Levy must have resulted from "outside intervention" because there was no other rational explanation. I alleged that Judge Cirillo poked me in the chest with his forefinger at a Philadelphia Bar Association function and accused me of "keeping him off of the Supreme Court."

Before I filed the Motion, I checked the Code of Professional Responsibility to make sure I had not gone over the line. I saw that the relevant sections all required that a representation or allegation must be "knowingly false" before it becomes a violation of the Code of Professional Conduct. While I didn't have any smoking guns, I had a wealth of circumstantial evidence to back up what I believed with all my heart and mind to be true. Certainly, no one could establish that my allegations were "knowingly false."

The shoe dropped in a letter to me dated March 12, 1993, from the Office of Disciplinary Counsel, which spoke of complaints filed against me by Judges Peter Paul Olszewski and Harry Bradley and an investigation into these complaints. A later complaint by Judge Cirillo would be added. All complained about the allegations in my Motion to Recuse in the Leedom/Spano case.

Studying the letter, I noticed the reference number C4, which identified the Pittsburgh office of the Disciplinary Counsel. That said it all. According to the Rules, the office with jurisdiction over an attorney is the office where the attorney practices. I was in District III, the Philadelphia suburbs. Justice Zappala was in Pittsburgh, District IV, and the appointment of John Doherty, who was also from Pittsburgh, as Chief Disciplinary Counsel, was Zappala's. This is the same Justice Zappala who had equated me to a cocaine smuggler and murderer in his Dissenting Opinion from my exoneration from the previous Disciplinary Board proceedings. Also, he had all but identified me by name in his Opinion in the Crime Commission subpoena case. There could be no question. Justice Zappala would use the power of his office not to fulfill his oath of office, but to punish and silence a critic.

Recognizing that the best defense is to go on offense, I filed a Petition for Extraordinary Relief in the Supreme Court seeking to block the investigation. Even though I was working full-time to get on the ballot for the Supreme Court race, and setting up a campaign team, and trying to build a political party across the state, I found time to prepare and file the Motion.

By unsigned Order dated October 14, 1993, during the heat of the Supreme Court race, the Supreme Court, without Opinion or revealing who voted on the Petition for Extraordinary Relief, dismissed it. Another unsigned Order!

I wouldn't let up. I sent a letter to the President of the Pennsylvania Bar Association with the sure knowledge that this very establishment organization would do nothing. I foolishly hoped that somewhere, somehow, somebody would see what was happening and say, "No more."

Finally, on November 22, 1994, Disciplinary Counsel filed a complaint against me, a Petition for Discipline. The Petition added two complaints other than those filed by Olszewski and Bradley. A count was added for the Cirillo complaint. Also added was an allegation that I had improperly disclosed Levy's confidential Disciplinary Board hearing by making reference to it in the Motion. Again, Levy kept his commitment to Larsen to dog me to the end.

The Supreme Court, through its Disciplinary Board, which it appointed and funded, had finally lashed me to its rack where I would remain for the next nine years.

But, for the moment, as Lee Atwater, campaign manager for Bush 41, used to say: "Just keep movin".

I followed that advice.

THE GOOD RUN

Summer and Fall 1993

A big stumbling block lay ahead of the Patriot Party and my candidacy for the Supreme Court.

Under Pennsylvania election law, a minor party candidate is required to obtain signatures representing two percent of the total votes for the leading candidate in the prior election in order to gain ballot access. Even though Ross Perot had received nine hundred thousand votes, nineteen percent of the vote, in the 1992 presidential race, the Patriot Party was still considered a "minor party" under the Pennsylvania Election Code. The authors of this legislation knew exactly what they were doing.

In Pennsylvania, judicial elections are held in odd numbered years when turnout is low. Governors and presidents are elected in even numbered years, when turnout is high. This means that in order to run as a minor party candidate in a judicial election, you need two percent from the higher-turnout prior election. Republican and Democratic Party candidates need only one thousand signatures.

I convinced the Patriot Party to challenge the third party signature requirement on due process grounds in Federal Court. We filed suit.

We drew Judge Edward Cahn, a fair and non-political Judge. Following the hearing, Judge Cahn agreed with us that the Election Code was unconstitutional and struck it down as applied to my candidacy. One week later, Judge Cahn ruled that we needed two percent of the votes for the leading candidate in the last odd-numbered year election, or twenty-nine thousand signatures, instead of fifty-six thousand. What a win! Among the headlines:

Surrick wins round over ballot rules

Surrick gains court victory

To end the charade of statewide election where the voters are blissfully unaware of the qualifications of judicial candidates, and Philadelphia and Pittsburgh control the outcome, I came up with a reform plan. I asked my friend, Tom Comitta, a municipal planner, to use census data to divide the state into seven judicial districts, one for each Supreme Court Justice. The Superior Court has fifteen Judges. There would be two Superior Court Judges elected from each of these seven districts, with the fifteenth moving through the districts as vacancies occurred. The nine Judge Commonwealth Court would have one Judge per district with two swinging through the districts. The districts I proposed were to be approximately equal population and would follow county lines. Statewide voting for appellate court Judges would give way to regional elections.

Armed with a large graphic of these districts, I took to the road in July with the goal of visiting all eighty-six daily newspapers and as many weeklies as possible. I wanted to stir up as much interest as I could, and hit on the idea of visiting the state's newspapers to get "earned media." I would never be able to afford TV ads in the last weeks of the campaign so I had to try to nurture a populist groundswell to have any hope of winning.

Meanwhile, the signature drive was working. To be safe, I wanted to gather approximately thirty-three thousand signatures by August 2 to ensure I made the twenty-nine thousand signature requirement set by Judge Cahn as some signatures would invariably be stricken. On August 1, the Patriot Party members, who had worked tirelessly to obtain signatures, converged on Harrisburg by car caravan, bus, and light plane. We counted, notarized, and packaged the Nominating Petitions, and the next day, I filed them with the Election Bureau. I was on the ballot!

The Harrisburg Evening News headlined:

35,000 sign Patriot Party petition

On August 4, no less than the *Wall Street Journal* noticed what was happening in Pennsylvania and covered our progress with a front-page story.

Over the summer, I visited every newspaper in the state at least once. What wonderful people! They listened to me, and gave me sorely needed ink. Newspaper editors in little towns like St Marys and Punxsutawney and Bradford and Warren listened, liked what they heard, and told their readers about me.

After an interview, *The Bradford Era* headlined:

Surrick says states high court a "disgrace," promises reform

Even some of the larger urban papers, such as *The Allentown Morning Call* and *The Harrisburg Patriot-News*, gave me time and wrote about what I was up to. But I couldn't crack *The Philadelphia Inquirer.* It ignored my judicial reform message.

Meanwhile, the Grand Jury was grinding away in Harrisburg supposedly looking into Larsen's charges that Justices Zappala and Cappy were "fix artists" who "specially steered" cases through the Supreme Court. It was becoming increasingly apparent that the Motion to Recuse filed by Larsen was becoming the vehicle by which his former comrades would destroy him. He had committed the unpardonable sin of an insider going public. Justice Zappala, with the aid of Senator Vince Fumo, and the corrupt establishment that I had been decrying for ten years, had enough of Rolf. Now that he had turned his sights on his colleagues, they finally all agreed: Larsen had to go.

They wouldn't focus on Larsen's charges of malfeasance in the courts. Instead, they discovered he used anti-depressants, and he had used his employees to purchase his medications to hide the fact that a Supreme Court Justice took Prozac. His medications would be his sip of hemlock.

On August 10, 1993, the Republican State Committee attempted to appeal the decision of Judge Cahn reducing the signature requirement from fifty-six thousand to twenty-nine thousand. This gave me additional coverage.

Surrick blasts GOP court challenge to his state court candidacy

Throughout all this hoopla and legal maneuvering, I continued to campaign and continued to receive superb press. The Pennsylvania Bar Association asked me to participate in its process of rating judicial candidates. This was the same bar association that had endorsed Larsen for retention in 1987, and Papadakos this year. I declined—only to get more press:

Surrick spurns state bar review

To make this more delicious, the Pennsylvania Bar asked the candidates for the Supreme Court to speak in Pittsburgh. I was the only candidate who received applause from the lawyers attending.

As if I didn't have enough on my plate, the Disciplinary Board's prosecution was ongoing. I thought long and hard and decided, even though Disciplinary Board proceedings are confidential, I had to take advantage of a little used provision in the Code of Professional Responsibility and waive confidentiality. I called a press conference and blasted the process as political, which was duly reported across the state. Some of the headlines were:

Discipline panel probes Supreme Court candidate

Surrick protests harassment

Patriot Party candidate discloses investigation

Justice candidate says probe political

Candidate wants probe public

I continued my attacks on Russell Nigro, the nominee of the Democrats. Russell Nigro was owned lock, stock and barrel by state Senator Vince Fumo. He was an easy target as one of Vince Fumo's minions. Russell just couldn't keep his foot out of his mouth. I linked Nigro with Fumo at every opportunity.

I found out that Nigro had called lawyers who practice before him and asked them to have their clients release a lien on a piece of real estate owned by Vince Fumo. What's more, when the press called him and asked him about it, he said he didn't see anything wrong with this practice. I wrote the Pennsylvania Bar Association and asked that they reconsider the "highly recommended" rating and threw in five cases where Nigro was entirely too lenient with drug dealers. My press release was picked up:

Surrick attacks Nigro in Supreme Court race

High court hopeful bashes Nigro

It occurred to me that the support I was getting, particularly from lawyers, made the rating system of the state bar association suspect. Was the small committee "qualified" recommendation of Nigro and Republican Castille controlled? I decided to conduct my own poll. *The Harrisburg Patriot-News* reported on September 14, 1983:

Third party candidate polls bar

A long-time critic of Pennsylvania courts; Surrick questions the qualifications of Nigro, a Common Pleas Court judge, and Papadakos, who is seeking retention in a yes-no vote. The Bar Association gave Nigro its highest rating, highly recommended, and endorsed Papadako's retention.

"The Bar Association's endorsements of these candidates is destructive of public confidence and a betrayal of the trust placed in these institutions by the lawyers," Surrick said.

I plowed on from courthouse to courthouse, newspaper to newspaper, radio station to radio station. With no money for TV ads, it was my only hope.

Meanwhile, the attempt by the Republican State Committee to appeal Judge Cahn's decision on the signature requirement was still out there. On October 4, 1993, the Court of Appeals for the Third Circuit heard argument on the Republican Party's appeal of Judge Cahn's Order. I had the growing Patriot Party out in force in front of the Federal courthouse in Philadelphia. Ron Castille was scheduled to appear. I prepped my group to chant, "What's the deal Castille?" It went back to the campaign when Frank Rizzo trounced Castille in a race for mayor of Philadelphia. Castille was a boozer, and he liked guns. On two different occasions, when angered, he had pulled a gun on someone. Rizzo capitalized on these incidents by making his campaign slogan, "What's the deal, Castille?"

When Castille arrived, he was greeted by a booming chant, "What's the deal, Castille?" He turned bright red and pursed his lips as he entered the courthouse. Inside the courthouse, the Circuit Court dismissed the Republican Party's Petition to Intervene. It was not Castille's day. I was on the ballot to stay. *The Harrisburg Patriot News* and *The Philadelphia Inquirer* headlined:

Judge Panel keeps Surrick on ballot

Surrick stays on ballot

Armed with this latest victory, I took to the road with renewed energy. I crisscrossed the state. Pennsylvania is very rural outside of Philadelphia and Pittsburgh and incredibly beautiful in the Fall. To drive over a mountain where the reds, yellows, greens and browns were a riot of color and drop down into a small, neat little town in the valley was memorable. Not all towns were that way. In Frackville, where in 1960, John F. Kennedy had promised to put the coal miners back to work, the mines were still closed and the coal miners' families were hardscrabble poor. In Sharon and Aliquippa, west of Pittsburgh, the steel mills were ghostly still, and the men spent their days in the local taproom. In these run-down towns, I thought frequently of Harry Chapin's *Midnight Watchman*, who *"watched the metal rusting and watched the time go by."*

I loved every minute of it. I felt I was doing something very important.

Life was good!

THE RACE TO THE FINISH LINE

October/November 1993

My car was really getting a workout. I would go west to Erie and then work back along the northern tier of counties, visiting Meadeville, Franklin, Oil City, Clarion, and DuBois. I then went over to St. Marys, Bradford, Tioga, and Sayre. Then I would drop down to Honesdale, Scranton, Wilkes-Barre and Allentown.

The middle and southern loops took me to Reading, Lancaster, Harrisburg, York, Sunbury, State College, Carlisle, Johnstown, Altoona, Uniontown, Washington, Latrobe, Pittsburgh and New Castle. No town was too small if it had a daily newspaper, or a radio station that would give me air-time. Actually, some of the weeklies gave me really good coverage. Editors and reporters greeted me warmly at each stop. Outside the urban areas, the media was open and eager to hear what I had to say. By talking about the domination of Philadelphia and Pittsburgh in state judicial elections, I struck a resonant chord. There is a rock-solid honesty in rural Pennsylvania that contrasts markedly with the cynicism and intellectual effetism of the press in the urban areas. In Pennsylvania's heartland, a reference to "The People's Republic of Philadelphia," would always get a response.

Among the many headlines the rural Pennsylvania press printed about my campaign were:

Supreme Court hopeful stops in Ellwood City
Supreme Court hopeful brings candidacy to Mercer

I left Ron Castille alone because I figured most Republicans would know, since I was from heavily Republican Delaware County, that I was probably a former Republican. Some might then feel they were not being totally disloyal by giving me a vote. One night in Scranton, at a League of Women Voters TV debate with my two opponents, I worked Nigro over unmercifully. I whispered to Castille, "How about getting into the act. I have him on the ropes." Castille, always wanting to appear to take the high road, whispered back, "You're doing just fine." I paid him back on the next question when he went into his law and order act. He bragged about the many convicts he, as District Attorney of Philadelphia, had sent to death row. I cut in to ask him, "How many are white?" In politics, law and order is the race card. I hate it.

It was time to visit the editorial boards of the major dailies. My interview with *The Allentown Morning Call*, the states fourth largest daily, was great give-and-take with journalists who were willing to listen and make up their minds on the facts. I was thrilled when they endorsed me.

The Sunbury Daily Item then weighed in for me, as did western Pennsylvania's *Pittsburgh Tribune-Review*, where Paul Koloski was the Editorial Page Editor.

Then came editor Jake Betz of *The Shamokin News Item:*

Surrick's plan is the answer

Bill Caulfield of *The West Chester Daily Local* voiced strong support.

On October 29, *The Pocono Record* published an editorial:

For Supreme Court, vote for reform

and endorsed me.

I had worked hard on Paul Golias of *The Wilkes-Barre Citizens Voice* and was rewarded by endorsement from that major newspaper.

Denny Bonavita, a bright and caring man, brought *The DuBois Courier-Express* into my column.

The Scranton Times told its readers to take a hard look at the "Surrick Plan."

I loved *The Pottstown Mercury's* ringing endorsement:

For state Supreme Court, vote for Robert B. Surrick

The best part of that editorial was their observation that:

"The most amazing thing about Nigro's campaign is how you can't even see Fumo's lips move when Nigro talks."

That left *The Philadelphia Inquirer* and *The Pittsburgh Post-Gazette,* the state's two largest daily newspapers, for me to tackle. My meeting with the *Post-Gazette* Editorial Page Editor, Mike McGough, and his staff, was cordial and low key. However, it was clear to me that they strongly opposed the "Surrick Plan," calling for regional election of the state's highest courts. Five of the seven Supreme Court Justices were from Pittsburgh. Western Pennsylvania is very parochial. The Pirates and the Steelers enjoy fan support that rivals religious fervor. Governors and senators most often come from western Pennsylvania. More to the point, twenty-one of the thirty-one appellate court Judges come from either Philadelphia or Pittsburgh, and most of them from Pittsburgh. It is a political fact that voters from western Pennsylvania vote for candidates from western Pennsylvania.

Accordingly, the *Post-Gazette* endorsement went to Castille, whose law and order message registered with the white working class neighborhoods of Western Pennsylvania. Of me, they wrote:

"Mr. Surrick is an accomplished attorney who has earned his stripes as a tireless critic of the judicial establishment. But his Ahab-like obsession with reform, however admirable, in our view, isn't a solid enough base for a Supreme Court candidacy."

The Philadelphia Inquirer Editorial Board meeting was a horror show. The paper's unions were about to go on strike, and the Board was on edge. David Boldt, the Editorial Page Editor, was cold, detached, and seemed to be in love with the sound of his own voice. Boldt's effete manner was that of a haughty intellectual. He didn't like the "Surrick Plan." While admitting the Supreme Court was in trouble, he didn't want change. Why should he? Philadelphia had the other two Supreme Court

Justices. It quickly deteriorated into a personal attack when Boldt suggested I was a "zealot." I challenged his label. He went to the dictionary and read aloud the definition of "zealot". He grudgingly conceded that it didn't fit me. I wondered to myself, had I acted like a zealot when I had supplied *Inquirer* reporter Dan Biddle with material which was instrumental in winning the *Inquirer* at least one Pulitzer Prize?

The *Inquirer* endorsed Castille, and dismissed me as follows:

Some may wonder why this newspaper is not endorsing Mr. Surrick, 60, who for years has been a courageous whistleblower on court abuses. It's our feeling that he has, unfortunately, spent too many years in the wilderness, and turned into a zealot.

I thought about what Boldt's predecessor, Ed Guthman, formerly Bobby Kennedy's press secretary, wrote on October 19, 1986:

"Surrick has a passion for justice, public accountability, and ethical conduct… The law is not a game to Surrick."

Who had it right — Boldt or Guthman?

I really thought I had a chance. The press had been good — the timing what with Larsen and Fumo was great, and I had a coherent message. I had garnered more than twice as many newspaper endorsements as my opponents combined. I had the backing of the Perot supporters. I had been all over the state while Nigro and Castille sat in Philadelphia raising money from lawyers who would practice before them.

I didn't have the money for TV. My opponents each spent over a million dollars on TV.

Money won. On November 2, 1993, I received five percent of the vote.

PENNSYLVANIA, LAND OF GIANTS

A Civics Lesson

January to December 1994

Was I wounded or feeling defeated receiving only five percent of the vote in the 1993 election?

No. I thought great progress had been made in articulating the problems with the Pennsylvania court system and the need for reform. I didn't know what reform, if any, was within reach, but I did know for sure that it wouldn't come via a third party. Third parties are valuable in advancing new ideas or pointing out problems but the power for change is through the two major parties.

I made the decision to continue the fight for reform because I truly believed — no, I knew — that our judicial system had been corrupted at many levels.

The first thing to be done was to create a vehicle to keep up the call for reform. Over the years, I had discussions with Phyllis Beck and Ned Spaeth, both Judges of the Superior Court. They had created "Pennsylvanians for Modern Courts", an organization around which groups could rally to address the problems in the judicial system in Pennsylvania. They were gold-plated establishment and totally unwilling to take a strong stand. They thought they could work within the system, which was naive in the extreme. Reformers come and go — the corrupt stay because their stake in the system is greater than the reformers. I had learned over the years that individual legislators did exactly what they were told by the leadership, and the leadership did what they were told by the political power structure. They had a system that suited them and there was no reason to change it. As for the judiciary, simply stated, the politicians and the trial lawyers needed to control the outcome of certain cases at all levels to preserve their wealth and their power.

There is another element of this political power structure that is hidden from public view. They all work together. Political affiliation really is secondary. Power is primary. They have to work together, when necessary, to keep the power in the hands of those who know how to play the game. Insiders like Spaeth and Beck, sense this and, as a result, position themselves as reformers but never directly challenge the real power structure by exposing corruption. They are what I call "feel good reformers," who never accomplish anything worthwhile, while giving the appearance that they are doing something. People like me who are willing to call corruption "corruption" are as dangerous to their game as I am to the power structure.

Being contemptuous of and wanting to needle them, I formed a non-profit corporation called the "Coalition for *Real* Judicial Reform".

I prepared a pamphlet entitled **Blueprint for Judicial Reform** and distributed it to the legislators and the media. I wrote op-ed pieces that appeared throughout the commonwealth. I kept the judicial system under public scrutiny.

Incredibly, the Grand Jury that had been empanelled by Attorney General Ernie Preate to investigate Justice Larsen's charges of case fixing by Justices Cappy and Zappala indicted Justice Larsen. *Inquirer* reporter Fred Cusick was right again! Here was a classic example of politicians from both parties coming together because their control was endangered. Larsen had been very powerful with tunnels to all the power structures. My criticism of him for ten years had blown his cover and his own arrogance had made him expendable, indeed even dangerous, to the network he had been part of for the last seventeen years.

Larsen was indicted and convicted under an obscure provision of the Criminal Code that prohibits the purchase and use of prescription drugs in another person's name.

Talk of impeachment moved from cloakrooms and antechambers to the newspapers. If Larsen had bothered to ask me, I could have told him he was toast. There was no one in Pennsylvania who had greater reason to wish this man ill, but I derived no satisfaction from his predicament. Remember, his downfall came about because he blew the whistle on two other Supreme Court Justices, and if it can happen to him, it can happen to anybody.

The House voted seven Articles of Impeachment. The Impeachment of a Supreme Court Justice received national attention.

What was really amusing about all this was that the legislators suddenly discovered that Justices were keeping votes secret; that they were using unvouchered expense accounts; they were engaging in political activity; and deciding important cases with unsigned Orders. At press conferences they professed shock.

Larsen's sentence after conviction on the criminal charge had included removal from office. This did not satisfy the long knives and his impeachment trial went forward in the Senate.

Meanwhile, the Supreme Court pretended it was initiating reform by doing away with the unvouchered expense accounts, the centerpiece of my 1993 campaign. The good-old-boy system closed around Justice Zappala who, now that Larsen had been eliminated, was the power on the Supreme Court.

I was told that documentary evidence of Zappala's case fixing had been given to the house managers. They ignored it. The legislature was on a mission, and that mission did not include investigating Larsen's charges of Zappala's case fixing. The mission was limited to bringing Larsen down.

To prove they were at the ready, the Court of Judicial Discipline, successor to the Judicial Inquiry and Review Board, piled on Larsen by bringing charges against him.

On Monday, August 8, 1994, the Senate of Pennsylvania, in its massive Connamara marble-lined, domed chamber, began the impeachment trial of classmate, Justice Rolf Larsen.

The Chester County Daily Local saw all this as a vindication of me and headlined:

Westtown attorney gets last laugh as Larsen goes to trial: Surrick's crusade for judicial reform receives validation

It sort of summed up the last fourteen years into two sentences:

...it was Surrick, the Westtown attorney with a personal crusade to reform the state's top court system, who lays claim to first raising public doubts about Larsen's fitness to serve on the court. Larsen took action against his critic, filing a complaint against Surrick with the state Disciplinary Board as well as a libel suit.

On October 4, in an historic vote revealing the corrupt state of affairs in Pennsylvania, the Senate voted to convict Larsen and remove him from office.

Strikingly, he was acquitted on the Article that charged him with falsely accusing Justices Zappala and Cappy of fixing cases. The Senate had found substance to this charge! He was also acquitted on the flimsy charge of misuse of prescription drugs, the charge on which he had been convicted in criminal court. Of the seven Articles of Impeachment, Larsen was acquitted on six. He was convicted only on the charge that he was fixing cases with PATLA leader Richard Gilardi, former Chairman of the Disciplinary Board. Gilardi's testimony that he met with Larsen to fix several of his cases was the clincher. To my knowledge, Gilardi never faced disciplinary action by the Disciplinary Board for his conduct. Why? Justice Zappala now controlled the Board.

In December, Ernie Preate, Attorney General of Pennsylvania, was indicted for selling his office to underworld gambling interests in his hometown of Scranton. In June, he went to jail.

As for the so-called reformers, the so-called honorable journalists, and the so-called moral leaders, they had come down on the side of Fumo and Zappala. The power had shifted but the game was the same.

A VERY GOOD RUN

Spring 1995

The Pennsylvania scene was not far from the last act of Hamlet with bodies littering the landscape. Larsen was down. Attorney General Ernie Preate was in federal prison. Ed Dennis, former U.S. Attorney, appointed as Special Counsel by Preate to oversee the Grand Jury, disgraced himself along with Jim Tierney, former Maine Attorney General, by going in the tank on Larsen's charges against Zappala and Cappy. Ed Dennis saw his reputation permanently diminished when he represented Preate in his criminal troubles. Dennis was accused by the U.S. Attorney of over-billing on Preate's legal fees, which Preate had charged off to the people of Pennsylvania. Zappala was hiding from questions about his involvement with his brother's bond underwriting business and his involvement with Senator Vince Fumo. Fumo was trying to lie his way out of the purpose of his visit to his pal Justice Zappala.

As 1993 came to an end, a number of favorable newspaper articles continued to roll off the presses about me.

Surrick leads good fight for judicial reform

headlined *The Easton Express* on November 9, 1993. The article began:

Bob Surrick looks like a genius these days. Or, if not brilliant, Surrick at least looks like one of the few lawyers in Pennsylvania with guts.

In 1995, there would be two open seats on the Supreme Court, and I reasoned that my name recognition would mean a great deal if I ran as a Republican. I had rejoined the Republican Party and decided to test the waters with an announcement of my intention to run. I was still news. *The Philadelphia Inquirer* wrote:

Ex-Patriot choice seeks court seat

Robert Surrick will seek the GOP nomination. He's been a longtime critic of Pa's judiciary

Playing off the successful national Republican campaign of 1994, I put together a campaign piece with my platform, which I called **Contract for Pennsylvania** on one side. On the other side of my literature, I reprinted some of the favorable editorials I had garnered.

The Supreme Court's bad press continued, this time with Chief Justice Nix taking the heat. The *Inquirer* headlined:

Nix is criticized by U.S. magistrate

The February 10, 1995, *Inquirer* article reported the U. S. Magistrate stated:

"The chief justice's mid-trial talk with a judge and prosecutor was improper."

I had been charging for years that Supreme Court Justices had been improperly intervening in lower Court cases. Here was another example. How many unethical and improper interventions never came to light?

In February, I went to the Republican State Committee meeting, not to seek endorsement (which I would never get) but to engage in guerilla warfare. Bill Winkler, a denizen of the nether world of politics and known for his ability to trash candidates, had signed on to my campaign and went with me to Hershey. Using some supporters from around the state, I sprung a floor motion to adopt regional election of appellate court Judges, the "Surrick Plan". The leadership of the party directed the rank and file to vote "no." The rank and file revolted and the resolution overwhelmingly passed. The convention nominated Sandra Newman and Mike Barasse for the Court.

I threw some punches at Sandra Newman, the wife of a wealthy plastic surgeon who made a fortune doing nose jobs on the Main Line. In 1993, their seven hundred and forty thousand dollar investment had purchased a Commonwealth Court seat. Now, they were trying to buy a Supreme Court seat. *The Associated Press* quoted me:

(Surrick) accused Mrs. Newman and her husband, Dr. Julius Newman, of trying to buy her seat on the high court. The Newman's invested nearly $740,000 of their money in her successful 1993 campaign for the Commonwealth Court.

I went back on the road, criss-crossing the state while Craig operated my headquarters. As always, the Disciplinary Board business was still hanging around.

Winkler, known in the trade as "The Prince of Darkness," was doing his job digging up information about Sandra Newman. He provided me with a smattering of information from the election records of Newman's expensive buy of a Commonwealth Court seat in 1993. We both knew that Sandra was capable of anything in her quest for power, and it was up to us to find it. I knew there was more. Suddenly, Winkler disappeared—he couldn't be found anywhere. As the weeks went on, I suspected he had hit pay-dirt in his research on Newman and the information might have been more valuable to her than to me.

I was getting good press in every town. Without serious dollars, it was the only way to get my message into the public arena.

In April 1995, *The Lewistown Sentinel* and *The Sunbury Daily Item* endorsed me.

The Philadelphia Bar Association held a debate, and I dominated. At one point, I sarcastically asked if the Supreme Court seats were for sale (referring to the mega-dollars the Newmans and others were spending), then I was in favor of auctioning them off from the steps of the capital in Harrisburg and giving the money to the poor. Sandy Newman's face contorted with anger.

While in Pittsburgh, I met with the editorial board of *The Pittsburgh Post Gazette.* They were civil, knowledgeable, and patient. They listened closely, but I knew they would not endorse me. I was not establishment. They wrote:

Also on the Republican ballot is Robert B. Surrick, an accomplished sixty-one year old lawyer from Chester County.... Mr. Surrick has already done a service to the Supreme Court with his nearly two decades of criticism of the court's aloofness and lack of accountability. The question is whether an outsider should become an insider; we think not.

As expected, *The West Chester Daily Local* and *The Allentown Morning Call* gave me a boost by endorsing me. *The Philadelphia Inquirer*, as expected, didn't endorse me. They wrote, rather oddly:

The crusader is West Chester lawyer Bob Surrick, the man who first blew the whistle on ousted Supreme Court Justice Rolf Larsen, and who has leveled frequent, justified criticism of the entire court. No question, Pennsylvanians owe Mr. Surrick a debt of gratitude for diagnosing the high court's woes — its penchant for secrecy, its reputation for political maneuvering, its perceived lack of erudition. But they don't owe him a seat on the court. Moreover, the man whose sailboat is named Maverick is not ready to serve on any team we can think of — certainly not among justices he has blasted for a decade. His value remains greatest as an outsider.

We now see the *Inquirer* and *The Pittsburgh Post Gazette* saying as a matter of policy, that you have to play the game to get their endorsement. Only insiders need apply.

In the Primary on May 16, 1995, Sandra Newman, who spent over a million dollars of her husband's money on the race, was nominated to one of the two seats on the ballot. I received three hundred and twenty thousand votes, twenty-six percent of the vote. I lost the second seat by only eight percentage points to the District Attorney of Lackawanna County, Michael Barasse, who was endorsed by the Republican State Committee and had the party apparatus and money at his disposal.

I had done the best that I could to focus public attention on the judicial system. I felt I had exposed the betrayal of trust and had made people look at it.

To what end?

LASHED TO THE RACK

The Hearing

Spring 1995

While the Primary race for the Supreme Court was in progress, I had my hands full. During the campaign, I kept the pressure on the Disciplinary Board by demanding a hearing before the May 16th Primary. The rules require a hearing within sixty days of the Petition for Discipline, but as usual, the Disciplinary Board was ignoring the Rules. There is something seriously wrong when you're forced to defend yourself in a forum where the Rules apply to you but not to the prosecutor.

The Disciplinary Board finally appointed a hearing committee. I immediately noted that it was designated a "Special Hearing Committee." Under the Rules, there are standing committees of three lawyers who are randomly assigned to cases in their district. Why a "Special Hearing Committee?" I raised holy hell with the Disciplinary Board and was told that all the standing committees were busy. If you believe that, I have some bridges for sale at discounted prices. The only thing "Special" about this prosecution of the foremost critic of the Supreme Court was that he was now firmly in their clutches.

The Special Hearing Committee consisted of Carol Ann Sweeney, Wallace Bateman, and Thomas Gowen. I didn't know any of them but suspected they would not have been appointed to the

Disciplinary Board unless they were seen as good soldiers. I assumed they would do what was expected of them.

I thought that this Special Hearing Committee should know something about me so I sent a letter to Disciplinary Counsel Sam Napoli, with a copy to the Special Hearing Committee. I attached one hundred and eighty-seven clippings of articles I had written and articles written about me.

I then attacked the delay in scheduling a hearing. In a letter dated May 1, 1995, I pointed out that Disciplinary Counsel Napoli had sought to delay the hearing by representing to the panel that Judge Olszewski, who was to be a witness, was unavailable due to recent open-heart surgery. I was livid. In the letter, I noted that I had called the chambers of Judge Olszewski and discovered he was back to work and hearing cases. Disciplinary Counsel Napoli had made a *knowingly false statement to a tribunal,* a clear violation of the just quoted language of the Rules of Professional Conduct.

It was only one of many lies from Sam Napoli. This was a different world from where I had lived. I would never knowingly lie or misrepresent to a tribunal. When I began practice, if a lawyer was known to play fast and loose with the truth, he or she was forever penalized by the ongoing disbelief of the adjudicator. Not so anymore. The new standard in Pennsylvania, and sadly, everywhere else, is whatever you can get away with is right.

I demanded that the hearing be public. Finally, the hearing was set for July 26, 27, and 28, <u>after</u> the Primary, not before as I had demanded, and as required by the Rules. They would never give me a public forum during the Primary campaign.

The date of the hearing arrived. I wanted to be respectful but also wanted the panel to know that I wasn't going to be pushed around. Carol Ann Sweeney, the chair, did her best to keep me in bounds but I had long since concluded that if these people knew no bounds, neither did I.

The only witnesses called by Disciplinary Counsel were the complaining Judges. Disciplinary Counsel left Arthur Levy home. Judge Bradley denied that the Leedom case was fixed. Judge Olszewski, now a Senior Judge by appointment of the Supreme Court, at first perjured himself by denying he authored the Opinion in the Levy case. When shown a letter that conclusively proved he wrote the Opinion, Olszewski changed his testimony and admitted he was the author. Judge Cirillo also committed perjury when he denied he knew me and testified he was not at the Philadelphia Bar function in 1983. When shown his calendar, which I had subpoenaed, he admitted he was there and conceded he probably met me.

The first witness I called was Jim Cavanaugh, a Judge on the Superior Court who sat on the panel that heard the Levy case that Olszewski dismissed on the basis of the so-called untimely Motion for Post Trail Relief. I had known Cavanaugh for years and thought he was a decent man. When I went to his chambers in West Chester to subpoena him, he thought it was a social visit and invited me in. When I presented the subpoena to him, he was fit to be tied. His Irish face turned purple. It reminded me of Justice McDermott at the deposition a few years back. I not only subpoenaed Judge Cavanaugh, I subpoenaed his records of the Levy Argument.

When he took the stand, he was asked about the Levy case. I pointed out that the Prothonotary's docket conclusively established that a timely Motion for Post Trail Relief had indeed been filed. When I tried to ask him about this, he said he didn't have any records and he didn't remember the case. In my mind, this was preposterous. Judges keep their records forever, for just this kind of eventuality. I was sure his records would show that, after the argument, the three-Judge-panel had decided the case in my favor. I was sure that Olszewski, who had been assigned the task of writing the Opinion, fabricated the untimely Motion theory in order to dismiss my appeal, and the other two Judges on the panel didn't bother to check the record. I was willing to give them the benefit of the doubt. I wasn't going to get anything from Judge Cavanaugh. Cavanaugh, in true Pennsylvania tradition, when other Judges are involved, circled the wagons. Edmund Burke had it right.

It is necessary only for evil to triumph for the good man to do nothing.

For three days, I dominated the courtroom in the Montgomery County courthouse. I testified at length about what I knew and when I knew it. The testimony followed a memo I had previously sent but was far more extensive and dramatic. I put some forty-five exhibits into the record, including notes of testimony, pleadings, and court Opinions. Disciplinary Counsel, Sam Napoli, was ineffective and the members of the Special Hearing Committee knew it.

The members of the panel were caught. They knew that the Disciplinary Counsel had not carried his burden of proof and knew that I had built an overwhelming record to support my defense that there was no *knowingly false* allegation, *false statement*, or even *misrepresentation* in my Motion to Recuse.

Before the hearing, I called *Inquirer* reporter Fred Cusick, who was professionally offended by my predicament. I had tried to reach Dan Biddle, but he wouldn't return my phone calls. Fred came to the hearing. I suspected it was on his own time. At the close of the hearing, I suggested we go for a beer. On our third beer, Fred told me that I had built an absolutely airtight case. He then went on, in his cynical fashion, to say that it wouldn't make any difference. They wanted me, and they would get me. From his great bearded jowls he laughed, "People like you can't be left on the streets."

On July 27, 1995, Cusick filed a story titled:

Frequent critic of high court is before the ethics panel again

Cusick wrote:

Judicial reform advocate Robert B. Surrick was back in court yesterday, fighting again for his legal life.

This is the third time since the early 1980's that Surrick has been brought before the ethics panel, which is known as the Disciplinary Board of the Supreme Court. Surrick spent most of the 1980s fighting a variety of charges filed with the board by Larsen. The charges were dropped in 1989. Larsen was impeached and removed from office in 1994 for having an improper discussion about two cases with an attorney who was a former chairman of the Disciplinary Board.

Surrick said he believes that if the charges against him are upheld, there is a good chance he will be disbarred.

He contended that the charges represent a vendetta by some in the state's judicial hierarchy upset by his criticism of the courts.

"There have only been 27 months in 12 years that I haven't been under investigation. None of it for the way I practice law, all for my criticism of the courts," he said.

The Rules required the Special Hearing Committee to file its Report within sixty days. I drew comfort from the fact that it would soon be over. What to do now? Go to Cuba. Why not? Maverick was docked in Key West.

JUSTICE STOUT

July 18, 1995

"Justice Stout — Bob Surrick — do you have a minute?"

Former Supreme Court Justice Juanita Kidd Stout was hurrying from her courtroom on the fourth floor in the Wanamaker Building in Philadelphia to her chambers across the square when I stopped her. We had never met but both knew a great deal about the other. Sam Klein was her attorney.

Judge Stout had been a Philadelphia Common Pleas Judge for nineteen years. In 1987, Governor Robert Casey appointed her to fill a vacancy on the Supreme Court. She was the first black female in U.S. history to serve on a state's highest court. She brought brains, uncommon common sense, and personal dignity to the office. A petite lady, and a native Oklahoman, Justice Stout spoke slowly and carefully. After her removal from the Supreme Court, she was appointed Senior Judge in the Court of Common Pleas in Philadelphia.

"Bob, I will always have a minute for you. What can I do for you?"

"Justice Stout, I know you know some things that ought to be made public. You are the person who has to do it. As you know, the Disciplinary Board is again pressing charges against me. It's important to me that the public have the full story about what's been going on."

"Whatever are you talking about?"

"I know about what happened to you as a result of your vote — your swing vote on a three-to-two decision — to dismiss the Disciplinary Board charges against me back in 1988."

"I don't know what you are talking about," she said, not unkindly, but with some apprehension in her voice.

"Let me be more specific. When Governor Casey appointed you, everyone knew you would reach the mandatory retirement age of seventy in March. Your appointive term would not end until the following January. It was understood that you would serve until January. The justification would be that you were appointive, and the mandatory retirement provision in the Constitution wouldn't apply to you."

"That's true. Go on."

"On March 6, your seventieth birthday, the day after your vote in *Disciplinary Counsel vs. Surrick,* Justice Papadakos walked into your chambers and invited you to your retirement party. Isn't that right? When you told him you weren't retiring, he said, 'The fuck you're not!' and walked out. The following week, Attorney General Ernie Preate brought a Quo Warranto action in the Supreme Court challenging your right to sit. I have information that the Quo Warranto Petition was written on a computer in the chambers of Justice Papadakos, and, of course, Justices Papadakos, Zappala, and Larsen voted you off the court."

"Bob, even if that were true, I couldn't talk about it. It would be harmful to the Court."

"Justice Stout, how much more harm can be done? These willful men have no regard for anything but their own interests."

"I can't do it, Bob, I'm sorry, but I just can't do it."

Suddenly, this very mild-mannered woman seemed to stiffen and she said:

"I have to go, Bob, but watch yourself. These are evil men who know no limits."

Unable to be angry with this fine lady, I, nevertheless, walked away disappointed. A woman who had fought oppression by the system her entire life because of her race and gender felt it more important to protect the already soiled reputation of the Court than to help one individual who was being battered by the Court, a Court that had just battered her.

LASHED TO THE RACK

Looking For An Exit

January 1997

Sam Stretton called me to suggest I run for the Superior Court. There were four open seats. Nominations would be at the Spring Primary in May. His reasoning was that in 1995, without money or party support, I had garnered over three hundred and twenty thousand votes, representing twenty-six percent of those voting. The people who voted for me were hardcore supporters. There would only be about seven hundred thousand people voting in the Spring Primary. If I held the votes I received in 1995, with five or more candidates running for four seats, I would surely be nominated to one of the slots. I felt hesitation.

"I don't know, Sam. I'm tired. I love to campaign but I don't know if I'm up to another statewide campaign. And then, there is the Disciplinary Board thing hanging over my head. You know, under the Rules, the decision of the Special Hearing Committee was due in October 1995. Now it's January, 1997, and nothing has happened."

"Bob, it's an outrage. During the '93 campaign, you had it hanging over your head, then in '95 it was still there, and here we are in '97, and it's still there. I think we should go to Federal Court and do something about it."

"You and I both know the feds aren't going to take a case when there's an ongoing state proceeding."

"Have you read the *Midddlesex* case? It holds you can have access to the Federal Courts if you can show bad faith, harassment or some other extraordinary circumstance. In your case, the Board didn't follow its own rules requiring a hearing within sixty days. Now the decision is fifteen months overdue. You have been under investigation or prosecution almost non-stop for fifteen years. If that isn't bad faith and harassment, I don't know what is."

"I don't know. Even if that's so, I'm out of money. I can't afford any more legal fees. I'm just about broke."

"Tell you what, Bob. I'll file a Complaint and go to one hearing for five hundred dollars."

"Let me think about it."

As I left Sam's cluttered office on High Street in West Chester, I thought about my financial situation. I needed money. Sam's logic was right on. I could win a Superior Court seat. If I could get the Federal Court to enjoin the Supreme Court and Disciplinary Board from chasing me, it would be great publicity and would really kick off a campaign.

I walked back into Sam's office and said:

"Prepare a complaint, Sam. Let's go!"

The complaint was filed in the United States District Court. We drew Judge Joseph McGlynn. McGlynn was an old Philadelphia political warhorse who had moved to the Federal bench from the corrupt Philadelphia Common Pleas bench. It was doubtful that McGlynn would ever find the Board guilty of bad faith or harassment. But, we had no choice. You play the hand you're dealt.

On January 22, 1997, we appeared before Judge McGlynn. As the hearing opened, Howard Holmes, the seriously overweight attorney representing the Disciplinary Board, announced that the Special Hearing Committee had filed its Report and that it had been mailed yesterday. Of course, I hadn't seen it. Sam asked for a copy. I quickly read the last page and then tried to spin through the other fourteen pages. My God, they found in my favor! They recommended dismissal of all the charges! Obviously someone had put some real heat on the supposedly independent Special Hearing Committee to get out a Report because of this lawsuit. One day before the hearing — after fifteen months — how obvious was that?

Judge McGlynn immediately took the position that there was nothing further before him. To his credit, Sam stood his ground and argued that there was such bad faith, such harassment, that the federal court must step in to protect me. He took the position that I had been hurt in the '93 and '95 campaigns by these proceedings dragging on and, as an announced candidate for the Superior Court in 1997, I should have the protection of the Federal Courts from further harassment.

McGlynn wanted to end it, but Sam asked to put on testimony. After a lot of discussion, McGlynn finally permitted testimony. I testified at length about the past fourteen years and put into evidence all the Rules that the Disciplinary Board had broken. I noted that Judge Newcomer, in this very courthouse, had directly questioned Disciplinary Counsel's motivation when he suggested that Disciplinary Counsel had a "secondary motive" in bringing the charges against me. It was all to no avail. McGlynn dismissed the lawsuit.

Shockingly, McGlynn then stated that he rejected "entirely any evidence suggesting that there was outside influence on Judges accused of misconduct in the Motion to Recuse." It wasn't even before him, but he took the opportunity to circle the judicial wagons to protect Bradley, Olszewski, and Cirillo.

I left Sam at the entrance to the Federal Court building so I could take the Report of the Special Hearing Committee to a quiet place and study it. A corner booth in a corner bar served nicely.

I couldn't believe what I was reading. I had received an honest count. The Special Hearing Committee made the following findings:

- *"The Respondent did not know that the allegations contained in his Motion for Recusal were false."*
- *"(N)or did Respondent lack a reasonable basis, within the normal pleadings practice in Pennsylvania to make the assertions contained in his Motion for Recusal."*
- *"Respondent had become a very outspoken critic of the Pennsylvania Supreme Court and... he was on the losing end of two extremely unusual decisions complained of in his motion only after he had been an outspoken critic of the Judiciary."*
- *"The evidence, as presented, indicated that the basis of the decisions against the Respondent appeared so out of the range of ordinary error that it could reasonably give rise to the suspicion that some improper influence had prevailed even if, in fact, it had not."*
- *"(T)he panel has concluded that this decision could reasonably give rise to the belief on Respondent's part that improper influence had been exerted. While*

we agree that the language used by Respondent was somewhat intemperate, we cannot conclude that he...did not have a reasonable basis, to make the assertions that he did, even if, contrary to his belief, they turned out to be false."

- *"Disciplinary Counsel cites several cases from outside of Pennsylvania where (an) accused lawyer admitted that he had absolutely no evidence in support of his allegations and that he essentially made up the allegations. This is a far cry from the substantial body of evidence produced by the Respondent as to his state of mind and as to the reasonableness of his belief in the averments that he made."*
- *"We therefore conclude that the Respondent did not violate the Pennsylvania Rules of Professional Conduct and we recommend the dismissal of all charges asserting the making of false statements in the Motion for Recusal.*

I was elated! It looked like I had finally reached the end of my problems. The state press thought so too. Fred Cusick filed a January 28, 1997, story headlined:

A state panel clears West Chester lawyer of ethics charges: The committee said legal reform advocate Robert Surrick did not break any rules

The *Philadelphia Legal Intelligencer* trumpeted:

Surrick cleared of triple complaints

The West Chester Daily Local News on January 29, 1997, published a long editorial entitled:

Lawyer wins another round

It wrote:

Surrick is hated by hacks of every stripe because he doesn't play the game. The payoff is that he has been under investigation for most of the past 13 years and his attempts to gain a judicial post are supported by neither major party. Nor has much been done to improve the quality and integrity of judges, aside from the removal of Larsen. Still, Surrick continues to throw his body before the juggernaut, for which we all owe him a debt of gratitude.

In my excitement, I didn't stop to be a lawyer. If I had, I would have been aware that the fat lady hadn't sung yet.

LASHED TO THE RACK

The Disciplinary Board

April 18, 1997

"May it please the Board."?

Reciting the time-honored lawyer's opening, I began my argument to a panel of the Disciplinary Board.

The Recommendation of the Special Hearing Committee had been just that, a recommendation. The Disciplinary Board now was required to hear argument and act on the Recommendation. This three-member panel would hear argument and make its Recommendation to the full Disciplinary Board, all appointed by the Supreme Court. The full Disciplinary Board would then make its decision. In spite of the overwhelming evidence in my favor, now on the record, and affirmed by the Special Hearing Committee, Disciplinary Counsel continued to argue that I should be punished.

I had filed what I believed to be an airtight brief. The findings of the Special Hearing Committee, which had the responsibility to find the facts, were so strong that I just didn't know how anybody could get around them.

Disciplinary Counsel, the hapless Sam Napoli, had argued first, having the burden to try and overcome the findings of the Special Hearing Committee. He was terrible. His sole point was that I had been reckless in my allegations against the three Judges. But that wasn't the standard. The standard, under the law, was that I would have had to make a "knowingly false" statement.

Napoli was so bad that John Doherty, Napoli's boss and Justice Zappala's alter ego, had to step in to try and rescue the case.

Suspecting where Napoli might go, I started my brief with the sentence:

Disciplinary Counsel, disingenuously, would have you believe that 'reckless disregard' is the standard by which the allegations in the Motion to Recuse should be judged. That is not and never has been the law of Pennsylvania.

I had to be careful. I was angered by the continuation of this charade but at the same time wanted to be highly professional. I kept it crisp and matter-of-fact with just a touch of aggression to let them know I believed this to be beyond the pale. At the conclusion of my argument I was sure I had carried the day.

Before the hearing, I called Fred Cusick and asked him to come to the hearing. Fred was in the audience. When it was over, I suggested we have the usual beer or two. Fred was his usual cynical self.

He asked me, "How do you expect to win anything in this kangaroo court?"

"I have the sons-a-bitches surrounded," I answered.

Fred had covered Harrisburg for a number of years and had learned that there are no limits with politicians. He watched Thornburgh make nice with his enemies and screw his friends. He had been splattered with state Treasurer R. Bud Dwyer's brains when Dwyer put a .357 in his mouth at a press conference and pulled the trigger. Dwyer had been convicted of bribery. The next day, upon sentencing, his pension would have been forfeit. Dwyer blew his brains out before sentencing to save his pension for his wife and children. In 1901, when Theodore Roosevelt passed through, "*Harrisburg was notoriously the most corrupt seat of state government in the nation*". One hundred years later, change was not noticeable.

Cusick believed that everyone in high or even low office in Pennsylvania was crooked, and all you had to do was dig deep enough and you would hit paydirt.

Fred filed an article that was published in the *Inquirer* April 19, 1997 edition, titled:

Lawyer again faces hearing on breach of the ethics code: A panel had cleared Robert B. Surrick earlier. The state is seeking to have that decision overturned

Cusick wrote:

Yesterday, John L. Doherty, chief disciplinary counsel, told the new three-lawyer panel that it should consider punishing Surrick with suspension or disbarment.

Such harsh penalties are usually reserved for lawyers who have swindled their clients or committed some other major infraction. But in the small world of the Pennsylvania judiciary, Surrick's offense may be viewed as more serious: He has attacked sitting judges.

The Disciplinary Board Report, under the Rules, had to be filed no later than June 18, 1997. Finally, on October 17, 1997, four months late, the Board entered an Order dismissing the charges. I quickly looked through the Opinion to see if they left any loopholes for Disciplinary Counsel to appeal to the Supreme Court. There were none. It should have been the end of the matter.

It wasn't. Disciplinary Counsel filed an appeal to the Supreme Court. The Supreme Court does not have to take every appeal. The Rules of Appellate Procedure provide that an appeal will be allowed, *"only when there are special and important reasons therefore."* In its Petition for Allowance of Appeal, Disciplinary Counsel did not allege any "*special or important*" reasons for the appeal.

The request for appeal was based solely on Rule 8.4(c) of the Code of Professional Responsibility:

Misconduct

(c) It is professional misconduct for a lawyer to engage in conduct involving dishonesty, fraud, deceit or misrepresentation

All prior cases in Pennsylvania interpreting this rule had required an intentional, or knowing misrepresentation. Neither the Special Hearing Committee nor the full Disciplinary Board found that I had intentionally or knowingly misrepresented any facts.

I immediately smelled a rat. Disciplinary Counsel could not win under existing law. For Disciplinary Counsel to seek allowance of an appeal, it could only mean that Doherty had been told to file the appeal by one or more Supreme Court Justices.

What were they doing? The facts were the facts, and both the Special Hearing Committee and the Disciplinary Board had said over and over again that I did not make a knowing or intentional misrepresentation.

Were they going to change the law and then try and apply it retroactively — ex post facto — to my case? I couldn't imagine this. It would be too obvious. It would be extreme judicial arrogance.

Several years later, when writing this chapter, I looked at the Disciplinary Board Opinion and noted the concurring opinion by Robert N.C. Nix III, the son of former Chief Justice Robert N.C. Nix, Jr., who had just retired. Nix, the younger, while agreeing with the dismissal of the charges against me, had decried the use of Rule 8.4(c) by Disciplinary Counsel. He wrote:

> *I have always been wary of the broad net that this section of our Rules might cast. This Rule should not, in my opinion, be used as a "catchall" for attorneys whose conduct is questionable but not a direct violation of any Rule.*

Only with the gift of hindsight could I understand the next sentence he wrote:

> *The majority's finding in this case takes a step in the direction of limiting the application of Rule 8.4(c).*

Nix, the younger, clearly still had access to the thinking of Justices on the Court and was trying to head them off at the pass; it was a courageous but futile effort.

THE LAST HURRAH

Spring 1997

Here we go again.

Sam Stretton had done the math. With four Superior Court seats open, all I had to do was keep the three hundred and twenty thousand votes I had received in 1995 to win one of the four Republican nominations in the May Primary.

Chester County Common Pleas Judge Jim MacElree was going to be the choice of the Republican State Committee for one of the slots. I decided that with my Chester County base, he was the one I wanted to target. If I defeated him, one of the slots would be mine. The Republican State Committee would meet in mid-February. To let everyone know that there would not be easy pickings in Chester County, I floated a trial balloon in December to keep my name in public view. It was the practice of judicial candidates not to announce until February but, as usual, I wasn't usual. *The West Chester Daily Local News,* on December 2, 1996, headlined:

Surrick kicks off next run: Early Superior Court Candidacy Defies Custom

My first break came when the Pennsylvania Bar Association, after much fanfare about a "new and diverse" Judicial Evaluation Commission, voted MacElree "not recommended." Jim is an arrogant man, the scion of an old established Chester County family who have been Judges and lawyers for the last century. He thought the nomination was his as a matter of birthright. He thought noblesse oblige — behavior considered to be the responsibility of persons of high birth or rank — meant that he was owed something. He apparently became offended and lost his temper when the interviewing committee asked him some hard questions. As a result, the Commission questioned his judicial temperament.

Son Craig re-activated my computer fax program, which had every state newspaper in its database, and I went to work. Judge MacElree had one of the many libel lawsuits by Judges pending against *The Philadelphia Inquirer.* Hoping to capitalize on the media's anger about Pennsylvania Justices and Judges suing their critics in their own courts, I wrote a letter to MacElree and faxed it to every newspaper in the state:

Dear Judge MacElree,

For over 10 years, I have spoken out against Pennsylvania judges bringing lawsuits against their critics in their own court system. Justice Larsen utilized this pernicious practice, which brings the entire judicial system into disrepute. I enclose copies of newspaper articles, "Judges Use Courts for Intimidation," (Phila. Inquirer 3/8/86), and "Surrick: Nix Judges Suing Critics," (Del. Co. Daily Times 3/17/86), which outline my long-held views on this subject. I hold the same view about your present libel lawsuit against the Inquirer. Your lawsuit must be heard by a colleague on the bench, which makes the process look bad.
More importantly, as you now are a candidate for statewide office, the Inquirer will be forced to cover a candidate who is suing it. Will it affect their reporting? I witnessed the chilling of coverage of Justice Larsen because of his lawsuit. Moreover, other newspapers will be covering you; a judge who they know is willing to use the judicial process of which you are a part, if you don't like what they write about you. You have created a bad situation, which only you can correct by immediately dropping the lawsuit. I call on you to end the lawsuit against the Inquirer without delay.

Very truly yours,

Robert B. Surrick, Esquire

As I mailed the letter, I thought about what Gene Roberts, former executive editor of the Inquirer, and later managing editor of The New York Times, said in a speech to his alma mater, the University of North Carolina at Chapel Hill:

We have no count of the number of leads that aren't being followed, the abuses of power and privilege that aren't being disclosed because editors cannot afford the time and expense that a libel suit brings. This is what should alarm us most of all — not the sound but the silence.

While I was trying to get MacElree to do the right thing, the Supreme Court did it again. Esther Sylvester, a Philadelphia Common Pleas Judge, had been indicted for receiving cash from the Roofer's Union. With the help of some slick lawyering and a touch of fabrication, Esther won acquittal in Federal Court. She claimed that a now-dead court officer had returned the cash. Nevertheless, the newly created Judicial Conduct Board recommended that she be removed from office for lying under oath. The Supreme Court ignored the Board and refused to discipline her. To show that extortionists and fabricators were alright in their book, the Supreme Court Justices, in 1992, made her Administrative Judge of the Philadelphia Family Court Division. Now, in 1997, the Court completed her rehabilitation by appointing her to the Court of Judicial Discipline, successor to the Judicial Inquiry and Review Board. She now sits in judgment on the ethics of other Judges.

It was no different from Arthur Levy's appointment to a Disciplinary Board hearing committee after he had obviously embezzled from Levy and Surrick. The indisputable fact is these corrupt Justices care not a whit about what people think. They will do as they damn please. With the likes of Sylvester and Levy, and others installed in their accountability system, they have obligated minions who will do whatever they want. That's power, Pennsylvania style. And the honest Judges and lawyers keep their mouths shut for fear of their own well being.

MacElree and the Republican establishment were not going to take the Bar Association's "not recommended" rating lying down. Enter the public-spirited Dick Sprague. He sought to intimidate the Commission. He demanded access to the notes of the interviewers of lawyers and Judges who had been promised confidentiality. The *Philadelphia Legal Intelligencer* reported, on February 14, 1997, that:

Sprague demanded, by 5 p.m. today, a copy of the rules governing the commission, the resumes of all commission members, their basis for selection, and method of appointment, and the vote of the commission on each of 11 candidates.... Sprague asked for investigating subcommittee reports....

Sprague's demand was made to PATLA leader James F. Mundy, now President of the Pennsylvania Bar Association. Mundy had been one of the witnesses subpoenaed by Sprague in the 1982 Larsen investigation with whom I clashed. A Larsen ally, Mundy had attended one or more of the so-called "Nights on the Town." It seems that Mundy had been another major rehabilitation project by the power structure. Mundy had been spiffed up and had worked his way to the top of the Pennsylvania Bar Association. The Supreme Court had previously put him in charge of the Disciplinary Board.

But I digress.

On the last day for filing, Gregory Cirillo, son of Superior Court Judge Vince Cirillo and a lawyer in Philadelphia, delivered sufficient signatures to Harrisburg to put his name on the ballot for Superior Court. There would now be six candidates in the race, four endorsed by the Republican Party, Cirillo, and me. I didn't get it at the time. I should have.

In 1993 and 1995, I had refused to meet with the Pennsylvania Bar Association's judicial rating committee. They were controlled by the pols and I couldn't afford the risk of something negative from an establishment organization. In 1997, the past President of the Pennsylvania Bar Association called and asked me to participate. He gave me his personal promise that I would be treated fairly. I took a chance and submitted myself to the newly formed Judicial Evaluation Commission. On March 25, 1997, the Commission released its rating of me, which stood in marked contrast to the "not recommended" rating given Jim MacElree. It wrote:

Bob Surrick, West Chester Republican. Recommended. The sole practitioner's intellect, knowledge of the law and broad-based legal experience has given him understanding of the appellate courts and is an aggressive advocate of judicial reform with a deep commitment to the law.

Gregory Cirillo did not submit himself to the commission. A puzzle.

It was time to mount my faithful charger, the 1987 Mercedes, now with two hundred and seventy thousand miles under its tires, and visit the newspapers around the state.

Editorials and news articles poured in which ranged between good and very good. Thirteen daily newspapers endorsed me. A sample of the headlines follows.

The Waynesboro Record Herald headlined:

Legislature should adopt Surrick plan

The Reading Eagle headlined:

Judge hopeful attacks system

The Lancaster Intelligencer bannered:

Judicial Reform: A new idea from Surrick

The *Wilkes Barre Times Leader* editorial noted:

Support Surrick's plan for the election of judges

The Gettysburg Times headlined:

Superior Court candidate urges judicial reform

The DuBois Courier-Express headlined and wrote:

Surrick deserves a seat on court

We think Surrick has made a legitimate case that he should get one of the Republican nominations.

That case is both relative (Surrick's qualifications) vis-à-vis the other aspirants and absolute (Surrick's vision) for where the scandal–tainted Supreme Court should go from here.

The Philadelphia Inquirer made it three for three in negative editorials about me. In a May 13, 1997 editorial, eschewing analysis and evaluation of my judicial reform platform in favor of pejorative prose, it opined:

Finally, there's the longtime critic of the state courts, West Chester lawyer Robert B. Surrick. Despite his "recommended" rating and all that he's done to expose the judiciary's shortcomings, he's a combative loner who seems wholly unsuited to sit on a court where consensus building is required.

On May 20, 1997, the people voted, and I found out what the pols were up to when they put Greg Cirillo on the ballot. Stretton's math was accurate. The four candidates endorsed by the Republican State Committee were in the mid three-hundred-thousand-vote range. Cirillo and I combined received almost four hundred and fifty thousand votes. But Cirillo had split my expected independent or non-organization votes. I received only two hundred and thirty-five thousand votes while he got two hundred and fourteen thousand votes. Without him in the race, I would have topped four hundred thousand votes.

I had to admire the political skill of the Republican Party, which figured out how to beat me.

MERIT SELECTION OF JUDGES

1998

Pennsylvania is one of a handful of states, eight at my last count that selects Judges at all levels in partisan political elections. Having run statewide for appellate court positions, I know something about the process.

First, it is clear beyond dispute that the voters are without a clue as to the qualifications of the judicial candidates. Voters will vote for a candidate if the candidate is from a county near where they live. They will vote based on name recognition regardless of how the name is known, good or bad. The voters elected John Flaherty to the Supreme Court because they thought he was Pete Flaherty, the popular mayor of Pittsburgh. Millions spent on slick TV commercials, not qualifications, carry the day.

Race plays a large part on elections. A "law and order" candidate blatantly appeals to those who believe all blacks belong in jail. In Pennsylvania, those voters are legion.

Money trumps qualifications. Supreme Court candidates now spend millions in a statewide race; millions in contributions from lawyers who will soon be arguing their clients causes before the successful candidate. The big edge goes to the trial lawyers, PATLA, in these races.

Political parties have abdicated their responsibility to support quality candidates. For proof, we need to look no farther than Justice Newman whose money spoke louder than her qualifications and Justice

Larsen whose PATLA pals engineered his support from both the Republican and Democrat State Committees, in spite of his scandalous behavior.

The organized bar has contributed to the corruption by rating "qualified" and then supporting unsavory candidates. Larsen, McEwen and Papadakos come immediately to mind.

Enter the do-gooders mouthing their mantra "merit selection." They argue, with considerable force, that statewide election produces mediocrity or worse. They urge merit selection as the solution to the ills facing our appellate courts. But is it? Let's look at merit selection.

Under a merit selection system, the executive, the Governor of Pennsylvania, would nominate from a list of candidates produced from a commission. Who picks these pickers is open to debate. The Governor's nomination from the list would be sent to the Pennsylvania Senate for its "advice and consent." This, of course, is modeled after the Federal system where the President proposes and the United States Senate disposes. Does that work. Does it take politics out of the process? The answer to that question is for all to see. Here's how it works in real life.

In 1997, President Clinton nominated Frederica Massiah-Jackson to the United States District Court for the Eastern District of Pennsylvania. Loaded with baggage from her tenure as a Common Pleas Judge in Philadelphia, this cynical merit selection nomination was based on race and gender, not qualifications. The baggage? How about telling a prosecuting attorney during a court proceeding to "shut your fucking mouth." Another court record revealed this nominee for high office telling a lawyer she "didn't give a shit" about his argument. A racist through and through, she had exposed undercover detectives in open court to black spectators, telling them to "take a good look at these guys…and be careful out there." Her bias for criminal (black) defendants was legendary and documented. Nevertheless, she lied about it to the Senate Judiciary Committee. What is so unfortunate about this nomination is that there were, in fact, several highly qualified black women available. They just didn't have the political support that Massiah-Jackson had. The Judiciary Committee held its nose when it reported this nomination to the full Senate.

It took a courageous and lonely outcry from John Morganelli, District Attorney from rural Northhampton Country, to expose the chicanery. Once exposed, others like Lynn Abraham, District Attorney of Philadelphia, joined the opposition. Finally, the Pennsylvania District Attorneys Association came out in opposition to the nomination.

Faced with this negative groundswell, prior to the vote of the Senate on March 17, 1998, Massiah Jackson withdrew. Her supporters were outraged. *The New York Times*, who never found a black woman it wouldn't support, called it a "judicial mugging." Other backers such as the NAACP, the Barristers Association of Philadelphia, the Philadelphia Bar Association, the Hispanic Bar Association, the Asian American Bar Association, and Senator Specter, her sponsor, screamed "foul." PATLA member and Philadelphia Bar Association Chancellor Mark Aronchick bitterly attacked Morganelli. For standing tall, Morganelli will become an obscure figure in Pennsylvania, his political career over.

One of Massiah Jackson's biggest supporters, Philadelphia Mayor Ed Rendell became Governor in 2002. With this track record, can anyone be confident that he will nominate Judges based on qualification? Do we want him controlling merit selection nominees?

How does "merit selection" work on a national level? The United States Senate has put in place new tests before giving its "advice and consent" to presidential nominees. First, the nominee must pass a litmus test given by the majority. Does the nominee favor or oppose abortion, the death penalty, injured plaintiffs, and so on. Next, the nominee must have enough votes to bring cloture to a filibuster. Otherwise, the nominee gets "Borked." This so-called merit selection nomination process has become totally politicized. It is confirmation or defeat dictated by special interest groups.

Would Pennsylvania be any different? History says no. The record says no. One need only look at the present process when there is a judicial vacancy in Pennsylvania that I have previously described. It has become a farce. It can be summed up in one example and a memorable phrase. Governor Casey nominated five lawyers to fill vacancies on the Philadelphia bench who did not have the support of the Democratic City Committee. John Herron was one of the nominees. An outstanding man of experience, and more importantly, character, Herron was voted down five times by the Pennsylvania Senate, a record. The powerful Senator Vince Fumo was quoted by the media brazenly saying, "that boy doesn't know how to play the game." So much for merit selection. I rest my case.

As a practical matter, merit selection will never pass in the Pennsylvania legislature. No legislator is going to go back to his or her district and tell their constituents "I just took away your right to vote for Judges." It's just not going to happen.

The solution? Elect from seven statewide districts, the Surrick Plan, described previously.

But, it is unlikely that any reform will occur. The power structure likes it the way it is.

LASHED TO THE RACK

That Rat That I Smelled Was A Rat

April 14, 1998

On April 14, 1998, the Supreme Court finally acted on the Disciplinary Counsel's Petition for Allowance of Appeal. The Court accepted the appeal and ordered my case be remanded to the Disciplinary Board, "for further proceedings in accordance with *Office of Disciplinary Counsel v. Rebert"* decided on April 1, 1998, two weeks before.

What the hell was *Office of Disciplinary Counsel v. Rebert?* When I looked at the Disciplinary Board Opinion in *Disciplinary Board v. Surrick,* I saw a citation to this Rebert case. *Rebert* was cited by the Disciplinary Board for the proposition that for a Rule 8.4(c) *misrepresentation* to be a violation of the Code, it must be intentional. That was the law according to the Disciplinary Board and certainly had been the law in all prior Pennsylvania cases.

The Supreme Court decision in *Office of Disciplinary Counsel v. Rebert* was not reported anywhere. I went to the Prothonotary of the Supreme Court on the fourth floor of City Hall in Philadelphia and asked for the Opinion. I was told it was a Disciplinary Board matter, and, as such, it was confidential, and I couldn't see it. Talk about Kafka and *The Trial.* The Supreme Court had sent my case back to the Disciplinary Board, "for further proceedings in accordance with *Office of*

Disciplinary Counsel v. Rebert," but I wasn't going to be allowed to see the *Rebert* Opinion.

I walked from City Hall to Sam Klein's office at 18th and Arch. I asked Ellen, his secretary, where Sam was. She said he would be back shortly. I told her I would wait. When Sam came in, I told him the catch-22 I was in, and he said he didn't believe me.

Let me take a moment for an aside. When I was riding high, I had a million friends whom I could call on, and I enjoyed total credibility. They believed what I told them. As time went on and the war stories appeared, "friends" jumped ship. The worst part was even my really good friends began to doubt the accuracy of what I would say. They had to practice law in the system. That's where they made their living to support their large houses, kids in private schools, and their BMWs. As a critic of the system, I had set myself apart from them. The words of Milovan Djilas, who put himself in deep trouble by saying the wrong thing to Stalin, were so true. Now in disgrace, he wrote in the Forward of *Conversations With Stalin* about a former comrade with whom he had endured political prison and so many other hardships. He noted:

> *He seemed to pity me, powerless to help me, while I did not dare approach him…for fear of forcing him into an inconvenient and unwanted fraternization with me.*

To his everlasting credit and again revealing a man of extraordinary courage and balance, Sam said, "This is bullshit. I'm going over to the Prothonotary and get the Opinion. Wait here."

About twenty minutes later, Sam returned with a wide grin. He asked:

"Weren't you charged with violating the Rules of Professional Responsibility for alleging in your Motion to Recuse that Arthur Levy was the subject of a confidential Disciplinary Board Hearing? Didn't they accuse you of violating the confidentiality of Disciplinary Board proceedings by making Levy's case public?"

"Yes, but the charge was thrown out. I proved that Arthur had himself waived confidentially by making reference to it in his Brief to the Superior Court."

Sam started really laughing.

"What's so damn funny?"

"You won't believe this. The Disciplinary Board screwed up when it put the *Rebert* citation in your Opinion. It violated the rule of confidentiality. In other words, the author of that Opinion, Gregory Miller, and all the rest of the Board who approved the Opinion, violated the Rules and should be subjected to the same charges brought against you. Here's what's really funny. The Supreme Court compounded the error by citing *Rebert* in the Order remanding your case to the Disciplinary Board. Now they don't know what to do. They can't give you the Opinion with Rebert's name on it. They all have violated Rebert's right to confidentiality big time."

"Stan Rebert is the District Attorney of York County. I know of him. He says and does wild things. Give me the phone-no-get Ellen to call him at the York County Courthouse."

A few minutes later, Ellen called on Sam's intercom, "Mr. Rebert on line two."

I picked up the phone and said: "Stan, I know that you know who I am. I have campaigned in the last three elections in York County and received substantial votes there. I need the Supreme Court Opinion in your Disciplinary Board case."

Without figuring out what I was up to, or more likely not caring, he readily agreed to fax it to Sam's office.

When the fax came in, we couldn't believe what we were seeing. In *Disciplinary Board v. Rebert,* the Supreme Court had changed the standard for a Rule 8.4(c) "misrepresentation" from an "intentional" misrepresentation of the facts, to "reckless ignorance" of facts.

"Sam, in the unlikely event you haven't figured it out, here's what's happening. This is a three-rail bank shot. Zappala and pals know it would have been too obvious to change the "misrepresentation" standard in *Disciplinary Board v. Surrick.* So they changed the Rule in *Rebert,* normally a confidential Opinion out of public view. They will then apply it to me. It's smoke and mirrors. They don't give a shit about Stan Rebert, it's about me. As soon as they get me, they'll let Stan go."

"I think you're right. Bring me your file. I am representing you from now on. This kind of thing has got to stop."

"Sam, I can't afford you."

"There will be no fee or cost to you."

The Philadelphia Inquirer, on April 19th, published this headline and sub-head:

Lawyer again faces hearing on breach of the ethics code.

A panel had cleared Robert B. Surrick earlier. The state is seeking to have that decision overturned.

On June 12, 1998, I received an Order from the Disciplinary Board. It ordered another hearing pursuant to "*the new standard*" established in the *Rebert* Opinion.

If I wasn't so damn angry, I would have been amused at this Disciplinary Board Order, which repeated the Supreme Court's violation in citing a confidential case. A "new standard" was to be applied retroactively? A "new standard" invented in 1998 to be applied to my Motion to Recuse filed in 1993?

It stunk to high heaven and got worse.

The Supreme Court then handed down another Opinion. In *Disciplinary Board v. Price,* the Court again changed the Rules. It abrogated a bedrock principle of constitutional law and reversed its own Rule that Disciplinary Counsel always had the burden to prove every element of its charge against a lawyer by clear and convincing evidence. According to *Price,* if a lawyer charges a Judge with misconduct, all the Judge has to do is deny the charge and now the burden of proof shifts to the lawyer to prove the truth of his statement. The Supreme Court had changed the Rules in two very significant ways prior to hearing my appeal. The changes, of course, were aimed at me and would bury me.

I knew now that there would be no stopping this Court, led by Justices Zappala and Cappy. *Vengeance is mine, saith the Lord* is a non-starter in the Pennsylvania Supreme Court.

As Bill O'Donnell was wont to say, "You have to be able to take a joke."

LASHED TO THE RACK

Who's Kidding Whom?

September 28, 1998

After the Supreme Court remanded the case to the Disciplinary Board, the Disciplinary Board entered an Order scheduling re-argument on September 28th to address the "new standard" set forth in *Rebert.*

As Sam Klein approached the podium, I noted that the make-up of the Panel had changed. Gregory Miller was still chair and Angelo Scaricamazza, a Fumo apparatchik who had consistently voted against me, was still sitting. Steve Saltz, who had previously voted for me had been replaced. Even though Saltz's term on the Disciplinary Board was up on April 1, under the existing Rule, procedures, and policy of the Board, he should have continued to sit on an ongoing case in which he had previously participated.

Miller introduced the Panel indicating that John Morris was the new member. Was I suspicious? You betcha! I was more than suspicious. I thought about John Rogers Carroll's admonition that "Paranoids are the only realists." After the Supreme Court changed the rules in *Rebert*, I knew we were playing a charade. The replacement of a favorable vote with another of their appointees confirmed my belief that I was not going to get an honest count.

Right off, the new member, John Morris, asked a series of lengthy questions. It was clear he had read the record and knew his way around the Code of Professional Responsibility. He asked about the inter-relationship of various sections of the Code as we entered the phony realm of lawyers arguing about how many angels can stand on the head of a pin. The issue was easy. It was not rocket science. Did I have a reasonable basis on the facts I presented to the Special Hearing Committee to make the allegations I had made in the Motion to Recuse? The Special Hearing Committee said I did and the Disciplinary Board had said I did. This was bullshit!

As Sam Klein was making a point, he referred to Justice Larsen, and Morris interrupted, saying:

Well, we all know about that. We know that Mr. Surrick had years in the wilderness — apparently because of his initial vote to throw Justice Larsen off. And much to the permanent disgrace of the Pennsylvania Bar and certain portions of the judiciary, nobody stood ready to do anything to relieve Mr. Surrick.

What in the name of sweet Jesus did this mean? Who was Morris? I was sure he was put on this panel to join Scaricamazza in burying me. But here he was recognizing the trouble that my Larsen vote had caused me and decrying, almost in the language of Edmund Burke, the fact that lawyers and Judges had stood by without coming to my aid. Was this guy throwing me a bone while helping to chain me to the seawall while the tide was rising? Or was he for real?

Later in the argument, he would ask questions which forced Disciplinary Counsel into untenable positions like:

Mr. Morris:

...unless you interrupt a fix in progress, you simply cannot say anything about it? That's your view?

Ms. Kistler:

That would be my view...

Later Morris asked:

So you are taking the fact that the Board and everybody says that Judge Cirillo never said that, and it is your determination that if Mr. Surrick put it in a petition, that was just a lie?

Ms. Kistler:

Correct

Mr. Morris

That one doesn't go down easy with me.

After the argument, I asked Sam Klein about Morris. Sam told me that Morris was a very capable trial lawyer. He had been First Assistant District Attorney under Emmett Fitzpatrick and knew his way around a courtroom. But what were his connections? Which Supreme Court Justice had put him on the Board? What were his ambitions?

Okay Bob, so Morris came into the hearing playing it straight. It would only be a matter of time before a little bird would whisper in his ear. He would change his mind. I would bet anything on that. Zappala and pals would not have gone to the trouble of changing the Rules in *Rebert* and *Price* just to let me have an honest hearing before the Board. No, Morris would do me in-of that I was certain as I walked out of what I saw as a polluted hearing room into bright fall sunshine in the City of Brotherly Love.

On April 1, 1999, the Disciplinary Board filed its Report. It found I had violated Rule 8.4(c) prohibiting attorney misrepresentation when I alleged that the Olszewski decision was based on outside influence. On the Bradley charge, the Board found I had sufficient basis to allege a "fix" and on the Cirillo charge, the Board found I had "sufficient facts" to support the allegation in my Motion to Recuse. The Board recommended I receive a "public censure."

This result was not unexpected in light of the contortions of the Supreme Court to change the rules of the game in the middle of the game. The Disciplinary Board had done the Supreme Court's bidding. Because it was a remand from the Supreme Court, the case would now automatically go back to the Supreme Court. I had no illusions about my fate.

But the shocker in the whole business was a Concurring and Dissenting opinion by John Morris. He completely misrepresented Sam Klein's argument by writing:

> *In the course of argument before the Board Panel, Respondent through his counsel, wisely conceded the untruth of the charges leveled in his recusal petition.*

No such concession was ever made. It was a misrepresentation of the record, pure and simple.

I didn't know it at the time, but six months earlier Disciplinary Board members John Morris and Angelo Scaricamazza had voted to dismiss the charges against Stan Rebert, even under the lower standard.

Nor could I know that Angelo Scaricamazza, the good soldier, would become Chairman of the Disciplinary Board on April 1, 2001.

My problem? How to make swimming in a cesspool fun?

ADRIENNE CALLS IT QUITS

November 1998

Recess! It felt like grade school. The mandatory Continuing Legal Education class was an unbelievable bore. As the lawyers moved for the exits, I went with the flow. Just outside I noticed an attractive young woman with a cell phone plastered to her ear. After using the men's room and getting a cup of coffee, I wandered back toward the hotel ballroom.

There she was—still talking. As I walked past her, she pushed the "off" button and put the phone into her purse. I looked at her and said:

"It will not be long before cell phones are implanted in babies heads at birth"

She smiled and said:

"We are working on that."

We walked back into the room together and I noticed her seat was in the very back of the room not far from mine. I hadn't noticed her as I had spent the morning reading the New York Times. The seat next to her was open so I picked up my coat and newspaper and moved beside her. We began a conversation that continued in hushed tones through the next hour's class. She was a very intelligent young lady and extremely articulate. The conversation, "sotto voce" was wide ranging and fascinating. At the end of the session, we exchanged e-mail addresses as the horde of lawyers rushed for the exits.

That night I sent her an e-mail and received a reply the next day. We arranged for lunch the following day. It looked like a very interesting situation. Over lunch, I was startled to hear that not only was she a lawyer; she was a pediatric plastic surgeon who specialized in burn repair, mostly in the inner city. I was very taken by this woman of substantial accomplishment. She lived in Upper Darby but began driving to my house in West Chester to accompany me on my daily three-mile walk. This went on through November into December. We both agreed that we had never been with another where the conversation flowed with depths and nuances that would fly by others.

On Christmas day, Adrienne came to the house in a hostess gown, obviously ready for a party somewhere. She held my hand and told me that there would never be anything other than friendship between us as she was living with an orthopedic surgeon and had been for years.

We continued our daily walks until I moved to Florida in April. At times, she would burst into tears and tell me about her failing medical practice. Because she did burn work in the inner city, pay from Medicaid and whatever insurance was available, was very slow. It barely covered the cost of her office. She told me that her medical malpractice insurance was skyrocketing—it was now almost fifty thousand dollars a year. She couldn't afford it. Her significant other had paid her last premium. She loved her work and apparently was the only one pasting these disfigured children, mostly black and Hispanic, back together.

While back in Florida, we kept in touch by e-mail and telephone. Her situation was getting worse. She couldn't ask her friend to continue to pay her malpractice insurance and she couldn't, under Pennsylvania law, continue her surgery without it.

In July, I had to go back to Philadelphia and arranged to meet with Adrienne for lunch at a downtown restaurant. She was distraught. She had closed her practice. I asked her who would take care of the inner-city kids, and she told me that there was no one else doing what she did.

It really didn't mean much to me at the time. Like most people, I had other things on my mind. So long as my Medicare and AARP supplement paid my medical bills, it was not a problem to me. The only health care crisis I now knew about was for inner-city kids with disfiguring burns. I knew that insurance costs were increasing dramatically as a result of malpractice suits against doctors and hospitals, but it wasn't touching me so I didn't focus on it.

PATLA lawyers were having a field day and the general public wasn't looking.

THE ROLE OF THE SUPREME COURT IN THE COMING MEDICAL MALPRACTICE CRISIS

1997-1999

There was gold to be mined in Philadelphia.

The trial lawyers knew that Philadelphia juries, mostly working class, with a lottery mentality, would produce big verdicts in medical malpractice cases. Consequently, cases from all over Pennsylvania flooded into the Philadelphia court system. But there was a procedural problem. A lawsuit had to be brought in the county where the cause of action arose. If the alleged malpractice happened in Bucks County, for example, the lawsuit should be brought in Bucks County. However, there was an escape hatch in the Rules. Where there were multiple defendants, a lawsuit could be brought in any county where any one of the defendants could be served. Because of the nature of the health care delivery system, with large hospital systems or group practices, doctors and hospitals services usually spanned many counties, almost always including Philadelphia. Therefore, if the alleged malpractice occurred in Bucks County, if any of the alleged tortfeasors had an office or any kind of a presence in Philadelphia, the suit could be brought in Philadelphia and was being brought there.

The insurance companies for the doctors and hospitals soon caught on to what was happening.. The Rules also provided that:

"For the convenience of the parties and witnesses, the court, upon petition of any party may transfer an action to the appropriate court of any other county where the action could originally have been brought."

Petitions for transfer began to flood in as the defense lawyers for the insurance companies wanted to avoid hostile juries in Philadelphia. Judges not in the thrall of the trial lawyers in Philadelphia began to transfer the malpractice cases to the counties where they belonged. The trial lawyers appealed these transfers.

Enter the Pennsylvania Supreme Court where the majority of the Justices were in the thrall of the trial lawyers. The test case, *Cheeseman v. Lethal Exterminator, Inc,* was not a medical malpractice case. This would provide cover for what was really happening. The Supreme Court nóted in *Cheeseman* that:

...all of the parties and fact witnesses resided in Bucks County; all of Kathleen Cheeseman's treating physicians resided in Bucks; and no significant aspect of the case involved Philadelphia.

Nevertheless, the Supreme Court reversed the trial Judge and the Superior Court's approval of the transfer of the case to Bucks County. Justice Newman, noted in a dissent:

"Today, this Court has again revised the test for change of venue petitions ...

She let the cat out of the bag by further noting:

Perhaps the perception the Philadelphia juries are more generous than those in Bucks County has influenced Appellants' (plaintiffs') *choice of forum."*

Justice Newman's Dissent was not to the result; she objected because the change of law was not applied to all of the pending cases where plaintiffs had appealed decisions transferring cases out of Philadelphia.

With the exits barred, the Philadelphia Judges pushed these medical malpractice cases through the system. The result was predictable. To be sure, there were verdicts for the defendants in many of the cases. A significant number of medical malpractice cases are spurious and can't be proved. The suits are started by hungry lawyers in the hope that the insurance carrier will pay something just to be done with the litigation. But the verdicts for plaintiffs were whoppers. In 1999 and 2000, there were forty-four medical malpractice verdicts of over one million dollars in Philadelphia, some up to forty million dollars. *The Philadelphia Inquirer* reported on September 2, 1999 that:

The state fund that covers most malpractice claims for doctors and hospitals in Pennsylvania paid out a record amount-$299 million-for lawsuits over the last year, due mainly to a surge in cases from Philadelphia.

The state fund referred to above is the so-called CAT fund, fully funded on a yearly basis by the doctors and hospitals. The unfounded potential liability in the CAT fund was approaching three billion dollars.

It would only be a matter of time before the medical malpractice problem would exacerbate into crisis.

LASHED TO THE RACK

The Supreme Court

November 15, 1999

The Supreme Court argument was scheduled for Tuesday, November 16, and I was meeting with Sam Klein to go over the legal argument he intended to offer the next day.

We met in his office with Carrie Flaxman, his attractive and very bright assistant. Sam started by reading some notes he had made. He told me that he was going to tell the Court that I conceded that the charges I had made against the Judges were untrue. I went ballistic! I have never had such a rush! In the first place, I believed with all my heart that what I had written in the Motion to Recuse was true. In the second place, the evidence I had presented totally justified what I had written. Most importantly, both the Special Hearing Committee and Disciplinary Board concluded that I was justified in the allegations. What in the world made Sam want to take this position?

"Sam, you concede that up front, and I can write the first sentence of the Court's opinion. It will be, 'Surrick admits his Motion to Recuse contained knowing falsehoods.' Jesus Christ, Sam, you still don't get it. You believe in goodness and honor and the majesty of the law and probably the fucking tooth fairy! These sons-a-bitches don't care what is right or what the truth is. They are on a mission to disbar me. The only way you can stop it is not to give an inch and beat them at their own power game. Show weakness and they will eat you alive."

"Calm down."

"No, goddamnit I will not calm down. These aren't grade school playground games. Zappala and Cappy want to bury me, and they will if we don't stand up to them. They are used to running over people. The only thing they understand is if you stand up to them and threaten to expose them."

Sam looked truly startled by my outburst. I was rolling.

"Look Sam, I know you have to practice in the system. I know that to do this, at some level, you have to believe in the system. If you don't believe, you can't do your job. You will walk around pissed off all the time. I understand that. I've been there. When I came to understand that the people running the system were corrupt to the core, and will only do what is right if they don't have a dog in the fight, my courtroom days were over. It's like trying to make nice with your wife when you know she's screwing your best friend. I am not asking you to convert or even try and understand what I am saying. I just want you to stand toe-to-toe with these bastards and not give an inch. If Zappala mistakes courtesy for weakness, he'll walk all over you."

"Bob, I—"

"No, Sam, I'm dead serious. I won at every level for the last fifteen years because I took no shit from anyone. I wasn't rude or arrogant, but I sure as hell stood my ground and let them know that I knew what they were trying to do."

Sam, always the diplomat, said:

"Bob, why don't you tell me what you really think?"

That broke the tension. I laughed. I knew that, in the end, he would do what had to be done and that, after our meeting, we would both be on the same page. Sam Klein is a decent and honorable man. A good man.

The next day I drove to Harrisburg and once again climbed the steps of the State Capitol. I first stopped in the newsroom on the second floor, and found what I expected at eight fifty-five a.m. – nobody. I had sent a press release about the argument but knew that I had become old news. Some of my reporter friends would be sorry that Surrick had troubles, but their editors would be disinterested in a story that now seemed longer than *War and Peace.*

I walked up to the Supreme Court Chamber on the fourth floor. As I entered, I saw Ron Castille, now Justice Castille, on his crutches, talking to a group of school children that had come to the state Capitol to see government in action. He had lost a leg in 'Nam and never let anyone forget it. We exchanged glances. There was no acknowledgement on either side. I mirthlessly laughed to myself as I wondered how much the kids believed, and how much Castille believed, about the honor and integrity of this mysterious and awesome Supreme Court sitting in a gilded chamber that was fit for the Hapsburgs.

I looked around the courtroom. I was the first case on the list. No reporters were present. I thought back about Fred Cusick at my house on the Fourth of July, 1980 and Dan Biddle's relentless quest for information from me during the eighties. I thought about the extensive material I had given him, and his Pulitzer Prize. Now I was alone in a silent world.

Sam Klein arrived, and we went into the hall to talk briefly. I then took my seat in the front row of the second section where I could hear, but not be in Sam's back pocket. The clerk entered and started as usual:

"Oyez! Oyez! Oyez! The Supreme Court of Pennsylvania, Chief Justice Flaherty presiding, is now in session. God save this Honorable Court."

My attention went immediately to Justice Zappala. His thick black hair was, as usual, well coiffed. In his black robe, he looked every inch the Godfather he had become. He sat quietly on the bench, not looking at me, seemingly concentrating on the attorneys before him. A balding Justice Cappy, Zappala's toady, looked, as usual, a little disheveled and out of place. I suspected that Zappala would load the gun, and Cappy would fire it.

There were half-a-dozen lawyers in the chamber who knew me, lawyers I had argued cases against, who declined to meet my eyes when I looked at them. When you're on top, you have a million friends. When you're down, nobody knows you.

Sam made a good argument, but I knew I was toast from the "get-go" from the questions Cappy and Zappala asked. It became perfectly clear that they were going to apply the *Rebert* "reckless ignorance" standard to me even though it didn't exist when I filed my Motion to Recuse. Worse yet, they were going to shift the burden to require me to prove my innocence, without giving me a hearing to do so. Of course, it was all done with back and forth exaggerated courtesy, and high-minded phrases, but I knew that I was about to be buried.

When the argument was over, I stood to leave and looked at the ornate, gilded and marble elevated bench where the Justices were sitting. Justice Newman saw me and turned to Castille. I could read her lips saying, "He's here!" I guess they all thought that since I was retired and living in Florida, I wouldn't bother to come up for the argument.

When we left, I saw Sam was seriously frustrated. It later dawned on me that Sam was approaching clinical depression as a result of the conflict between his principles and the reality of what the court system had become. I told him he did a great job, and gave him a ride to the train station. He didn't want to ride back to Philadelphia with me. Enough was enough, already. I understood.

I figured about four months for an Opinion. I was right on target.

While driving back to West Chester, I thought about the last sixteen years of non-stop prosecution by Disciplinary Counsel and my need to keep going, absorbing punishment while winning each and every time. Why did I keep going? Maybe Robert Service had someone like me in mind when he wrote *GRIN:*

There's nothing to be gained by whining
And you're not that kind of stuff
You're a fighter from way back
And you won't take a rebuff
Your trouble is that you don't
Know when you've had enough.

DE NILE REVISITED

December 14, 1999

Sam Klein had called and I returned the call.

"Ellen, is Mr. Klein in?"

"Sam's on another line. Wait just a minute Bob, and I'll put you through. By the way, how's Sandy?"

Sandy had been the love of my life for the last five years.

"It's over, Ellen."

"What do you mean, it's over?"

"Just what I said. Knowing Sandy, there's no way I will ever see or hear from her again."

"Bob, she loves you. She'll be back."

"Not a chance. She…"

"Sam's free, I'll put you through. Bye."

"Sam, what's up?"

"You won't believe the conversation I just had with John Morris," Sam said. "You remember John Morris was on the Special Hearing Committee after the Supreme Court sent your case back to the Disciplinary Board for rehearing to apply the *Rebert* standard. I was walking back to the office and bumped into him. His office is in my building. Well, he started talking about why he voted against you. He said he knew 'The Bradley case was fixed,' probably by Larsen. And he said, 'Nobody believed Cirillo.' Then, he said you went 'Too far on Olszewski.'"

"Hold it Sam. Wait. Didn't Morris write a Concurring Opinion in the Disciplinary Board Report? He did. I have it right here. Wait a minute. Here it is. He wrote:

*I strongly disagree with the majority's failure to find an additional violation regarding Surrick's statements concerning the trial judge (*Bradley*) and another judge of the Superior Court (*Cirillo*).*

Sam, if you live to be one hundred, you will never see duplicity on this scale again. When he was talking to you, he probably forgot what he wrote. Wait a minute. You said he told you that there 'probably was a fix in on Bradley.' Listen to this. He wrote in his Opinion:

Second, Surrick not only trumpeted his unsupported charge of a "fix" but then he proceeded with even greater license to invent a scenario as to how and why the case was fixed. This scenario...involved various local political figures acting in the supposed interests of another Superior Court judge whose alleged interest in filling a vacancy on the Supreme Court was somehow connected to why the trial judge decided the case incorrectly. Inasmuch as Surrick now concedes that the case was not fixed, his scenario of <u>how</u> it was fixed can only be viewed as ruthlessly bizarre.

Godamnit, Sam, how can he know that all this sleaze is going on, the fixing, and lying, and then vote against me? It doesn't make sense. From what you're telling me, he knew that what I wrote in the Motion to Recuse was accurate. How can he pick an isolated incident and say 'Surrick crossed the line here,' when he knew the deck was stacked; that the system was rigged? How can somebody say that Surrick was right that Larsen was trying to fix cases against him — and then find me guilty on a pissant point that I was right about anyway! Sam we both know that Olszewski ..."

"Calm down Bob, I wasn't going to tell you because I knew you would go ballistic. I—."

"You're goddamn right, I am ballistic. You and I both know that when the *Rebert* case came out, I was dead. When the Supreme Court changed the Rule in *Rebert*, they did it to get to me. They couldn't change the rule in my case because it would have been too obvious. But changing it in *Rebert* changed the Rule in the dark. The *Rebert* case was supposed to be confidential. We both know that Morris would not have been put on the panel unless he'd do what was in his best interest. It stinks!"

"You're right, it stinks."

"Sam, you and I have talked about this in the past. Guys like Morris are very pragmatic. They'll do whatever they have to do to protect themselves and get ahead in the system. They can know something is bad and go into complete denial! They have no understanding of what Georges Clemenceau wrote about the Dreyfus court-martial:

When one man's rights are violated, every man's rights are jeopardized.

He knows there is lying and fixing going on, yet he votes with the liars and fixers. Doesn't he have any conscience?"

"Bob, I know that you won't understand this, but most men do what they feel they have to."

"You're right, I don't understand, never will, and don't want to. Sorry I'm yelling at you."

Oh well, thirty pieces of silver for one little kiss still goes a long way!

LASHED TO THE RACK

The Coup De Grace

March 25, 2000

Let's review the bidding.

On August 11, 1992, I filed a Motion to Recuse in the case of *Leedom v. Spano and Surrick*. On November 22, 1994, the Office of Disciplinary Counsel, appointed by the Supreme Court, filed a Petition for Discipline alleging I had violated the Code of Professional Responsibility in the Motion to Recuse by making knowingly false charges against Judges Bradley, Olszewski and Cirillo. In spite of the Rule requiring a hearing before a three-lawyer, fact-finding committee within sixty days, I didn't get a hearing until one-hundred and eighty days later on July 26, 27, and 28, 1995. In spite of the Rule requiring the Hearing Committee to file a Report within sixty days, the committee didn't file until I took them to Federal Court eighteen months later in January 1997.

The Special Hearing Committee found that I had a reasonable factual basis for the allegations in the Motion and recommended dismissal of the charges. On review of the Report of the Special Hearing Committee, the Disciplinary Board agreed that I had a reasonable factual basis for what I wrote, and on October 17, 1997, dismissed the charges. Disciplinary Counsel appealed to the Supreme Court.

On April 1, 1998, the Supreme Court decided the *Rebert* case, changing the standard by which attorney representations are to be judged. Two weeks later, the Supreme Court remanded my case to the Disciplinary Board to be judged in accordance with the new, and lower, standard announced in *Rebert.* The Disciplinary Board caught on and found that I had violated the "new" standard and recommended that I receive a public reprimand. I appealed the retroactive application of the new standard, (which didn't exist in 1993 when I filed the Motion to Recuse), to the Supreme Court. The case was argued before the Supreme Court on November 16, 1999, at which time the Court considered the evidence in the record taken on July 26, 27, and 28, 1995, under the "new" standard announced on April 1, 1998. The Court also changed the burden of proof placing upon me the burden of proving my innocence. I would not be allowed a new hearing to offer such proof even though I now had a new burden. It was Kafkaesque.

So here I am, eight years after filing a Motion to Recuse, waiting for the Supreme Court to hammer me. I had become numb — in a sort of catatonic state about the whole thing.

The phone rang and when I picked it up, I heard Sam Klein say:

"Bob, I have bad news. Let me read it to you. Cappy wrote it."

This Court is presented with the question of whether the evidence is sufficient to establish Respondent's culpability on two charges that he violated Rule 8.4 (c). The precise issue to be resolved is whether Respondent acted with reckless disregard for the truth when he leveled accusations of case fixing against certain jurists in a pleading filed in the Superior Court. For the reasons set forth herein, we find that Respondent did violate Rule 8.4 (c) on both counts and that the appropriate discipline is a five-year suspension from the practice of law.

"Are you there, Bob?"

"Yes. Can you fax the Opinion? Did they slam me?"

"They did. Do you want me to read it.

"Might as well."

We do not find that public censure would be sufficient to address the measure of Respondent's wrongful conduct. Although we have concluded that Respondent acted recklessly rather than intentionally in this matter, the impact upon Judge Bradley, Judge Olszewski and the judicial system as a whole, is the same. Respondent's predilection to unprovoked character assassination, whenever he receives an adverse ruling, exhibits conduct that is clearly unprofessional and calls into question his ability to continue practicing law in a fit manner. Respondent, in preference for his personal conspiracy theories, recklessly, and carelessly, disregarded the truth when he called into question the integrity of the judicial system by declaring the system is subject to the whim and manipulation of one person. Respondent's conduct was inexcusable and unprofessional. His defense of this conduct does not allay our concerns with his fitness to practice law; rather it arouses them.

"Sam, did Cappy point to any part of my testimony that he said was untrue or even reckless under the new standard?"

"No. He dealt only in generalities. Nothing specific because there wasn't any testimony that he could point to that wasn't true."

I couldn't help thinking about that day in 1956 — forty-four years ago — when I visited the Media Courthouse and was so moved by the majesty and dignity of the courtroom. Here seven Supreme Court Justices had desecrated the concept of the Rule of Law to silence a critic, a critic who believed with all his soul in the Rule of Law. A majority of the Justices, Castille, Nigro, Saylor and Newman certainly knew that the process had been perverted by the change of the rules in the middle of the process. Their willingness to go along with the Zappala vendetta raised the age-old question. In any polity, when does compliance with injustice become complicity? It was obvious that the silent Justices had crossed the line. In crossing the line, they betrayed their oath of office. And as certain as night follows day, they had fashioned various forms of denial to assuage their guilt, if they had any.

"Are you there, Bob?"

"Yes, Sam, I am. I keep thinking about that Judge in England — I think his name was Jeffries — he would sentence pickpockets and minor criminals to death by being chained to the seawall on the Thames at low tide. Then he would have his lunch in a pub with a view of the seawall, watching the tide come up and drown the poor wretches. Are Cappy and Zappala any different?"

"Don't go there, Bob."

"I won't, Sam. I am well aware that anger corrodes its container. But for the moment, I have to wonder how they live with themselves."

While the press did not attend the hearing, the Opinion of the Supreme Court was so harsh that it was finally picked up. On March 25, 2000, the *Inquirer* published a story that headlined,

Lawyer who blew whistle suspended:

Robert Surrick helped get a Pa. Supreme Court justice impeached. The court said the facts are not related.

The article began:

A lawyer who helped spearhead efforts that led to the impeachment of a Pennsylvania Supreme Court justice has been suspended from practicing law by the state's high court.

While the *Inquirer* was continuing to write about my predicament, at least in a superficial way, its reporters would not dig behind the story. They had become publishers of handout news releases. There would be no more investigative pieces about corruption in Pennsylvania Courts. The heady eighteen years of Gene Roberts and seventeen Pulitzers were over. Before and during the impeachment of Rolf Larsen, the *Inquirer* signaled that it would give Zappala and his cohorts a pass.

Meager journalism had become the rule.

THE DISCIPLINARY BOARD OF THE SUPREME COURT

June 2000

In 2003, HALT, a nonprofit good government group in Washington that limits its scope to analyzing and rating attorney accountability systems in the fifty states, rated Pennsylvania's Disciplinary Board last-dead last! Was this news to me? Hell no! I had been claiming for years that the Disciplinary Board, under the complete control of the Supreme Court and PATLA types, had become a political arm of the Court, giving passes to the chosen and their cronies and punishing enemies.

In the 1993, 1995 and 1997 campaigns, I had decried the low estate to which the Board had fallen and outlined specific proposals for reform. I was a lonely voice in the wilderness. The lawyers and so-called leaders of the bar, as usual, ignored the obvious, just as they ignored the obvious and supported the Retention Election of Justice Larsen in 1987 and Justice Papadakos in 1993.

The inherent and fatal defect in the attorney discipline system is grounded in the 1968 Constitution that created a unified judicial system under the <u>complete and total control</u> of the Supreme Court. A practical reality of governance is found in the enduring truth of Niccolo Machiavelli's maxim in *The Prince* that power corrupts and absolute power corrupts absolutely. As the Larsen led Supreme Court degraded, that complete control over the attorney discipline system became a path to perdition.

During these campaigns, speaking to reform of the attorney discipline process, I proposed that the power of appointment of the Disciplinary Board be removed from the Supreme Court. I proposed a fifteen member Disciplinary Board made up of the Presidents of the county bar associations on a rotating basis. I suggested this would be a much less risky proposition than relying on a politically elected Supreme Court. Under my proposal, the Board, not the Supreme Court, would promulgate the Code of Professional Responsibility and appoint the hearing committees.

I also proposed the creation of an Office of Disciplinary Counsel headed by Chief Disciplinary Counsel who would be selected from a list of three attorneys proffered by the Disciplinary Board to the Chief Justice, the Governor and the Attorney General. The appointment would be for a fixed term. Chief Disciplinary Counsel would staff his or her office.

Under my proposal, the Supreme Court would be final arbiter of all appeals from the Disciplinary Board.

All proceedings would be open to public scrutiny.

Would this be perfect? Nothing is perfect. But a lot more people would have to be corrupted than seven Supreme Court Justices for the system to malfunction as it now does.

Will this kind of reform happen? I doubt it. The pols, the special interest groups, and the Judges like it the way it is. Their attitude would be: Forget the dreadful rating of HALT; it's ours to control and we like it the way it is.

In the unforgettable phrase coined by departed *Inquirer* columnist Steve Lopez:

Pennsylvania, Land of Giants

It was time to move to Florida.

MAYBE — JUST MAYBE

September 19, 2000

The Board meeting dragged on.

I had been elected to the Board of Directors of Sombrero Country Club in Marathon, Florida, in February. I immediately became embroiled in controversy over the financial situation of the club. It was clear to me that if spending continued at the present level, we were in for a hefty assessment and dues increase. With many of the members on fixed income, and others who only used the club for two or three months a year, I was concerned that we would price ourselves out of a limited market and begin to lose members.

I spoke out about what I saw as a serious problem and, in return, the Treasurer and Finance Chairman told the Board I didn't know what I was talking about. It became intensely personal. Lynn Voit, a local artist whom I had dated, and a member of the Board, went so far as to publish a letter calling me a discredited lawyer who had been suspended for five years by the Supreme Court of Pennsylvania for making *"wild accusations not unlike my complaints of fiscal irresponsibility at the club."* Bad news travels fast.

Anyway, I was nervous. I had to catch a plane at Ft. Lauderdale at four, and was due in the United States District Court in Philadelphia the next day. The District Court had issued an Order requiring me to show cause why the Federal Court should not follow the Pennsylvania Supreme Court and suspend me for five years. Such Orders are routine, and almost always result in the Federal Court following the highest state court's attorney discipline.

Sam Klein and I both saw this as a chance to get out of a corrupt state court system into the Federal Court. Sam had filed a brief and the hearing was scheduled for four p.m. the next day.

The flight up was god-awful. What is normally a two-plus-hour flight became an eight-hour ordeal. Philadelphia was socked in and we were diverted to Atlanta. Craig was still waiting for me when the plane finally landed at the Philadelphia airport after midnight.

Before the hearing, I went to the pressroom in the Federal Courthouse and talked with Shannon Duffy, the Federal Court reporter for *The Legal Intelligencer*. I knew he would be interested. He had covered many other stories in which I was involved; the Stretton hearing before Judge Newcomer; the successful 1993 ballot access challenge before Judge Cahn; and the hearing before Judge McGlynn, when I had tried, unsuccessfully, to block the Disciplinary Board's prosecution over the Motion to Recuse. Duffy admired my willingness to throw my body in front of a speeding train. He didn't understand that my vote to remove Justice Larsen in 1983 had started a series of prosecutions over which I had no control. I could only defend myself and go on offense when I had the chance.

I was elated with the panel of three Judges assigned to hear argument. All were civil-rights sensitive and understood the deeper meanings of the First Amendment. Sam made an understated but cogent argument on my behalf. My elation turned to pure excitement as the argument progressed. As an experienced trial lawyer, I recognized where the panel was going, and it was beyond my wildest hopes!

I can't adequately express the feelings that coursed through me as I realized I was finally going to get a fair hearing. It was clear that these three Judges were offended by the shenanigans of the Pennsylvania Supreme Court.

I couldn't believe it when Judge Padova actually forced Disciplinary Counsel to concede that I had never been given a hearing on the charges on which I was suspended. And that I had never been given the opportunity to come forward with evidence to meet the new burden of proof decreed by the Supreme Court.

Could this nightmare be ending? Finally, maybe, just maybe, after all these years of harassment and prosecution, I would have a hearing where the deck was not stacked.

When we left the courtroom, Sam and his assistant, Carrie Flaxman, were jubilant. They saw daylight! Sam, a deeply sensitive man, and Carrie, a very bright young lawyer, knew something important had happened.

However, as the Pennsylvania Dutch are wont to say, "The proof of the pudding is in the eating."

I'll wait for the pudding, thank you!

HOW SWEET IT IS

February 7, 2001

The phone rang and I picked it up.

"Bob, will you please get off the damn phone? I'm trying to send you a fax."

"Okay, Ellen."

Ellen Kauffman, Sam Klein's long-time secretary, could be very direct. I had called her several days before asking for a copy of the Cappy Opinion in *Disciplinary Board v. Surrick.*

I let the fax activate, and the copy began to come through. I became curious as the pages piled up. I didn't remember the Cappy Opinion being that long. I picked up the pages that had come through and saw to my amazement the caption for the United States District Court for the Eastern District of Pennsylvania. I hurriedly scanned the fifteen or so pages I now had and saw the factual background of my case was being outlined in minute detail. No clue as to which way the case was being decided. It was exquisitely nerve-wracking to take the pages, one at a time, as they were slowly printed; four pages a minute. Come on, come on, I thought as I scanned each page for a clue.

Then, on page thirty-three, finally, the words I had been looking for.

"Mr. Surrick has not waived his right to be treated fairly by this court."

The District Court was not going to follow the Pennsylvania Supreme Court! I spun through the remaining pages to see the strength of the language. Judge Stuart Dalzell wrote a Concurring Opinion wherein he observed:

Surrick's professional catastrophe is thus of grave First Amendment moment to the Bar and to the public.

. . .

While a courtroom is, to be sure, not a free speech zone on the order of a public square or the Internet, neither is it an alien place to core First Amendment values, as this case illustrates. Judges are public figures and their impartiality and ethics are matters of profound public concern.

He then footnoted:

See 22 Judicial Conduct Reporter...reporting that between 1980 and the end of 1999 no less than 266 state court judges had been removed from office as a result of judicial proceedings. Indeed in 1999 alone, two of thirteen judges were removed because of ex parte communications. It is well past the time in Pennsylvania when one could reflexively attribute such improper communications to lawyers' hyperactive imaginations.

I was numb! I had gotten a fair shake! Seventeen, going on eighteen years! One-fourth of my life!

I spent the next three hours on the phone with lawyers, reporters, Sam Klein, Sam Stretton, and others. It was a smorgasbord of congratulations and legal analysis.

On February 9, 2001, Shannon Duffy of *The Legal Intelligencer*, reported:

Panel Recommends Bob Surrick Be Allowed To Appear in Federal Court

Attorney Robert Surrick has been suspended from practicing for five years by the Pennsylvania Supreme Court, but the U.S. District Court in Philadelphia is leaning heavily toward allowing him to continue practicing there due to the unfairness of the process that led to his state court suspension.

The Philadelphia Inquirer missed the story. Finally, I sent Fred Cusick a copy of the Opinion and the Legal Intelligencer article. Ten days after the fact, on February 17, 2001, the *Inquirer* headlined a story:

U.S. panel says Pa. Infringed lawyer's right

Cusick wrote:

In a decision released last week, the federal judges said that they found the state Supreme Court had effectively changed the rules in Surrick's case in the middle of the disciplinary proceeding that led to his suspension.

Speaking for the panel, Judge Louis H. Pollak said the Supreme Court's methods were not the kind on which the federal court "can confidently rely."

The three-Judge panel of the United States District Court had slammed the Pennsylvania Supreme Court. I doubt that this had ever happened in the history of attorney discipline in Pennsylvania.

It was historic. I felt eternally grateful that the system had finally worked.

LASHED TO THE RACK

Disciplinary Counsel Calls It Quits

February 10, 2001

Two days after receiving the good news from the three-Judge panel, Sam Klein called again.

"Are you still celebrating, Bob?"

"Sam, you know how high I was after receiving your fax. It just doesn't get any better. It would be really hard to articulate what I felt. You know my overly heightened sense of right and wrong. The release that I felt when I received the news was enormous."

"Well, I have some more good news. Disciplinary Counsel will not file objections or exceptions. They have thrown in the towel."

"Does this mean what I think it means? That Disciplinary Counsel is saying that there's no viable basis to find fault, legally, with the Pollak Report?"

"That's exactly what it means, Bob. It's over. You've won. Of course, the entire twenty-some Judge court will have to sign off but between the stature of the panel and the absence of objection of Disciplinary Counsel it will be pro forma. Not a chance in a million that the full Court would ever reverse the panel."

"From your mouth to God's ear."

"It's done — over."

"One final question, Sam. Who can I sue for eighteen years of embarrassment, misery, and the destruction of my practice?"

"I knew you would ask that, and I already have two assistants on it."

"You know how I feel about you, Sam, so I leave it at that, thank you. I won't activate your homophobia again by telling you I love you."

"As you like to say, Bob, it just doesn't get any better."

A FEDERAL FIASCO

April 2, 2001

"Bob. Don't pick up. Sam wants to fax you something."

"What is it Ellen?"

"Don't know but Sam is pretty upset."

"Okay. Send it now. I won't pick up."

The phone rang and I let the fax kick in. The pages started to come through and I saw it was an Order from the United States District Court for the Eastern District of Pennsylvania. I assumed it was an affirmation of the Report and Recommendation of the three-Judge panel. Sam had been working for weeks researching my right to sue the Pennsylvania Supreme Court and Disciplinary Counsel for the egregious denial of my fundamental right to procedural due process and the damage it had caused, both professionally and monetarily. When Disciplinary Counsel admitted at the hearing that I had never been given a hearing on the charge on which I had been suspended, it was all over as far as I was concerned. However, Sam had hit a wall in his research. It seemed that the Supreme Court had judicial immunity from suit, no matter how corrupt its actions. The immunity was total and all encompassing, and the immunity extended, by judicial Order, to Disciplinary Counsel.

I started to read the Order and when I reached the end of the first paragraph, I was breathless. The pit of my stomach ached and my mouth was so dry I couldn't utter a word. The Order read:

...after consideration of the Report and Recommendation of the three-judge panel of this Court dated February 7, 2001, and the appended concurring opinion, and the record in this matter, and the Court having voted not to adopt the Report and Recommendation or the concurring opinion, it is hereby ORDERED that the Report and Recommendation and the appended concurring opinion are marked NOT ADOPTED.

How could this be? The three-Judge panel consisted of really heavyweight Judges on the Eastern District bench. This Order was not only an affront to them, it was an unheard of and unprecedented "in your face" insult, the likes of which I had never seen in thirty-five years of practice.

I dialed Sam. He was as dumbstruck as I was. He asked if I had read the whole Order and when I told him that I had not, that I was too shocked by the first paragraph to go on, he said:

"Not only did they insult the panel by reversing them, they trashed them by firing them and ordering a new panel to adjudicate what the penalty should be now that they have adopted the Supreme Court's finding that you violated Rule 8.4 (c)."

"Jesus Christ, Sam, who voted? When did they vote? What the hell is going on here?"

"I don't know. But read on. The Order requires further filings to be under seal, in secret, outside of public attention. It really stinks, Bob. I am sick at heart. I always believed Federal Court Judges were apolitical because of their lifetime appointment."

"That's your virginity showing up again, Sam. Grow up! They still take phone calls. Zappala is obsessed with getting me. Off the top of my head, I can name a half-dozen Federal Judges who will take calls. Their appointment to that Court was political. Many want to go up to the Circuit Court of Appeals. They don't cut their ties to their political pals. I know for a fact that Eddie Becker (Chief Judge of the Court of Appeals for the Third Circuit) talks openly about his ties to the ward leaders in Philadelphia. Who voted and how?"

"Bob, don't go there. I don't know who voted, when they voted, what the vote was. It was all done in secret. All I know is that Dalzell, Padova and Pollak were really trashed. It's an insult beyond my experience."

"Let me go to my sources, Sam. I'll find out what happened."

"Call me with whatever you get."

I picked up the phone and called Shannon Duffy at the pressroom in the Federal Courthouse. When I told him what had happened, he was speechless. Never in his long experience had he seen anything like this.

"Shannon, can you find out what happened here? I know you have sources. Sam and I can't believe this and we would really like to know what happened before we consider our next move."

"Let me nose around, Bob. The Order doesn't give any information about what happened. I'll be back to you."

I began to go to my sources and found that there was reluctance on the part of anyone in the Federal Courthouse to talk. However, between my sources and a return call from Shannon, I was able to piece together what had happened.

When the twenty-some Judges met, they voted not to accept the Report and Recommendation. It was a single vote margin! Then, on a motion to dismiss the three-Judge panel and replace it with another, it was a tie vote. Chief Judge Jim Giles cast the tie-breaking vote to create a new panel. I knew most of these Judges. I had known Giles in the past when he was a junior lawyer with the Dilworth firm. Giles and Jay Waldman were political animals. So were Bob Kelly from Delaware County, Curt Joyner from Chester County, and Anita Brody from Montgomery County. It appeared to me that Zappala had pulled out all the stops to overturn the three-Judge panel. As Fred Cusick once observed, people like me "can't be left on the street."

I called Sam back and told him what I had found. He was busy and couldn't talk. A few hours later, in the evening, I received the following e-mail from Sam:

I HATE the practice of law. When associates, young and innocent, ask me what is going on here, it is very sad that I cannot give them any reasoned answer. This does it for me — I'm getting out.

I was very upset. It was one thing for me to have to take this bullshit but I didn't want Sam to get emotionally involved. Many, many times I had told him that you can't practice law in a corrupt system if you admit to yourself that the system is corrupt. A certain amount of denial is necessary to keep going. I e-mailed him back and asked him to call. He called back right away and I told him not to get upset — leave it to me to get upset. His only response was:

"Bob, I have to mentor young lawyers here. What do I tell them?"

Judicial corruption is like a stone dropping into calm water. There is the splash at impact but the ripples keep going with complex effect on everything they touch.

I felt great sadness for Sam. The realization that anything can be fixed at any level was more than he could handle. I knew that but tried not to let the moral issues get in the way of surviving based on asserting my legal rights. Sam was still back struggling with the fact that some Judges, Judges obligated to uphold the Rule of Law, are corrupt and evil people. The dichotomy between what he wanted to believe and was trained to believe, and the real world was tearing him up. He was stressed beyond his ability to handle it.

LASHED TO THE RACK

Another Federal Court Hearing

May 22, 2001

I met Sam in the Federal Courthouse at Sixth and Market Streets before the scheduled four p.m. hearing. Our talk was stilted and desultory. He didn't want to talk. I didn't want to talk either. Neither of us wanted to be there. We both knew that something terribly wrong had taken place and his faith in what we had been trained to respect had been badly shaken. Mine was gone. At four o'clock we took our seats in the courtroom. Judges Buckwalter, Brody and Reed entered a side door and took their seats on the bench. For an instant I wondered if all three had voted against me. Of course they had. They were appointed by Chief Judge Giles who was the tie-breaking vote on removing Dalzell, Padova, and Pollak from the case.

Buckwalter opened by making it clear that the panel didn't want to hear any argument that Surrick was not guilty of violating Rule 8.4(c). The only issue to be discussed was whether or not the Federal Court should adopt the five-year suspension ordered by the Supreme Court of Pennsylvania.

Sam made a strong argument that seemed to shake a couple of the Judges. He pointed out that I had been cleared of the main charges, i.e. making false statements to a Court, making false statements to a Judge, and bringing the judicial system into disrepute. He pointed out that never in the history of Pennsylvania had a lawyer been found guilty of violating Rule 8.4(c) standing alone — that it always had been coupled with the direct violation of a substantive rule — and that Rule 8.4(c) had been changed between the time of my hearing and the time of the Supreme Court's application of it to me. This brought frowns. He was really pointing out the absence of due process that had been found by the prior panel. Sam also pointed out that on five previous occasions, Disciplinary Counsel had recommended to the Special Hearing Committee, the Disciplinary Board, and the Supreme Court, that I receive a public censure and was now arguing that I should receive a five-year suspension. Disciplinary Counsel was making this argument after declining to challenge the Pollak panel's conclusion that I had not been treated fairly by its employer, the Pennsylvania Supreme Court.

Judge Lowell Reed, demonstrating his circle-the-wagons mentality, went after Sam about the horror of accusing Judges of fixing cases. He kept saying that this kind of charge made all Judges look bad and that it should not be tolerated under any circumstances. Sam pointed out to him that I had been exonerated of the charge of "bringing the judiciary into disrepute." Reed shook his head like a wounded bull and continued to say that this kind of accusation could not be tolerated. At this point, I knew it was Kabuki theater. The result was preordained.

Disciplinary Counsel made a weak argument, mis-stating the facts and the law in an effort to make me look like the Rasputin of the bar. I was once again listening to Bill Cherry making his jury speech in the Spano case, calling me names, but by now I had become immune to the angst of being called bad names in public.

To my surprise, Judge Buckwalter said he wanted to hear about my character. When Sam asked if he wanted to hear it from me, he said, "Yes". I walked to the podium.

"May it please the court," I started and went on to say:

"I suppose Governor Thornburgh had confidence in my character when he appointed me to the Judicial Inquiry and Review Board, which has oversight responsibility for the conduct of all Judges in Pennsylvania. I guess Common Cause/Pennsylvania thought my character was sufficient when in 1987 it awarded me its Public Service Achievement Award for my efforts to bring about judicial reform. I suppose some of the voters in Pennsylvania thought my character was okay when, without party support or money, I received twenty-six percent of the vote for the Supreme Court in 1995. I guess the editors of the thirteen newspapers who endorsed me for the Supreme Court thought I had decent character. No one has ever questioned my honesty, integrity or character before this. Or the way I practice law. My only question about myself is whether I should have agreed to serve when asked by Governor Thornburgh or whether I should have voted to remove Justice Larsen, because if I hadn't done either, I wouldn't be standing here today."

A GOOD GUY

May 29, 2001

When I walked into Guy Smith's office on State Street in Media, the secretaries greeted me with real warmth. Guy had frequently told me that I was a real hero to these women for my stands on judicial reform. Well, if the truth be known, he was the real hero. He was a totally stand-up lawyer in Delaware County, which put him in a class all by himself. Guy was a bear of a man, standing over six-feet-four, with a confident manner born of a certainty about what was right and wrong, both legally and morally.

"Surrick, get your ass in here," he bellowed from the conference room where he was working. When I walked in, he gave me a handshake that bent a few fingers and motioned for me to sit down in a chair across the conference table from him.

"What the hell are you doing in Media?" he asked.

"I've been to Bakers' Print Shop to see one of my true loves, Cindy Baker. Last week, I was back in Federal Court. That's why I'm here in Pennsylvania."

"Why Federal Court? I read in the *Inquirer* some time back that you blew Disciplinary Counsel out of the water in Federal Court."

"I did. But a funny thing happened when Alexander Graham Bell's machine started to ring off the wall in certain Federal Court Judges' chambers. The whole bench had a meeting, reversed their three-

Judge panel, fired them, and ordered me to appear and tell a more compliant panel why I shouldn't be suspended for five years."

"I don't fucking believe it. You were in the clear. Everyone knows you got a kangaroo hearing from the Supreme Court. Jesus, they are really pulling out all the stops to get you."

"Guy, I came to see you because you know what is going down around this county, and I want to know how my brother got appointed to the Federal Court. It makes no sense to me. I hear he had undecided cases on his desk for more than five years. I heard that Vince Cirillo had hauled him up to the Superior Court and chewed his ass out about his inability to make decisions and write Opinions. And as far as I know, McNichol and Sexton, who only understand power, think he is ineffective. What gives?"

"Bob, I don't know. Frank Hazel is McNichol's boy, and he was first in line. All of a sudden, something happened and Hazel was gone, and your brother was standing first in line. The strange thing is nobody's talking. Usually, after a while, someone gets drunk or someone gets super-pissed about something, and the story begins to leak. Not here — there's nothing on the street. Frank Hazel's not talking, no one's talking."

We switched subjects and began to talk about Delaware County politics. Somehow, we got back to a story Guy had told me years before about a Friday afternoon around four p.m. when he was a young assistant in District Attorney Steve McEwen's office. Steve handed him about ten files involving criminal indictments and told him to go to the Orphan's Court courtroom on the third floor, well off the beaten track in the courthouse. When Guy arrived, he found Judge Catania sitting on the bench and Jim McHugh at defense counsel's table. McHugh was a criminal defense attorney. While a bit of a Damon Runyon character, he was smart and plugged in to the political system. Catania told Guy to call his first case. Guy fumbled around, not understanding what was going on. He called one of the files, a driving under the influence case, and McHugh stood up and made a motion to dismiss the criminal charge on some ground or other. Catania immediately agreed and ordered the charge dismissed. And so it went until the ten criminal cases were forever concluded. Guy chuckled and said, "I'll bet you anything that those files no longer exist and they have been long since deep-sixed."

After a few more stories, Guy asked about Barclay. I told him that I had seen Barclay about a month ago at "Diddy" Cramp's funeral. Diddy was John Cramp's daughter who had died a very untimely death.

I related that Judge Dalzell was heard to say that he just met Barclay when Barclay came on the Federal bench, and he understood the brothers were very different kinds of people.

Guy snorted, "Different? Light years. I remember when Barclay was inducted for his second ten-year term, he didn't thank his wife or family, he publicly thanked those crooks Sexton and McNichol. He kissed their asses in public. Bob, I'll keep my ear to the ground. It was good to see you. Keep the bastards honest!"

Sometimes, meeting and talking to an honest man can do wonders for your spirit.

THE RUMBLE REACHES THE LITTLE GUYS

April 2001

I needed some medical attention. I went to see Lance Sweeney, a general practitioner in Brogue, Pennsylvania, near where I was staying. Lance is a short, middle-aged man with a kindly smile and direct blue eyes. He radiated a caring and thorough professional manner. He wanted to know all about me, the person. What I had done with my life, what caused me stress, how much I drank, did I smoke, how many brothers and sisters, what were my parents like? I was pleased that he was taking the time to find out not only what was bothering me medically but also what made me tick.

During our conversation, I also asked questions of him. He had come to rural southern York County because he wanted a real family practice. He had between four to five thousand open files at any one time. He knew the families, their history, and their needs. He felt strongly that a doctor couldn't adequately treat an individual just with medical skill and drugs—you had to treat the whole person—and a significant part of which, at times, was the emotional overlay to a medical problem.

I told him of my concern about what was happening to the health care delivery system and that I was researching it and intended to write about it. He became very animated and started talking very rapidly. I had struck a nerve.

"Bob, I don't know what I am going to do. I work sixty hours a week, which I don't mind. I love my work even though the income is shrinking and the cost of maintaining an office is going up. But the worst is my medical malpractice premiums are going out of sight."

"Lance that is just what I am focusing on. It has to do with the ascendancy of the so-called trial lawyers—at least that's what they call themselves. The medical malpractice verdicts against doctors, hospitals, nurses, laboratories, etc. are skyrocketing. The trial lawyers have gained control of the judicial system to the extent that they have a fail-safe at every level to protect their verdicts."

He thought for a moment and answered:

"What's the point of giving everything I have to the practice when it becomes an economic drag. Damnit, Bob, what I do is worth more than thirty to fifty thousand a year net—hell, I can make double that with a corporate job somewhere without all the headaches of trying to run an office and medical practice in a rural area. But these farm people need me."

"Lance, it has been coming for a long time. The specialties are getting hit hardest first. The premiums for surgeons, anesthesiologists, orthopods, are off the chart. I know a plastic surgeon in Philadelphia who at age forty-two quit. She tells me that doctors are fleeing Pennsylvania in droves. The guy she is living with, an orthopod, is in practice with eighteen other orthopods in Delaware County. They do eighty-five percent of the surgery in Delaware County and are thinking of closing their doors. Apparently, their malpractice carrier will not renew their insurance at any price and by state law you can't practice without insurance."

Wistfully, he responded:

"Let me tell you a story. I used to deliver babies—twenty-five to thirty a year. It was part of staying close to families—treating the whole person—all that—but I don't deliver babies any more."

"I am sure I know the answer but you tell me."

"Simple math—I would get around twelve-hundred dollars for a delivery which included pre and post natal care. When the malpractice insurance premium for my obstetrical practice exceeded the gross fees I was receiving for those services, it was time to pack it in."

"You, my friend, have just seen the future. It can only get worse. At least you don't have to practice in Philadelphia."

"I wouldn't," Lance said, as he handed me a month's supply of Protonex for my reflux. It appeared that he raided the drug salesman to have free drugs for his patients-a throwback he was, that's for sure.

Sooner or later he might have to pack it in—it sure as hell was not going to get any better—and the four to five thousand patients who he had caringly cared for would have to scramble.

Ah, the majesty of the law.

LASHED TO THE RACK

A Federally Funded Abortion

June 15, 2001

Sam had called late in the day and told me that the District Court had filed Opinions and Dissenting Opinions in *Disciplinary Board v. Surrick*.

"What do they say?"

"They suspended your license for thirty months. I'll let you read it first—and when you do, come scrape me off the fucking ceiling."

The fax started to print and the Opinions came through. I read, and I read, and I read. Forty years a lawyer and I had never seen anything even close.

Judge Dalzell, in a Dissenting Opinion, wrote:

The court's unsought action to reach such an unwarranted result is odd and disquieting.

. . .

Indeed, those who believe, as I do, that the First Amendment protects values at the core of our polity will share my particular disquiet that Article III (lifetime*) judges could be so unnerved by the possible application of those values in this extreme* *case that they have acted as they have where there really is no case and only controversy of their own making.*

That, sports fans, is Judge-speak for the fix was in.

Let me put it in order. First, there was the Amended Report and Recommendation written by the substituted panel. There were neither findings of fact nor discussion on the merits. They merely decided that the suspension of my Federal Court license should be thirty months, not five years.

Then, there was an Order signed by Chief Judge Giles suspending me for thirty months.

Then, there was a Dissenting Opinion by Judge Pollak, joined in by Judges Fullam, Newcomer, Green, O'Neill, Padova and Kauffman. Judge Pollak recounted the history of the case and called for affirmance of the decision of the original three Judge panel. He pointed out that the majority of the Judges, in overturning the original Report and Recommendation failed to:

...file an opinion or other written statement explaining its disagreement with the (first) Panel's...submission.

Next, there was the nine-page Dissent by Judge Dalzell, in which he blistered his brethren on the United States District Court for the Eastern District of Pennsylvania. In ringing language he decried the Court's action, taken by the *narrowest majority* that makes

...a lawyer's filing of a motion to recuse a professionally suicidal act.

Dalzell contrasted the five-year suspension that was recently imposed upon former Pennsylvania Attorney General Ernie Preate by the Supreme Court and the Surrick five year suspension. The difference? I allegedly made an "unintentional misrepresentation" in a pleading. Preate, the chief law enforcement officer in Pennsylvania, took bribes from gambling interests, a felony, and served fourteen months in federal prison. The comparison spoke volumes about the integrity and culture of the Pennsylvania Supreme Court.

Lastly, there was an unlabeled filing by Chief Judge Giles attempting, *on behalf of the court,* to justify the votes taken on April 2, 2001, that overturned the original Report and Recommendation of the first three-Judge panel and replaced the panel with more compliant Judges. Giles wrote that:

Judge Pollak acknowledged that the report had not concluded that Mr. Surrick was deprived of his federal constitutional right of due process…

Giles wrote on:

Indeed Judge Pollak expressly states, "We find it unnecessary to determine whether the state disciplinary proceedings were, taken in the aggregate, so fundamentally flawed as to yield to the conclusion that the state procedure was so lacking in notice or opportunity to be heard as to constitute a deprivation of due process.

The duplicity of this out-of-context quote is beyond cavil when reading what Judge Pollak further wrote, which Chief Judge Giles deceitfully omitted. Pollak wrote:

And it is clear to us that the processes of charge and proof that obtained in the state proceedings, even if constitutionally sufficient for the purposes of the Commonwealth, have not built a record and led to a judgment on which this court, in the performance of its independent responsibility to determine whether discipline should be imposed on a member of our bar, can confidently rely…

Having determined that, the state disciplinary proceedings resulting in the imposition of severe discipline upon Respondent Surrick do not provide a proper basis for this court to impose discipline.

That's as bad as it ever gets. Judge Pollak is a decent man and this distortion of his writing has to leave him wondering whether anything is sacred with some of his colleagues.

Citing the only other basis for overturning the first three-Judge panel, Chief Judge Giles asserted:

Indeed, Mr. Surrick admitted at state disciplinary proceedings that he had no objective factual basis for the accusations he made.

This so-called admission is, if possible, even worse than the gross distortion of Judge Pollak's Opinion. It is simply a total fabrication of the record. It never happened!

Judge Katz filed a Dissent to the second three-Judge panel. If Judge Dalzell lacerated his colleagues with the skill of a high priest with an obsidian knife, Judge Katz meat-axed the court with the following observation:

I respectfully dissent. I believe the discipline imposed is excessive and a gross overreaction, resulting in a grave injustice within the meaning of the Rule. On balance, it does more harm to the institution than to Mr. Surrick.

In all, nine Judges of the United States District Court dissented. It was unprecedented.

In spite of my anger, I had to laugh. Here were twenty or so Federal Judges running in different directions and pissing on each other in public. Reports, Amended Reports, Opinions, Dissents, written Dissents, etc. It was like *The Gang That Couldn't Shoot Straight.*

The Legal Intelligencer wrote:

A Divided Federal Bench Votes to Suspend Surrick

In an issue that seems to have bitterly divided the judges of the Eastern District bench, the full court voted to impose a 30-month suspension on attorney Robert B. Surrick—rejecting the previous recommendation by a three judge panel that Surrick undergo no discipline since his five year suspension by the Pennsylvania Supreme Court was the result of an unfair process.

Sam Klein was so angry that, without telling me, he filed an appeal to the Court of Appeals for the Third Circuit. Could it be that we were headed for the Supreme Court of the United States?

I had to ask myself, was the judicial system, which I so revered for so many years, always like this? Or was my prediction in 1981 that we were sliding into the Judicial Dark Ages prescient now that the District Court had proved itself just as corruptly political as the Pennsylvania Supreme Court?

STAN THE MAN

September 19, 2000

"May I speak to Mr. Rebert's secretary," I asked the receptionist at the office of the District Attorney of York County.

After spending several years in shorts and a golf shirt, I was back in a suit, blue striped button down shirt, highly polished wing tipped cordovans, braces and a matching tie. It really felt good. I still loved being a lawyer—the ambiance of a courthouse—the confident feeling of knowing you are good at what you do—the majesty of the law. How is it that I still get these feelings when at another level, I know of the sleaze, including case fixing, that goes on in these majestic buildings.

As I was musing about the fine line between denial and being schizo, a very attractive middle-aged woman opened the door and said "Mr. Rebert will see you now."

"I didn't know Mr. Rebert would be in," I answered. "Yesterday, when I was talking to him, he said was going to Harrisburg today."

"He got back early," she said as we entered Stan's office.

Having never met Stan, I was a little surprised by his appearance. I had been told he had multiple sclerosis and was failing. He seemed young, alert, with a devil-may-care look in his eye. Remaining seated, he took my out-stretched hand and said: "The file's on the conference table. Take whatever you need."

I couldn't believe it! I knew Stan was loose but giving me his confidential file was far more than expected when I called to ask him what happened to his Disciplinary Board proceeding. I felt sure the Board would give Stan a pass after Rule 8.4 (c) had been changed and applied to me. The file he offered was a treasure trove.

Rebert had been charged by Disciplinary Counsel with twice lying or misrepresenting to a Judge that he had given defense counsel investigative material that defense counsel was entitled to have under a Court Order. It was no ordinary criminal case. It was a high-visibility capital murder case where a young female had been brutally murdered. Stan, who had personally taken charge of the file, was pushing hard for the death penalty. The material withheld was a statement from a felon who Stan had planted in the jail with the defendant to gain an admission to be used at the trial. The felon had given statements at two separate times. Stan had only turned over one without revealing to the Court or defense counsel the existence of the other.

Stan took the position that he was under the impression that defense counsel had both statements. But if he had merely looked in his file (at the inventory of documents turned over, before he represented to the Judge that defense counsel was in possession of all required material), he would have seen that such a representation was not true. It certainly could be argued that the pressure of seeking a "murder one" conviction led Rebert to knowingly play fast and loose with the truth.

But this was another charade. The Supreme Court had ruled in *Rebert* that a misrepresentation was established when an attorney *deliberately closes his eyes to facts which he has a duty to see.* Did Stan Rebert have a duty to look at the file in his hand? In a case where a man's life was at stake?

His file further revealed that, on remand, the Disciplinary Board, without re-argument or further hearing, ignored the "new standard" of "reckless ignorance" and dismissed the charges against Stan Rebert, finding that his conduct was "not intentional." John Morris voted to dismiss.

Unlike in *Disciplinary Board v. Surrick,* Disciplinary Counsel chose not to appeal.

The file also revealed the taxpayers of York County had paid his fifty thousand dollar legal fee.

The system was working very well, thank you.

THE PENNSYLVANIA TRIAL LAWYERS ASSOCIATION

(PATLA)

On September 17, 1970, a group of lawyers, disgruntled with the Philadelphia blue-blood law firms having their way with their hand picked Judges, formed the Pennsylvania Trial Lawyers Association a/k/a PATLA.

At first, PATLA's growth was slow. They were lawyers who represented plaintiffs in personal injury claims on a contingent fee basis. It was a rag-tag bunch, mostly from Philadelphia, who had been shut out of the Philadelphia Bar Association leadership. They knew they needed to get control of the selection of Judges.

Control of the Disciplinary Board was of equal importance. In the 1950's and 60's, the Board of Censors of the Philadelphia Bar Association (this was before the creation of the Disciplinary Board of the Supreme Court) had declared war on the plaintiffs' lawyers. These plaintiffs' lawyers were mostly Jewish. The bluebloods saw them as ambulance chasers and worse. The prosecutions of these lawyers for alleged ethical infractions began to look like a pogrom. PATLA saw control of the attorney disciplinary process as absolutely necessary for their survival.

Along came Rolf Larsen. In 1977, with the help of this group, Larsen became a Justice of the Supreme Court. Larsen saw, in the growing power of a group dedicated to seizing control of the judiciary, a perfect vehicle for his ambition to control the Supreme Court and become Chief Justice of Pennsylvania. PATLA leaders saw in Larsen the ability to open the doors to a system heretofore closed to them. It was a marriage of convenience, but it also was a love match. An outsider all of his life, Larsen bonded with these outsiders as they did with him.

It was about this time period that the so-called trial lawyers discovered that there was a sea-change taking place in the medical community. For significant witness fees, doctors became available to testify against other doctors. Actually, it was happening in all professions as the litigation moneypot dramatically increased. Expert witnesses in malpractice cases became an offshoot of the oldest profession.

After Larsen's election, their first order of business was to gain control of the attorney discipline process. The Board was funded out of the budget of the Supreme Court and appointed by the Supreme Court. All appeals were to the Supreme Court.

Early on, there was a scattering of PATLA members appointed to the Board. Harold Randolf, Tom Foley, and Bill Archbold, PATLA members, were very much in the minority but were invaluable to PATLA because they learned the workings of the Board and set the stage for the take-over when the time came.

With Larsen's ascension to the Supreme Court, and his horse-trading with other Justices over appointments to the Board, not considered a plum, it was only a matter of time until he and PATLA had control. This process can only be understood by understanding that Larsen and PATLA knew where they were going. To his fellow Justices, who had no agenda, the appointment to the Board had little meaning. It was a stealth attack, perfectly executed.

Bob Daniels, a plaintiff's lawyer from Philadelphia, and PATLA leader, was and is a close confidant of Larsen. He gained control over the Board in 1984 when elected Chairman. The chair, as in many groups with part-time members, has enormous power. The chair controls what the other members see, the timing of events and meetings, sets the agenda for meetings, and sees to it that the staff does what he or she wants them to do. From that point on, PATLA members owned the chair or vice-chair. The staff, including Disciplinary Counsel, did their bidding.

Since Daniels, there has been a parade of PATLA leaders taking the chair of the Disciplinary Board. Leaders such as Jim Swartzman, Jim Mundy, John Tumolo, William Keller, Murray Eckell, Richard Gilardi,

Phillip Friedman, James Powell, Steve Saltz, and William Caroselli. Other PATLA soldiers appointed to the Board were Jim McDonald, George Douglass, Robert Kerns, Leonard Sloane, Mark Shultz, Mark Aronchick, Christine Donohue and Charles Cunningham.

While PATLA membership represented less than ten percent of the lawyers in Pennsylvania, from Daniels on, over two-thirds of the Disciplinary Board Chairman were PATLA leaders. PATLA and Larsen could now protect their own and punish their enemies at the bar.

PATLA members poured huge amounts of money into judicial races. It became common in the 1990's for millions of dollars to be spent on a Supreme Court race, money that came from the same trial lawyers who would argue their cases before Judges or Justices they elected.

But putting like-minded lawyers on the bench, Judges and Justices who saw the world as they did, who would protect large verdicts and contingent fees, was not enough for PATLA. They decided that they needed control in the legislature. They registered as lobbyists and began to lobby for legislation that expanded the liability of manufacturers, property owners, and most of all, doctors and hospitals.

Although legally required to report expenditures, PATLA lobbyists failed or refused to report money spent on lobbying until 1996 when Common Cause began to make noise about lobbying reform. So in 1996, for the first time, PATLA admitted it spent dollars lobbying legislators when staff member Mark ("let's go party") Phenicie reported he spent $3,547.00 and his assistant John Prevec reported he spent $2,107.00 on meals for legislators. In 1997, Phenicie reported $4,904.00, Prevec $651.00, and former Senate leader Ed Zemprelli reported $278.00. In 1998 staff lobbyists Phenicie and Prevec reported spending $6,675.00 on meals for legislators.

In 1999, legislation was finally passed that put some teeth into reporting requirements. As a result, in 2000, PATLA reported spending $331,005.00 on lobbying, and in 2001 it reported $546,242.00. For the first quarter of 2002 alone, PATLA reported spending a whopping $428,084.00 on buying favor for their legislative agenda that was now focused on the heath care delivery system's deep pockets. By now, PATLA was awash in money. It had almost four thousand members, paying between $50.00 and $290.00 a month for dues. In the year 2000, there were at least thirty lawyers giving over $200.00 per month; fourteen members giving between $150.00 and $199.00 per month and

144 members giving up to $149.00 per month. Over four hundred lawyers gave up to $100.00 per month in 2000. While not reported anywhere, it is likely that lawyers like Jim Beasley, who garner multiple multi-million dollar verdicts each year, kick in very substantial dollars.

History also teaches that whenever there is an imbalance of power, someone gets hurt. That imbalance now exists and is the driving force behind our present health care delivery crisis. It put the small plane manufacturers such as Cessna, Piper and Lycoming Engines in Pennsylvania out of business. Products liability cases have increased the cost of everything we buy. Class action lawsuits have destroyed whole industries. Where will it go and how will it end? I see no end in the foreseeable future. Legislators want to be bought. They need the money and special interest support to get reelected. Tort reform is unlikely to happen, and if it does, it will be spotty. The PATLA lawyers, and those they support, will, when they become Judges, foster and sustain large verdicts. The money is rolling into PATLA. It is a juggernaut without equal in Pennsylvania and its methods and tactics will be replicated in every state.

Pogo knew.

"We have met the enemy and it is us."

. . .

On August 23, 2002, the Supreme Court of Pennsylvania struck down the Lobbying Disclosure Act, the legislation advanced by Common Cause, which required lobbyists to reveal gifts and gratuities to, and expenses on behalf of legislators. One need only look above a few paragraphs to see the tremendous effect this Act had on the reporting of lobbying expenditures by PATLA.

Ignoring precedent, much like the 1988 decision calling off the General Election, the Court decided that the Act infringed upon its right to regulate lawyers. How dare the legislature require that lawyer/lobbyists reveal their expenditures to legislators! The Opinion by Justice Zappala was tortured and devoid of intellectual honesty but it served its purpose. PATLA was free to buy votes without leaving a trail. Was this a set-up? You tell me.

Barry Kauffman, Executive Director of Common Cause/PA called the decision "A serious blow to open government." He went on to tell me that in his travels around the country, the decision *"was universally ridiculed by good government organizations."*

A corrupt Supreme Court had done it again. Justice Stout was right. Right and wrong were meaningless concepts.

"They know no limits."

THE INQUIRER STRIKES BACK

January 28, 2002

Jim Beasley. The name strikes terror in the hearts of the pinstriped worthies occupying the Knight-Ridder boardroom. After all, he has become a sort of partner in its flagship newspaper, *The Philadelphia Inquirer.* Tony Ridder was heard to say about libel suits that the self-insured Knight-Ridder could no longer afford the cost, signaling that investigative reporting of politicians and Judges would be a thing of the past.

Beasley's presence across the table from an editor is enough to have the effort of an able investigative reporter gutted. That's why top notch journalists such as Bill Miramow, Tony Roche, Ric Tulsky and Mike Pakingham are now with the Baltimore Sun. Beasley has earned the fear. Winner of a thirty-four million dollar verdict for the intrepid Dick Sprague, six million for Justice McDermott, and a seven million dollar settlement for *Inquirer* reporter, Ralph Cipriano, whose investigative report on Cardinal Bevilacqua was rejected for fear of a libel suit. When it ran elsewhere, Executive Editor Max King was asked why the *Inquirer* hadn't run with the story. He inartfully said that parts of the story were not true. Beasley made him eat those words.

The *Inquirer* caved to Beasley. They did it, for all the world to see, on the front page of its January 28th edition.

First, a prominent action photo of Beasley, his son, and associate Slade McLaughlin, plotting their course of action. Then the headline and sub-headline:

Defendants in this case: bin Laden and associates

Phila. Lawyer James E. Beasley filed suit for two relatives of Sept 11 victims. He is seeking millions in frozen assets

When America went to war with Osama bin Laden and the Taliban last year, Philadelphia personal injury lawyer James E. Beasley did too: He sued them for wrongful death and racketeering.

In a tack that almost no one else has taken, Beasley, renowned for winning big verdicts in complex civil cases, filed suit in New York in November on behalf of two relatives of World Trade Center victims.

Since then, while the U.S. military has been on the trail of bin Laden, his al-Qaeda network and the Taliban, Beasley has been on the trail of their money.

So Beasley, with tens of millions of *Inquirer* money in his bank account, is, to the *Inquirer*, a hero after all. I don't get it! Stu Ditzen wrote this puff-piece, in the guise of a news story. In 1992, Ditzen wrote the same kind of alleged news article making Justice Zappala into some sort of saint. In doing so, he ignored the seamy connection between Zappala and his brother's bond underwriting firm, Russell, Rea and Zappala, and Senator Fumo. In Zappala's case, at least everyone knew that Zappala had become the enemy of Justice Larsen who was the enemy of the *Inquirer*. The enemy of my enemy is my friend. Why is the *Inquirer* now making nice with Beasley? It is too obscure for me. But one thing I do know, both articles represent a form of journalistic prostitution.

The *Inquirer* has not only been chilled, it now panders to its tormentors.

THE ONSET OF THE DARK AGES

October 2001

God, I love Sam Klein.

This statement once made directly to him, caused him to look at me a little funny. But, what the hell, it's true. In addition to being a nationally recognized legal expert on the First Amendment, he is a man of honor and decency that sadly is a rare combination in this money chase which once was the legal profession. As one who revered the profession, I put Sam at the top of my Pantheon for those who are willing to take the road less traveled.

Why do I feel this way today? Let me tell you.

While trying to get some data to back up my contention that the print media has been chilled, in general, and particularly as it relates to investigative reporting on the judiciary because of the plethora of libel actions brought by Judges in their own court systems, I called Kathryn Hatton, General Counsel to *The Philadelphia Inquirer*. Kathryn had formerly been a partner of Sam's at Kohn, Savett, Klein, and Graf. I will never forget the day she arranged for me to speak to the Philadelphia Bar Association. Halfway into my remarks on the slide of the judiciary into the Dark Ages, PATLA supporter Raymond Kremer, a brilliant but terribly flawed Philadelphia Common Pleas Judge, interrupted the proceedings by ranting loudly, over and over again, "do not believe this man, the truth is not in him," while he stomped from the room. Kremer had recently written an Opinion upholding a three million dollar personal injury verdict against the Southeastern Transportation Authority. Bob Daniels, PATLA leader and Larsen advisor, was plaintiff's attorney. On appeal, Richard Sprague would present the case to the Supreme Court on Daniels' behalf.

At first, Kathryn refused to give me the requested list of suits by Judges against the *Inquirer* and sister paper, *The Philadelphia Daily News.* Later she relented and sent me a list of six lawsuits. I knew it wasn't complete, but it was a start.

Gene Roberts had agreed to read my manuscript so I thought a comment from him on the subject might provide further corroboration to my perception that the media had been chilled. I drafted a note to Gene as follows:

Dear Gene,

I have been attempting to determine the number of libel suits brought by judges against their critics in Pennsylvania and against the Inquirer in particular. While my research is not complete, the numbers are alarming. The question becomes what has been the effect of these lawsuits on the ability or willingness of the print media to investigate and report on the "abuses of power and privilege" in the judiciary.
It seems to me that you are in a position to provide insights that are more than theoretical into this issue. Any comments you would care to make, either on or off the record, would be very much appreciated.

Bob

Before sending the note to Gene, I e-mailed it to Sam and asked if it was too "superficial." Sam, even though engaged in a six month trial in Wheeling, West Virginia, responded at once and e-mailed me back, as follows:

It is superficial, mainly because you have identified only one part of the problem. It is not only Judges, but perhaps even more importantly, public officials who have repeatedly sued—Mayors Rizzo and Green, Presidents of City Council Street and Coleman, District Attorneys Fitzpatrick and Sprague, US Attorney Curran, State Senators Fumo and Carn, and the list goes on and on. These folks are all part of the same political process as the judges. When the judges feel attacked they want to take it out on the media, and suits by others in the political process give them the opportunity to do so. This gives impetus to some of their own to sue. The sad fact is that the judges, there to protect constitutional rights, cheered and threw a party when the McDermott and Merriweather verdicts came in. No one paused for a moment to think about what it meant for the public; rather, it was a victory for "us" over "them."

In this environment, a paper concerned about its bottom line, as any paper must be, is in real danger. Reporting on judges is restrained, but maybe even more important is that reporting on public officials is restrained – if they sue, they get to go before judges who feel the same way about the media and they all feel a common bond. In my view, it is the "common bond" that is the most frightening, because as a defense lawyer you know walking into virtually any courtroom in Phila that the judge has a dear friend who has sued or wanted to sue the press. They hardly even stop to give the traditional lip service to the First Amendment—they start off with the notion that the press is unfair and slanted, and has done more harm than good to the public.

I don't believe that the press has made a conscious decision to back away from reporting, but the caution is there and some stories are just not worth the risk. Some, like Beasley, would say that is a good thing—that their lawsuits have brought responsibility to the media. I say—look at the record—the Penna judicial system was a disgrace since at least the Larsen years, and the papers covered it. It may be even worse now (perhaps because it is a bit more subtle, but not by much), and there is hardly a word.

Well, I'm starting to be like my friend Bob—ranting and going all over the place. The bottom line is that I think there is something important to say, but it is a tad bit more complicated than just the judges. I wonder how an editor feels when a public official like Fumo sues and the case goes before a judge who 1) Fumo put on the bench; 2) is a product of a political machine, and owes debts to folks who can be hurt badly by Fumo; 3) is a dear friend and political associate of another judge who has sued; and 4) has himself consulted or been represented by Fumo's lawyer. There is a real concern there that may actually threaten the very existence of the paper, and no one cares.

Sam said it all. Right on target except for his defense of the mental state of the print media. I agree with him that the press has not made a "conscious decision to back away from reporting." It reports, albeit defensively, indiscretions by public officials including Judges which come to light by accident. But it is clear the *Inquirer* has made a conscious decision to abandon <u>investigative</u> reporting of public officials.

There will be no more hard hitting series like **Disorder in the Courts** and **Above the Law** where Gene Roberts unleashed highly competent reporters to get the facts on the sorry state of the judiciary. And get the facts they did. The Pulitzers were earned and deserved. The spotlight on wrongdoing focused by the *Inquirer* infuriated the Justices and Judges who would never forgive and never forget. But the overriding benefit was that someone told the people.

There are almost forty thousand lawyers in Pennsylvania. Every lawyer in active practice knows what has happened to Bob Surrick. The twenty-year saga of lawsuits and disciplinary proceedings has received ample press. The chilling effect of this was recognized by Judge Dalzell when he wrote:

While a courtroom is, to be sure, not a free speech zone on the order of a public square or the Internet, neither is it an alien place to core First Amendment values, as this case illustrates. Judges are public figures and their impartiality and ethics are matters of profound public concern. Lawyers are the sentries for the public when they detect judge's breaches of these minimal standards. In that role, lawyers must have some Times-like "breathing space." Here, where a lawyer's loss of a recusal motion has meant the loss of his job for five years, an apparently unprecedented sanction on lawyer recusal speech in Pennsylvania—that breathing space has disappeared for him, and through him, for all Pennsylvania lawyers. Surrick's personal catastrophe is thus of grave First Amendment concern for the bar and public.

Sam Klein, in the brief filed in the Third Circuit, wrote as follows:

Vigilance in protecting Mr. Surrick's First Amendment rights is particularly important here, where his speech was critical of the institutions that ultimately decided to punish him—and to impose unprecedented harsh discipline upon him. The courts should be the protectors, not punishers, of citizens' First Amendment freedoms: particularly here, where the speech being penalized was set forth in a Motion for Recusal—a vehicle attorneys are permitted to use to attempt to ensure that partial jurists do not preside over their cases. These motions are often looked upon with disfavor—the actions taken against Mr. Surrick as a result of his motion may, as Judge Dalzell noted, have the effect of deterring future litigants from filing such motions.

All of the lawsuits and disciplinary proceedings initiated against Mr. Surrick—including this one—have been based on his controversial speech. Speech about public affairs, public officials, and the Pennsylvania judicial system, and his speech about the very court that suspended his license. After years of trying to punish Mr. Surrick for his critical speech about the judicial system, his detractors in the Commonwealth have now succeeded. Imposition of reciprocal discipline for conduct: (1) rooted in the First Amendment; and (2) not shown to have involved either knowingly false statements or false accusation against a judge, or conduct prejudicial to the administration of justice, amounts to a grave injustice. By failing to recognize this, the District Court abused its discretion.

Richard Sprague and Jim Beasley have made millions out of the cottage industry they have created—suing and chilling the media. The fact that they provide "courtesy" representation to Judges accused of misconduct exacerbates an already untenable and frightening situation.

The upshot! The media has been chilled by the judiciary, and the lawyers have been chilled by the Supreme Court.

Are there solutions to these problems? Of course there are. And the cure is not rocket science.

As for the media's problem with the crushing weight of lawsuits by Judges, the answer is to give judicial immunity by constitutional right. Forget the jumble of judicial immunity by common law. In return for constitutional judicial immunity, take away the Judge's right to sue for libel or slander, as I first advocated in a speech to Common Cause in 1987. I advocate this even though Judges such as Raymond Kremer have used their written Opinions for political, even venal purposes. An example is a vicious Kremer Opinion accusing David Marion, one of the attorneys in a case before him, of "perjury". He delivered the Opinion to *The Legal Intelligencer* just before the election for Chancellor of the Philadelphia Bar Association. Marion was the leading candidate and the *Legal* article almost cost him the election. In spite of this kind of abuse of judicial office, on balance, if the print media is free to report, the greater good is served.

As for the real and present danger to a lawyer acting as a sentry, apply the *Sullivan v. New York Times* test to lawyers' representations about Judges. Require that there be a showing of malice or knowing falsehood before sanctions against his or her license can be imposed.

Will this happen? I doubt it. There are too many vested interests. The only hope for change is that sooner or later the system will become so dreadful that a person, or group, with stature and courage, will risk their status and fortune to make it a better world for all who follow.

Lord only knows, I tried.

...

On October 21, 2001, I received the following e-mail from Sam Klein:

As for the proper standard, I am of the view that Sullivan doesn't go far enough. I know you won't believe this coming from Sam Klein, but the proper standard should be absolute protection. A judge has absolute immunity to say anything he wants from the bench, even if known to be false and uttered for improper motive. A judge who wants to hurt an attorney to keep him from winning an election for chancellor of the bar can write an opinion on the eve of the election calling the candidate a perjurer, knowing it is false and writing it for the sole purpose of securing the defeat of the candidate. Yet, the lawyer has no remedy, and neither does the public who may have been deprived of the service of a fine candidate due to the mischief of the judge. We give judges this protection, knowing that at times innocent people are harmed, because we want our judges to be able to express themselves freely, without fear of being sued. We hope they will act responsibly, but if they don't, that is the price we pay for getting free thought from our judiciary. The same should be true for lawyers, acting within the system, when they make statements about issues of public concern-filing motions to recuse as they are obligated to do when it is in the interest of their client, and pointing out wrongdoing by elected public officials who have what is in effect a lifetime term of office. Because lawyers are in the best, and perhaps the only, position to know what is really going on in the system, they should be free to speak out without fear of punishment. If they are wrong, or evilly motivated, that is the price a judge has to pay so that the system can function well.

So you look at the character of the speech—if it is a false representation of fact about when the accident happened or whether service was made, punish the lawyer. If it is about public affairs and the performance of a public official in office, then it should be protected.

Crazy thoughts—no one will ever accept them—but I have thought about this for some time and believe it may be the right resolution. Sure, I know that there are those who will contend, with sincerity, that such a rule would permit malcontents to destroy the system with false and malicious charges. But my guiding principle is that you cure bad speech with more speech, not punishment which leads to suppression.

John Peter Zenger may have died two centuries ago but those, like Sam Klein, will carry the torch of freedom forever.

ONLY THE GOOD DIE YOUNG

March 25, 2002

On arrival back in York today from Florida, I checked my e-mail and found the following from Sam Klein:

Bob—got a letter from the circuit court today advising that the case was removed from the Feb 26 submission list and will be relisted at the convenience of the court—never heard of this before…

Recalling John Rogers Carroll's admonition that paranoids are the only realists, I tried to call Sam but only was able to get his voice mail.

First the shenanigans in the District Court—now we had highly unusual maneuverings in the Circuit Court. I finally reached Ellen and she faxed me the letter. The letter revealed that six days after the case had been assigned to a three-Judge panel for disposition, it was removed, without explanation, from the panel and placed in limbo. I checked with lawyers who are familiar with Court of Appeals practice and like Sam, they had never heard of anything like this happening.

Then my world collapsed. Ellen called to say that Sam had died within the last hour—a massive heart attack. I couldn't control my tears. Sam stood beside me, for everything I had been fighting for, for twenty years. My friend, confidant, lawyer and conscience. I was in shock.

Forget my case—the important constitutional issues—I thought only of the Dedication I had drafted for this book:

Sam Klein, quintessential lawyer, honorable and decent man

I just couldn't accept that Sam was gone. The void was a black hole.

The next day, I picked the *Inquirer* obit off the net:

Samuel Klein, 55, libel cases lawyer

Samuel E. Klein, a widely respected lawyer who devoted much of his career to defending news organizations in libel cases and fighting to keep government proceedings and records open to the public, died at his Chestnut Hill home yesterday of an apparent heart attack.

Mr. Klein, a partner in the Dechert firm in Center City, had gone to work yesterday morning but soon returned home, telling his wife Rebekah, that he didn't feel well. He was stricken not long afterward.

Word of Mr. Klein's death spread rapidly through the legal community.

"Sam Klein, in my opinion, was the finest First Amendment lawyer in the United States," said James E. Beasley, who had done battle with Mr. Klein in several major defamation cases. "He was just a remarkable individual. I don't think he had any peer in First Amendment work."

In 1972, Mr. Klein, then a young associate in the law firm of the late Harold Kohn, began doing legal work for one of Mr. Kohn's client, the Inquirer.

Mr. Klein formed a close bond with Gene Roberts, then the newspaper's editor, and began spending long hours in the newsroom getting to know reporters and editors.

"When we needed someone to look at a story before the first edition, being the young kid on the block, he got the job," Roberts recalled yesterday. "I would say he went from being a green lawyer within five or six years to being one of the most knowledgeable attorneys in America about First Amendment law."

Roberts said Mr. Klein "didn't look for reasons not to put something in the paper," but tried to shape sensitive or controversial stories to make them sound.

Mr. Klein was a graduate of Temple University and Temple's law school.

He eventually became a named partner in the Kohn law firm. In 1992, he left to join the Dechert firm.

In recent years, Mr. Klein had worked as a defense lawyer for the tobacco industry as well as working for news media clients.

Katheryn Hatton, legal counsel for Philadelphia Newspapers Inc, publisher of the Inquirer and the Daily News, said of Mr. Klein: "Sam was a classic Philadelphia lawyer. He cared deeply for his clients, worked tirelessly on their behalf, and radiated integrity."

Richard A. Sprague, who litigated a 23 year libel case against The Inquirer, won a $34 million verdict in 1990 and settled the case for an undisclosed sum in 1996-said yesterday that Mr. Klein, his longtime adversary in the case, was "one of the finest, finest people" he knew.

"If ever there was a lovely human being who was a lawyer and highly principled man, it was Sam Klein," Sprague said "He handled himself the way a lawyer should, which you don't often see today. He stood for principle."

In addition to his wife, a son, Jared, and a daughter, Zoe, survive Mr. Klein.

Contact Stuart Ditzen at 215-854-2431

Gene Roberts, as usual, had it right. Sam, as the *Inquirer* legal counsel, "didn't look for reasons not to put something in the paper." This observation by Roberts spoke volumes about Sam's passion for openness in government. More to the point, it spoke to the *Inquirer* under Roberts being committed to fearless investigative reporting. Of course, what Roberts was really saying is that the policy of the *Inquirer* has changed out of fear of lawsuits and their effect on its bottom line. *The Philadelphia Inquirer* now looks for reasons not to tell the public what is really happening out of fear of a lawsuit. Roberts was repeating, in a subtle fashion, his North Carolina speech. What we all must worry about is:

not the sound, but the silence.

Wherever Sam is, he must have winced when he read the obituary and saw the *Inquirer* turn to Sprague and Beasley, their chief threats to investigative reporting, for Marc Antony-like observations about the fallen. Make no mistake, Sam had great respect for the legal skills of Beasley and Sprague—and contempt for what they were doing to a free press and the legal system.

Once again, Stu Ditzen and the *Inquirer* making nice with Beasley and Sprague nauseated me. It isn't like there were no lawyers or Judges of stature to call upon who saw the world as Sam did, who could speak to Sam's contributions to the legal system and those whose lives he touched. Beasley and Sprague represent everything Sam fought against his whole life. While Sam understood clearly what Beasley and Sprague were, Beasley and Sprague would never understand Sam and what his life was all about.

The Goldstein Funeral Home on North Broad Street was packed to overflowing. The service started forty-five minutes late because of the number of people trying to crowd into the chapel. Beasley and Sprague were not there. Among the speakers was Dan Biddle. He spoke of the years when at press time the newsroom would be packed with reporters while Sam huddled with Gene Roberts to give legal clearance to another investigative reporting coup—and of the roaring cheer when a grinning Sam walked out and gave a thumbs-up.

At the service, my eyes were moist, but I kept control. Graveside was another story. When the Rabbi intoned the Kaddish, The Prayer for the Dead, *Yit-qa-dal ve yit ka dash…,* I could no longer hold back. I waited until everyone left and sobbing put a handful of dirt on the polished wooden casket and said goodbye.

I shall never see another like him in my lifetime.

. . .

From the cemetery, I drove back to Sam's house in Chestnut Hill. It was a lovely home in a very old, upscale neighborhood. While Sam and Rebekah had been to my house when I married Bobbie, I had never been to Sam's. He was a very private person. Ellen greeted me at the door and filled me in on how the family was taking it. I went inside to speak to Rebekah. The house was crowded with people mourning Sam's untimely and sudden death.

Spotting Bob Heim, Sam's partner, across a dining room table spread with ham, turkey, and the like, I approached him and was greeted warmly. I thought I might as well clarify my status as Sam had been representing me pro bono. In response to my question, Heim, the Chair of the Litigation Section, said:

"It would dishonor Sam's memory not to follow to the end something Sam cared so deeply about. The Dechert firm will take care of you."

In the present world of the money chase, Heim is a throwback—a beacon of honor, character and integrity that shines brightly in contrast to the darkness from the lawyers and Judges who are unfamiliar with these words.

REFORM—PENNSYLVANIA STYLE

March 2002

The lobbyists for the Pennsylvania Medical Society and the Pennsylvania Trial Lawyers Association were ratcheting up the rhetoric. They were blaming each other for the medical malpractice crisis and questioning the motives of each other.

The legislature postured, pretending serious debate over important legislation. It was a charade. The possibility of real tort reform was never on the table. The issues being debated in the General Assembly were at the margin of the medical malpractice morass. Secondary issues such as the collateral source rule, informed consent, preservation of records, and a statute of repose were at the center of the debate. PATLA had won the battle before it even began by blocking consideration of a sweeping overhaul of a broken system of adjudicating medical misadventures. The Bill that was passed in mid-March would apply a very small band-aid to a very large, hemorrhaging artery.

There were those who saw clearly that the legislation was a farce. House member Thomas A. Tangretti was quoted:

In the struggle to enact a law that pleased every special interest, the Legislature lost sight of its main goal: making it financially possible for physicians to continue practicing in Pennsylvania while maintaining safe and accessible health care for patients.

. . .

The new law may postpone another malpractice crisis for a few years, but . . .the General Assembly will be addressing this issue again soon enough.

. . .

The current crisis was caused by skyrocketing malpractice premiums in the private insurance market. …Four years ago there were more than a dozen private malpractice insurance companies operating in Pennsylvania. Today five of those companies are bankrupt and several others are not writing any new policies.

Pennsylvania is not alone in this crisis. Recent media accounts report similar problems in New Jersey, Ohio and California.

Alfred W. Putnam, Esquire, a partner in Drinker Biddle & Reath, wrote a Guest Commentary for *The Legal Intelligencer* that nicely captured the crisis and the faux reform as follows:

Emergency Surgery Needed for Medical Malpractice Bill

Yes, it is true that our friends in Harrisburg have passed a new medical malpractice "reform" bill. And it's true that all sides are lauding the "reform" in the hope that we can convince the insurance industry that malpractice litigation in Philadelphia will be much better now so there's no need to double everybody's premium.

It is not true, however, that time will tell whether the new law helps. If it doesn't, unfortunately, insurance carriers are not stupid. They know full well that nothing has changed. And they —like a lot of doctors— are simply getting out of town while they still can.

The truth is that the "crisis" has only started. A number of carriers (St. Paul, Zurich, Princeton) have simply stopped writing medical malpractice insurance in this region. Others are either insolvent (Reliance, PHICO, PIC, PIE, Frontier) or are being "rehabilitated" (Legion, Villanova). That doesn't leave many bidders for business that nobody really wants. So the sky is the limit.

Two years ago, the medical malpractice premium for the Main Line Health System –on whose board I sit— was about $6.5 million. Last year, it was a little more than $12 million. In the New Year that will start July 1, it will exceed $21 million. And that, by the way, is for less insurance than we used to carry because the amount of insurance we used to carry is not available in Pennsylvania at any price.

There are consequences, of course. For instance, the increase in the malpractice premium that Main Line Health will pay for the coming fiscal year is larger than the projected operating margin of all the Main Line Health hospitals (Lankenau, Bryn Mawr, Paoli and Bryn Mawr Rehabilitation Hospital), combined. That's money that is no longer available to invest in staff, programs, technology, or buildings.

Perhaps our friends in Harrisburg will not miss those things. As for other less fortunate hospitals that were losing money even before the premium doubled, perhaps our friends in Harrisburg will not miss them.

In fairness, it should be said that the doctors have it worse than the hospitals. The increase in the latest quotes are usually in excess of 100 percent. Some physicians can't even obtain quotes. Depending on the specialty, an annual insurance premium can exceed $150,000 in Pennsylvania but come to less than $25,000 elsewhere – making for a good time to go.

Of the approximately 50 ob/gyn specialists we had at Main Line Health two years ago, 20 have either left or curtailed the services they offer. So we still have 30 – for now. Twenty percent of the orthopedic surgeons in our region left or stopped practicing between 1997 and 2000.

I don't have the latest numbers, but I gather they're worse. And you can't really recruit young people, of course. The combination of low reimbursement and skyrocketing malpractice premiums makes Southeastern Pennsylvania the last place in the country where any good young physician would want to settle down.

So, anyway, I'm glad to hear that the "crisis" is over. And I certainly don't plan to call anyone names. After all, I myself make a good living practicing law and plan to continue to do so. But let's all stay healthy, OK? Or at least make some out-of-state friends.

All of the statistics, all of the anecdotal evidence, all of the physical evidence such as shuttered hospitals point to southeastern Pennsylvania being the epicenter of the malpractice verdict explosion. The average medical malpractice verdict in Philadelphia is over one million dollars. Already, over seventeen hundred doctors have fled Pennsylvania. But the trial lawyers cannot and will not ever admit this—to do so would cause analysis of the root causes of the problem. So, after the Putnam article, which factually describes what is happening, the trial lawyers trot out Beasley, the younger, to muddy the waters. He wrote in *The Legal Intelligencer:*

There's no question that physicians are being squeezed "big time" but it's not a local phenomenon and it's not limited to medical malpractice insurance.

Putnam and his friends at Lankenau can keep looking at this as a local tort-based problem and never reach an acceptable solution or recognize it is a national problem.

He then went on to blame the greedy insurance companies for the problem.

Several days later, the *Inquirer* editorialized about the ever-increasing medical insurance premiums. Taking their cue from Beasley and the trial lawyers, they wrote:

It's a national problem that will require national solutions.

It may be that the medical malpractice crisis has become a nationwide problem because it has spread throughout the states. But by taking the position that it is a national problem, cover is given to Pennsylvania legislators to do nothing. No need to clean up our problem, let the federal government take care of it. What they are really saying is, have the federal government increase the Medicare payments to doctors and hospitals to relieve the dollar squeeze and leave the trial lawyers alone. Or have the federal government fund the insurance carriers. What is not being said is that the trial lawyers need to be reined in. Does anyone think that the trial lawyers would not fight to the death against caps on pain and suffering or punitive damage verdicts? Only the doctors and hospitals can change the system by spending more money on legislators than the trial lawyers.

The capitulation of the *Inquirer* to Beasley and the trial lawyers was now complete. Somewhere in that great bar association in the sky, Sam must be throwing up.

Who are the biggest losers in this game of chicken? Those that are always the losers, the poor. The rich will always find quality medical care. The poor will have fewer doctors, if any, to treat them, and the hospitals will no longer have the wherewithal to carry the charity load.

And the biggest winners? The trial lawyers who will still have a trough at which to gorge.

In the first quarter of 2002, during the so-called legislative debate over medical malpractice odds and ends, PATLA reported spending four hundred and twenty-eight thousand dollars on legislative lobbying. It was an enormous dollar outlay (almost equal to the outlay for the entire prior year) to preserve the status quo. But that was chickenfeed compared to the forty percent contingent fees on multi-million dollar medical malpractice verdicts that will now continue.

While it is true that not all four thousand members of PATLA will obtain multi-million dollar verdicts in medical malpractice cases, it surely is true that the rising tide of plaintiffs' verdicts in one sector will raise all boats in every other sector.

Who foots the bill? Only those who buy anything, need medical care, drive a car, ride public transportation, read newspapers, fly airplanes, whatever.

There is now no stopping PATLA in Pennsylvania and, as Al Putnam noted in his *Intelligencer* piece, the Pennsylvania Model has begun to surface in other states.

The Pennsylvania Model. Hijack the judicial system and buy the legislature with the profits is foolproof. It only takes a handful of Judges and lawyers to map a plan and execute it.

. . .

Throughout 2003 and into 2004, the medical community and their supporters lobbied legislators to pass a Bill to amend the Pennsylvania Constitution to remove the provision which barred any limitation on jury verdicts which would pave the way for caps. Both the House and Senate passed Bills by wide margins. To the uninitiated, it looked as if this proposed Constitutional Amendment had passed. But not so. This is Pennsylvania. The legislators, owned by the trial lawyers and PATLA, created minor differences in the Bills passed by the House and Senate. The Bills then had to go to a conference committee where members from each body would pretend to be seriously addressing the differences in the Bills. Then the conference committees report was sent back to the House and Senate Judiciary Committees. In the small hours of the morning on July 2, 2004, the Senate Judiciary Committee met and by a 10 to 4 vote, tabled action on the Bill thereby killing it. Because of the requirements to amend the Constitution, the earliest caps could now become a reality in Pennsylvania is 2007.

I had to laugh at Senator Stewart Greenleaf's explanation for his vote to table the legislation. He said he would not vote for caps unless there was a provision excluding catastrophic injuries. That wasn't what was before the Committee but a fig leaf is a fig leaf, however small.

If you listened carefully, you could hear the doctors packing up.

SIR, HAVE YOU NO SHAME?

May 12, 2002

On Sunday, May 12, 2002, *The Philadelphia Inquirer* headlined and wrote:

Temple law scholarship honors Samuel E. Klein

A $100,000 memorial scholarship has been established at Temple University's Beasley School of Law in honor of noted constitutional lawyer Samuel E. Klein, who died in March at age 55.

The scholarship will be awarded annually to a student in financial need who demonstrates outstanding academic achievement in the area of constitutional law, particularly in the area of First Amendment rights. The Scholarship is endowed by James E. Beasley, a frequent opponent of Klein's in the courtroom. Both men were graduates of Temple's law school

Klein was best known for his representation of news organizations in libel cases, and his efforts to keep government proceedings and records open to the public.

Beasley School of Law? Sound bizarre? It is. Operating out of the Beasley Office Building, Jim Beasley had taken some of the millions he had earned from suing (and silencing) the *Inquirer* and, through the medium of a massive donation, had the Temple University School of Law named after himself. As Dick Sprague has represented Peter

Liacouras, President of Temple University, I suspect his influence and Beasley's money carried that day. So now, Temple Law School with its tens of thousands of graduates no longer exists and the Beasley name will go on forever.

Not satisfied with trading on his own name, now he was trading on Sam's name.

Ozzie Myers, the south Philadelphia congressman who went to jail for taking Abscam money, said it best:

"Money talks and bullshit walks."

SELLING OUR SOULS

Ellen was on the phone.

"Bob, Brian Hirsh who now has your file told me to fax an Order from the Circuit Court to you. Don't pick up. Let it ring through to your fax machine."

The phone rang and after my fax machine recognized a fax was coming, it began to print. I looked at the single sheet with puzzlement and a touch of disbelief.

ORDER

At the request and direction of the Court, it is hereby ORDERED that Howard J. Bashman, Esquire is appointed to file a brief as amicus curiae in the above-entitled appeal in support of the District Court.

The amicus brief shall be filed and served within forty (40) days of the date of this order.

The fax cover sheet had Brian Hirsch's internal number at Dechert so I called him. He seemed to be a bright, pleasant young man who was in awe of Sam Klein. He related he had clerked in the Circuit Court. When I asked him if he had ever seen this kind of an Order before, he told me that he had not. Again, believing that paranoids are the only realists, my voice began to rise. Much like Sam, he broke in and stopped me.

"It's this simple, Bob. The Circuit Court would never reverse the District Court without a brief supporting the District Court. For whatever reason, the Circuit Court cut Disciplinary Counsel out of the process. When the three Judge panel looked at our brief, it became clear that there were serious constitutional issues."

"Brian, they cut Disciplinary Counsel out because Disciplinary Counsel did not file Exceptions to the Pollak panel Report and Recommendation. They accepted it! It would be tacky in the extreme for Disciplinary Counsel to have previously thrown in the towel and accepted a finding that I did not receive even minimal due process in the Pennsylvania Supreme Court and now be expected to argue that I should be disciplined."

"You may be right about that but the bottom line is that it is a good sign."

"As the Yiddish expression goes, Brian, 'from your mouth to God's ear.' I'll believe it when I see it."

In due course, Bashman filed an amicus (friend of the court) brief as ordered. I was shocked and disheartened by some of the disingenuous, dishonest and/or frivolous arguments he made. At one point in his brief, Bashman made the assumption that because nine Judges filed written dissents and twenty-seven Judges participated, the vote was "17 to 9". Judge Pollak, in his written Dissent filed with the Clerk and docketed for all the world, including Bashman, to see, noted the vote was 14 to 13. That this is beyond dispute was established in Judge Dalzell's Dissent wherein he wrote that the vote was by the "narrowest majority". Why did Bashman do what no careful lawyer would do? He is a very capable lawyer. I would find out in due time.

Bashman then went on to argue from a *Pennsylvania Law Weekly* article I had written (which was not in the record) that since I was no longer practicing and was living in Florida, I didn't have "standing" to challenge the imposition of discipline. Another argument which raised my blood pressure was that because the second panel in the District Court had provided that the thirty month suspension would run from the date suspension was imposed by the Pennsylvania Supreme Court, the suspension only had a few months to go so it was not worth taking the Courts time to hear and decide my appeal.

Just when I thought things couldn't look worse, they did. Edward Becker, Chief Judge of the Third Circuit, even though prohibited from political activity, is known to maintain his political connections. His insensitivity to maintaining an appearance of judicial rectitude was there for all the world to see when *The New York Times* reported on May 24, 2002 that the Senate Judiciary Committee had approved a Bush appointee to the Circuit Court as follows:

Judge Smith was put over the top when Senator Joseph R. Biden, Jr., Democrat of Delaware, said he was voting for him because he had lobbied on the nominee's behalf by Judge Edward Becker, the chief judge of the Third Circuit.

Mr. Biden had been Judge Smith's most vocal opponent on the committee.

Becker's lobbying of Biden was a clear violation of the Code Of Judicial Conduct that prohibits a Judge from "engaging in political activity." What struck me dumb was Senator Biden's public acknowledgement of Becker's political activity. We know it goes on but to admit it publicly is another story.

To place all this in context, Federal Judges are appointed by the President and must be confirmed by the United States Senate. The way it works is as follows. When a vacancy occurs, for example, in the District Court for the Eastern District of Pennsylvania, the political leader from the county whose turn it is to have the appointment, submits the political choice to the Senator who then submits the name to the President. The President then appoints, and the Senator goes to bat for the appointee in the Senate. It is a political process. The Federal Judge owes his lifetime job to his county party leader and Senator.

Recall Judge Dalzell's "disquiet" that a majority (*narrowest*) of his colleagues, Article III Judges, Judges with lifetime appointment, would act as they did in rejecting the Pollak Report and Recommendation. When told of that vote of the District Court, Dick Sprague was heard to say, "And they (Federal Judges) like to think they are less political than state court Judges—ha!"

Would Chief Judge Becker take a phone call from Senator Biden or other politicians? Of course. Did some of the District Court Judges who voted against me take phone calls? Of course. The visibility of these calls was what Judge Katz was referring to in his Dissent when he penned:

On balance, it (the vote) *does more harm to the institution* (the Court) *than to Mr. Surrick.*

Becker's violation of the Rule prohibiting political activity and the indifference of his colleagues to his conduct vividly portrays the absence of morality and rectitude that permeates every facet of our life today. It's not just the leaders of Enron, Worldcom, Adelphia Communications, Global Crossing, Tyco, etc. It permeates our institutions, our courts, our legislators, our churches—it's everywhere. A few months back, I was lamenting this state of affairs with my friend Rick Sander, Co-Chairman of the Board of Janney Montgomery Scott. I reminded him that when we both started out, a client complaint would mortify us. I suggested that now it's just seen as a cost of doing business. Regretfully, he agreed that the loss of shame in the professions is endemic.

This decline in moral values is nowhere more graphically evident than in a cursory examination of the Arthur Anderson debacle. Until recently, accountants and auditors were independent and their word was law with the client. They were the guardians of corporate and individual probity. Over time, they sold their souls to the company store. Only a few years back, it would be beyond belief, unthinkable, for an accounting firm to countenance and indeed, participate in turning operating expenses into capital assets to make their masters' stock options more valuable.

It's not just the obvious dumbing down of our people, and the coarsening and vulgarization of our culture that began in the Viet Nam era, it's the loss of meaning of words such as integrity and character. A close friend, a Judge, who taught ethics at a major law school, recently told me that he stood by dumbstruck as his students debated whether or not it would be worth it to lose a hard earned license to practice law "if the hit was big enough."

Most discouraging to me is the certain knowledge that in today's morality, John McNichol or someone on behalf of Justice Zapalla such as his compadre Vince Fumo, could call Arlen Specter and tell him "Surrick's a bad guy," and Specter could call any number of Federal Judges he has put on the bench over the years and pass along the word. Chief Judge Becker owes Specter. It's that simple. Would my head be payback?

I was now in the nineteenth year of litigation since I voted to remove Justice Larsen. Once again, Bill O'Donnell's voice came to me from his grave:

"Bob, you have to be able to take a joke."

MORE OF THE BIG CHILL

June 3, 2002

In 1987, Judge Ronald B. Merriweather of Philadelphia started a libel suit against Philadelphia Newspapers, Inc. owner and publisher of *The Philadelphia Daily News.* Philadelphia Newspapers, Inc is also the owner and publisher of *The Philadelphia Inquirer.* Knight-Ridder is the parent company of these and other newspapers. Plaintiff Merriweather's attorney? None other than the ubiquitous Mr. Sprague.

On June 3, 2002, a special panel of Judges, all from jurisdictions distant to Philadelphia, set aside a five-hundred-thousand dollar jury verdict in favor of Merriweather. The *Pennsylvania Law Weekly* headlined:

C.P. Panel Sets Aside Defamation Award to Philadelphia Judge

Publisher prevails in 15-year fight over story that implied case-fixing

What's the story here? It's that the *Philadelphia Daily News* has been in costly litigation over an investigative story for fifteen years, and the fat lady hasn't even warmed up her vocal chords. This was just another decision of the Court of Common Pleas. Next stop, the Superior Court-again! After that, probably the Supreme Court. How many more years? How much more in legal fees? Who knows? What is clear is that years ago the *Philadelphia Daily News*, because of these lawsuits, gave up investigative reporting on the judiciary, and it is unlikely that this corporate policy will change any time in the near future. The Knight-Ridder Board may be slow learners but Tony Ridder, who writes the checks, isn't.

I called Bob Heim, who represented the *Daily News* to confirm that Sprague had again taken an appeal in this case. He had. I asked him how much Knight-Ridder had paid Dechert Price and Rhoades in legal fees in this case over the fifteen years. Of course, he wouldn't tell me. My guess, based on thirty-five years experience, not less than a million dollars to date. Once again it is:

... *not the sound but the silence.*

While reading the Merriweather account in the *Law Weekly*, the adjoining story caught my eye.

Trial Court May Compel Reporters
To Disclose Unpublished Info

Decision viewed as narrowing the
scope of the Shield Law protection

The case involved two reporters, *Philadelphia Inquirer* reporter Mark Bowden and *Philadelphia Tribune* reporter Linn Washington. *The Philadelphia Tribune* is a small newspaper that serves the black community. These reporters refused to give up unpublished statements from a source. The reporters were held in contempt and fined forty-thousand dollars each; one hundred dollars a minute, for the time they sat in court and asserted their statutory right, as newspaper reporters, to protect their sources and what the sources told them.

On appeal to the Superior Court, that court, with now Senior Judge Peter Paul Olszewski writing the Opinion, upheld the lower court's finding of contempt which narrowed the application of the Shield Law but remanded the case to the lower court for further hearing on the fines. Even the Superior Court could not stomach a fine of one hundred dollars a minute.

From his grave, I heard Sam murmur to look at what he had e-mailed me last year. I went back and looked at the e-mail Sam had sent:

It is not only Judges, but perhaps even more importantly, public officials who have repeatedly sued - Mayors Rizzo and Green, Presidents of City Council Street and Coleman, District Attorneys Fitzpatrick and Sprague, US Attorney Curran, State Senators Fumo and Carn, and the list goes on and on. These folks are all part of the same political process as the judges. When the judges feel attacked they want to take it out on the media, and suits by others in the political process give them the opportunity to do so. This gives impetus to some of their own to sue. The sad fact is that the judges, there to protect constitutional rights, cheered and threw a party when the McDermott and Merriweather verdicts came in. No one paused for a moment to think about what it meant for the public; rather, it was a victory for "us" over "them."

In this environment, a paper concerned about its bottom line, as any paper must be, is in real danger. Reporting on judges is restrained, but maybe even more important is that reporting on public officials is restrained—if they sue, they get to go before judges who feel the same way about the media and they all feel a common bond. In my view, it is the "common bond" that is the most frightening, because as a defense lawyer you know walking into virtually any courtroom in Phila. that the judge has a dear friend who has sued or wanted to sue the press. They hardly even stop to give the traditional lip service to the first amendment—they start off with the notion that the press is unfair and slanted, and has done more harm than good to the public.

As usual, Sam had it right. The malice of the Judges for the media mocks the Rule of Law.

So, what's new? The disregard and disrespect for the majesty and nobility of a legal system that protects individual and institutional rights, a system that people have given their lives for, is new. It wasn't always this way.

I know—I was there fifty years ago.

THE SPREAD OF THE PENNSYLVANIA MODEL

July 1, 2002

By happenstance today, while in the coffee shop at Johns Hopkins Hospital in Baltimore following prostate cancer surgery, I picked up *USA Today*. The front page carried the following headline

Fed-up obstetricians
Look for way out
Insurance rates drive some off:
Others drive away

The article was about obstetricians leaving Las Vegas or closing their obstetrical practice under the pressure of skyrocketing malpractice rates. In a box on the right hand side, *USA Today* sub- headlined

Malpractice crisis brewing

Underneath, it wrote:

The American College of Obstetricians and Gynecologists is warning that rising malpractice insurance premiums are threatening the availability of doctors to deliver babies in nine states. The American Medical Association adds three more to the list where doctors are moving or dropping services because of high rates.

The states? Pennsylvania, New York, New Jersey, West Virginia, Ohio, Georgia, Florida, Mississippi, Texas, Nevada, Washington and Oregon.

The article included a half-a-dozen anecdotal stories of doctors with large practices who either left for more rural areas, like Maine, or closed the obstetrical side of their practice and refused to deliver babies while continuing the gynecological side, an area on which the trial lawyers hadn't yet focused.

This very serious article was not without its silly moments. Consider the following Beasley-like comment:

Reno attorney Bill Bradley, past president of the Nevada Trail Lawyers Association, blames the 'very vile nature of the insurance industry' not a lack of tort reform, for the rise in malpractice premiums in his state.' Instead of settling a claim, insurers often prefer to go to court where even bigger judgments are levied against their clients,' he says. 'The insurers use these judgments to support higher rates,' he says.

Sure Bill. And the Jews caused the Holocaust to get sympathy.

"SOMEBODY IS GOING TO DIE"

On July 7, 2002, *The Philadelphia Inquirer* headlined:

High costs shrink maternity care

The second and subsequent paragraphs reported:

In the last two years, Philadelphia and its Pennsylvania suburbs have lost seven out of 39 maternity units, including two this summer. The latest losses—at Methodist Hospital and Mercy Hospital of Philadelphia—were directly related to soaring malpractice insurance premiums.

. . .

The malpractice crisis has hit ob-gyns particularly hard because they tend to have big practices—doing 15 or more deliveries a month is not unusual—and get sued for unhappy outcomes, even if they may not be at fault.

. . .

"Obstetricians pay $800 to $900 in insurance costs per delivery. They are reimbursed about $1,600 for that delivery and nine months of prenatal care," said Andrew Wigglesworth, president of the Delaware Valley Healthcare Council." How do you run a practice on that?"

. . .

"Eventually, patients will be harmed. I believe somebody is going to die because they won't be able to get access to medical care," said Nancy Roberts, chairwomen of Lankenau Hospital's ob-gyn department. An obstetrician who deals with high-risk pregnancies, Roberts stopped delivering babies a year ago to reduce her malpractice costs

There are unseen losses to Pennsylvania in this crisis. We have seven medical schools in the state, some of them world class. What graduate in his or her right mind would opt to practice here? In fact, in February, 2004, twelve-hundred students from six medical schools signed a letter to Governor Rendell expressing their intention to leave the state upon graduation.

Recently I was asked by a very bright man, who is deeply concerned about the destruction being caused by the trial lawyers, whether or not this book or any book with similar information would cause the public to rise up and demand reform. My answer was an emphatic no. Why? There are a number of reasons.

First, the trial lawyers have cleverly tapped into a public distrust or at least dislike of insurance companies. When Beasley or Bradley blame the insurance companies for the problem, it resonates with a large segment of the public.

Secondly, not enough people have been hurt. The problem in the health care delivery system has not yet spread far enough and wide enough to touch a majority of our citizens.

Thirdly, it is the poor who will feel it first and be affected most adversely. The affluent will be inconvenienced but they will find quality health care. But the pregnant inner city black teenager will have problems getting any health care, much less quality health care. And like it or not, damn few people will spend much time worrying about a pregnant unmarried black inner-city teenager.

Lastly, few members of our society will worry about the plight of doctors. Again, the trial lawyers have cleverly engaged in class warfare. It is hard to find a doctor who does not complain about his or her medical malpractice premiums in terms of his or her economic well-being.

The trial lawyers are well funded and organized. That will carry the day for years. The media, at least in Pennsylvania, and in newspapers such as *The New York Times*, is not about to take on the trial lawyers.

Change will only happen when a growing number of dead babies and dead in-the-alley black inner city pregnant teenagers catch the attention of Oprah.

This situation, growing more acute by the day, does not result from market forces, a shortage of doctors, or inadequate resources. It is caused by one factor and one factor only. The trial lawyers are sucking millions of dollars out of the system—dollars that would otherwise be available for health care.

And the band plays on.

THE NATIONAL TENSION

On August 25th, 2002, The New York Times Sunday edition, headlined in its lead story:

RISE IN INSURANCE FORCES HOSPITALS TO SHUTTER WARDS

CUTS IN OBSTETRIC WARDS

Trauma Centers also Hurt— Malpractice Costs Leading To Reduced Services

Around the country this summer, at least half a dozen hospitals have closed obstetric wards, others have curtailed trauma services, and a string of rural clinics have been temporarily shuttered as a result of soaring costs for medical malpractice insurance.

. . .

In the last few weeks, the only trauma center in Las Vegas closed for 10 days:

. . .

In all, more than 1,300 health care institutions have already been affected according to a survey by the American Hospital Association.

"It is likely that this is going to get much worse," said Carmela Coyle, the senior vice president for policy at the hospital association. "We're likely to see more closures of services."

So far no deaths have been attributed to the cutbacks, but hospitals say risks to patients are rising.

In a full one-half page analysis on page 18, the *Times* further noted:

The costs have become truly staggering. Premiums for doctors have doubled and tripled, in some cases rising to as high as $200,000.00 a year…

In Philadelphia, for example, the cost of malpractice insurance at Thomas Jefferson University Hospital, which operates several hospitals, doubled this year to $32 million. (Ed. Note: The cost has gone from $7 million to $32 million in just five years).

…from 1995 to 2000, the average jury award jumped more than 70 percent, to $3.5 million, and a few claims since then have run to more than $40 million…

In this multi-page story, not once did *The New York Times* mention the role of the trial lawyers! In point of fact, the *Times* is not about to take on what is perhaps the most powerful lobby in America. The trial lawyers fund Democratic candidates at all levels. The *Times* almost always endorses Democratic candidates. *The New York Times* has become part of the problem.

The cat leaped out of the bag two weeks later. Highly regarded Texas Supreme Court Justice Pricilla Owen had been nominated by President Bush to a vacancy on the Court of Appeals for the Fifth Circuit. She received the highest rating from the American Bar Association, an organization with a decidedly liberal bent. She should have been a shoo-in. The trial lawyers moved on the nomination. On a 10 to 9 party line vote, the Democrats on the Judiciary Committee voted to defeat the nomination. Senators Kennedy, Leahy, and other

Democrats, whose re-election campaigns are funded by the trial lawyers, tipped their hats to that group by justifying their vote, inter alia, on the basis that she hadn't shown sufficient "judicial concern for injured plaintiffs." Just as Justice Rolf Larsen sold the Pennsylvania judicial system to PATLA, for ambition, President Bill Clinton sold the soul of the Democratic Party to the national trial lawyers for money. The trial lawyers massive contributions would elect Democrats and the Democrats would protect the trial lawyers' turf.

The crisis is building and will be fought out for years to come with the national trial lawyers having the edge—it's called money. Following the Pennsylvania Model, the national trial lawyers will hijack Congress and the Executive to prevent national reform of the system. President Bush may propose reform legislation such as was enacted in Texas while he was Governor, but the salons in Washington will only "talk" reform while protecting their contributors. In 2004, the trial lawyers would be successful in nominating one of their own, John Edwards, as the Democratic Party's candidate for Vice President. Edwards, an accomplished trial lawyer, piled up a personal fortune of forty million dollars suing doctors and hospitals. His election would insure that the fox would be in the henhouse.

Seven-year locusts come to pillage only once every seven years. The trial lawyers will be here 24/7, each and every year for the foreseeable future.

THE LAST HEARING?

Fall 2002

Bashman's amicus brief was filed in April. When the Circuit Court failed to assign the case for disposition in May, June, July and August, I began to get nervous. A little bird in the back of my head kept warning me that Bashman, in his brief, had raised the issue of the Federal Court suspension being over on October 24th. He suggested, without citing any legal authority, that the appeal would become moot at that point.

Through August, on a weekly basis, I contacted Brian Hirsch and asked why nothing was happening. His answer was the same each time:

"Bob, this is not unusual".

Brian had clerked in the Circuit Court and was a true believer in the honesty and integrity of the Judges on that Court. For my part, I had no reason to believe in the honesty and integrity of any Court.

Finally, we received notice that the case was scheduled for argument on December 18, 2002—almost eighteen months after Sam Klein filed the appeal and over ten years after I filed the Motion for Recusal.

Meanwhile, I had asked Bob Heim, Chair of the Litigation Section at Dechert, who would be arguing the case before the Third Circuit? I told him that this was an important case and I hoped that he would assign an experienced attorney. To my utter amazement and everlasting gratitude, he assigned Jeff Weil, one of their top litigators.

I met with Jeff and Brian Hirsch and was reassured that the case would get their full attention. Never did I anticipate the extent of the effort. Once Jeff got a handle on the case, he took it as a personal challenge to right the wrong he perceived. He called almost daily to nail down a fact and understand the twenty-year history of what had happened. He filed Petitions to supplement the brief that Sam wrote and add additional evidence to the record. He worked tirelessly to ensure that he could answer every potential challenge to the appeal from the assigned three-Judge panel. As an experienced lawyer, I stood in awe of his commitment to this case, a case where Dechert would earn no fee.

December 18th arrived. No one will ever understand the anxiety I felt as I realized that almost twenty years of prosecution by Disciplinary Counsel was about to be brought to an end, one way or the other.

The panel consisted of Judges Roth, Cowen and Fuentes. As Jeff began his argument, Judge Roth peppered him with questions, mostly about procedure and the technical aspects of the case. My heart sank. This usually portends that the Judge is about to ignore the merits, merits that in this case overwhelmingly preponderated in my favor. Jeff did a superb job of answering these questions and bringing the argument back to the merits.

Then the worm seemed to turn when Bashman took the podium. Judge Cowen hammered him with questions which Bashman either could not answer or responded to weakly. It was clear to me that Judge Cowen was familiar with every aspect of the record and was deeply offended by the absence of due process I received from the Pennsylvania Supreme Court. At the end of his argument, Bashman went personal. He noted that the District Court suspension was over and told the panel that "Surrick was only here to exact his pound of flesh from the Pennsylvania Supreme Court," a gratuitous comment that incensed Judge Cowen.

When the argument was over, I was shaky and disoriented. It was not only the stress. Three days later I underwent brain surgery for a subdural hematoma.

A week later, *The Legal Intelligencer* headlined and wrote:

Surrick Asks 3rd Circuit Panel to Overturn Suspension

For the past few years, attorney Robert B. Surrick has been trying to convince the federal courts that his five-year suspension by the Pennsylvania Supreme Court in March 2000 wasn't a fall from grace as much as a push.

So far, he isn't winning the battle—but he's coming darned close.

Surrick's case sharply split the judges of the Eastern District of Pennsylvania, and as was clear from appellate arguments last week, it looks like he's headed for another split vote by a new set of judges on the 3rd Circuit Court of Appeals.

Even though this long running saga involved serious First Amendment and due process issues, the *Inquirer* had stopped covering it. They had forgotten the immortal words of the great French statesman and civil libertarian, Georges Clemenceau, that:

When one man's rights are violated, every man's rights are jeopardized.

As noted by Dick Sprague, Federal Judges like to think they are better than their state court counterparts. Indeed, Judge Dalzell, in his Dissenting Opinion to the bizarre secret vote of the District Court, which overturned the finding of the Pollak panel that due process was lacking in my case, pointed out *no fewer than 266 judges on state courts around the country have been removed from office as a result of disciplinary proceedings.* Are Federal Judges free from corruption?

The Associated Press wire service reported on June 6, 2003 as follows:

Federal judge wrongly took part in affirmative-action case

The AP wrote:

The federal judge whose majority opinion sent an important affirmative-action case to the Supreme Court improperly intervened in the appeal…

Chief Judge Boyce F. Martin of the U.S. Court of Appeals for the Sixth Circuit in Cincinnati provided the crucial vote in a 5-4 ruling in May 2002 that upheld affirmative action in college admissions policies.

The review found that Martin named himself to a three-judge panel that was to hear the case even though court rules specify that assignments are made at random. Martin, named by President Jimmy Carter in 1979, also delayed for five months a request to have the full appeals court hear the case, ensuring the exclusion of two conservative judges, who were planning to retire.

After these judges went on senior status, which meant they could not participate in the full court appeal, the Sixth Circuit took over from the special panel and ultimately made its 5-4 ruling.

Is the Federal bench corrupt? Of course not! Are some Federal Judges corrupt? It would seem so. In 2001, there were 766 ethical complaints lodged against Federal Judges. Many complaints don't stick because they are heard by—you guessed it—Federal Judges. In spite of Judge Martin being caught red-handed, no discipline was recommended.

While Judge Dalzell described the judicial discipline experience in the Federal Court as "happier", he nevertheless noted that since 1980 there were forty-four cases where discipline was imposed on a Federal Judge for misconduct including three removals from office by impeachment.

The evidence supports the conclusion that the corrupt and the corruptors also inhabit the Federal bench.

As Judge Dalzell also noted:

The conduct of which Surrick complained in his written motion, therefore, is scarcely unknown either in Pennsylvania or in the other state courts…

Social and judicial injustice exists at all levels of government. First, it must be recognized and acknowledged. That is the major hurdle. Then, the Cowens, Dalzells, Pollaks and Padovas of the judicial world must take the lead in stamping it out, even if it means openly condemning colleagues in both state and Federal Court who violate their oath of office.

PATLA BUYS A GOVERNOR

December 31, 2002

Pa. warns doctors not to quit

This headline from the December 28th *Philadelphia Inquirer* covered a story about a December 20 letter the Secretary of the Commonwealth, C. Michael Weaver, sent to all licensed physicians in the Commonwealth warning them of the consequences of a stoppage of practice threatened by the doctors as a result of skyrocketing medical malpractice premiums. He threatened:

"A stoppage of practice may be detrimental not only to your patients, but also to your practice, your standing amongst colleagues, as well as your license should your conduct be found to constitute abandonment."

Several days later, Governor-elect Ed Rendell appeared on *CNN* to answer questions about the growing crisis. Rendell had been elected with six million dollars in contributions from the trial lawyers. The trial lawyers contributed more money to Rendell than any other special interest group in Pennsylvania. He owed them big time.

On CNN, Rendell first blamed the insurance companies for refusing to write medical malpractice coverage in the face of multi-million dollar losses. He didn't identify the cause of the losses. Next, he blamed the Insurance Commissioner for failing to regulate the insurance industry. Then he suggested that it was the CAT Fund that was not being managed properly. He stated that those who would blame the court system "were missing the mark." The words "trial lawyer" never passed his lips.

During this deceptive performance, what I had been waiting months to hear slid onto the table. Rendell mentioned that the three hundred million dollar shortfall in the CAT Fund could be made up from surpluses in health-care insurer funds. But make no mistake; it will ultimately be from general revenue. What a solution! Doctors would get some relief from skyrocketing insurance premiums, the trial lawyers could continue to rape and pillage the health care delivery system, and the taxpayers and those insured would ultimately pay for it.

THE CRISIS SPREADS

January 2, 2003

On January 2, 2003, *The New York Times* carried an article entitled:

West Virginia Doctors Protest Insurance Costs

The paper reported:

Almost all surgery was cancelled today after more than two dozen surgeons started a job action to protest the cost of malpractice insurance.

. . .

The hospitals are keeping emergency rooms open, but with the exception of plastic surgeons they have almost no emergency surgeons available.

. . .

In Pennsylvania, a similar halt in work was avoided today after Gov. elect Edward G Rendell promised to fight for $220 million in aid for doctors.

On January 28, 2003, *The Baltimore Sun* headlined:

More than 800 Florida doctors, dozen in Mississippi, stop work

On January 30, 2003, *The New York Times* reported as follows:

Unless It's an Emergency, The Doctor May Not Be In

As New Jersey braces for a work stoppage by doctors on Monday, physicians are canceling appointments; emergency rooms are planning for a sudden influx of patients, and many residents including the governor-are beginning to fret about disruptions in health care.

. . .

The doctors seemed in no mood yesterday to relax either their threat or their demands that the Legislature enact a $250,000 cap on jury awards for so-called pain and suffering damages for victims of medical malpractice.

New Jersey's trial lawyers are adamantly opposed to any such cap, and Mr. (Governor) *McGreevey has expressed sympathy with lawyers' opposition to curbs...*

This is only the beginning. At first I thought if Pennsylvania cleaned up the problem, it would be the end of it. But it has spread too far, too fast, and too deeply. Only federal legislation putting caps on pain and suffering and punitive damage awards and removing medical malpractice litigation from the state court systems will end the problem. There is no time for fifty states to fashion reform legislation that would surely be opposed in each state by the trial lawyers. However, the constitutionality of this kind of sea change in federal regulation, heretofore the province of the states, is dicey. And such legislation, if it ever could be passed over the opposition of the trial lawyers, would surely be litigated for years through the Supreme Court of the United States. Will Congress act? Bearing in mind the politics, it is problematic at best. Last year the trial lawyers infused the political system with nineteen million dollars in contributions to Democrats. In Washington, money talks and bullshit walks. Even if Congress acts, it will be in the face of thirteen states that have a constitutional prohibition against limitations on jury verdicts. In Pennsylvania, this prohibition would have to be overturned by a Constitutional Amendment that must pass two sessions of the legislature and be voted "yes" by the electorate in a General Election.

When Rolf Larsen sold the Pennsylvania court system to the trial lawyers, the genie was let out of the bottle. The trial lawyers in the other states quickly caught on.

The problem, caused by a judicial system and legislators obligated to the trial lawyers, appears politically intractable.

Let me put it this way. Which legislator(s) will lead the charge for caps on verdicts for pain and suffering and punitive damages in the face of almost certain defeat for reelection after choosing to become a target of the trial lawyers?

Frankly, I don't know any.

PRESIDENT BUSH ENTERS THE FRAY

January 16, 2003

On January 16th, 2003, President Bush spoke on national television from Scranton, Pennsylvania. The next day, *The New York Times* headlined in a front-page article:

WITH A NEW PUSH, BUSH ENTERS FRAY OVER MALPRACTICE

Bush called for caps on jury verdicts for pain and suffering and punitive damages, the engine that is driving the huge verdicts. He cited California where caps on these items were installed in 1975. California doctors' medical malpractice premiums are generally about one-third the national average.

In a sub headline, ever protecting the trial lawyers, the *Times* muddied the waters as follows:

Some Experts Say Poor Returns On Investments Play Bigger Role In Insurance Costs

Proving beyond doubt his commitment to the trial lawyers, Governor-elect Rendell was quoted:

. . .

jury awards were a just a small part of the problem and that the best thing the federal government could do to help doctors would be to increase their payments under Medicare.

In other words, give the doctors more taxpayer dollars to pay medical malpractice premiums and let the trial lawyers continue gorging at the trough.

This duplicity, in the face of evidence from California that caps work, says it all about our elected officials. They will lie and dissemble to their constituents with no penalty in order to curry favor with those driving the cash train.

What's wrong with this picture?

. . .

By 2003 the shortfall in the CAT Fund, now called the MCARE Fund was becoming a serious problem. Rendell and the legislators did the bidding of the trial lawyers and solved the problem with taxpayer dollars. They enacted a twenty-five cent per-pack tax on cigarettes to raise two hundred and fifty million dollars to make up the shortfall. The taxpayers were now funding the trial lawyers pillage of the health care delivery system. But the Rendall solution was a band-aid on the MCARE Fund's three billion dollar unfunded liability. The chickens will come home to roost.

FEAR IS THE FOOD THAT NOURISHES POLITICS

April 1, 2003

Today, the local store where I pick up my daily *New York Times* didn't have one so I grabbed *The Philadelphia Inquirer.* I saw that Matt Ryan, Speaker of the House, had died. There was an editorial entitled *A Good Man Gone.* The *Inquirer* wrote:

With Irish charm and gentlemanly finesse, House Speaker Matthew Ryan untangled many a political knot in more than four decades of representing Delaware County …

His body lies in state today beneath the rotunda of the Capitol…Not since Abraham Lincoln's body lay in state in 1865 has a public figure been so honored.

…

Mr. Ryan was noted for his negotiating skills and fairness.

The editorial was notable for what it didn't say.

My history with Matt goes back forty-three years. We both came to the bar in Delaware County in or about 1960. Matt was an ex-Marine, good-looking and had married well to the daughter of attorney Joe Mullray, a power in the Republican Party. We were both insiders; he through Mullray and me through brother-in-law John Cramp. In those years, we saw ourselves on the same team, the powerful Delaware County Republican Party. Matt was a good man in the sense that he was a good friend to many, a man of his word, and a hail-fellow, well met. But that was his private persona. I will speak only to his public persona.

Eventually, we went different directions. He was selected by the Republican Party to become a member of the state legislature and I became a maverick. His seat from Newtown Township was one of the safest seats in the legislature, leaving him free to campaign and raise money for other Republican candidates around the state. That wins friends and influences people.

By 1980, he was well on his way to becoming Speaker of the House, and I was well on my way to becoming a critic of the system. In the Chapter *I Would Be Chief Justice But For That Nigger*, I detail how close Matt had moved to the center of power. He was in a position to threaten Governor Thornburgh's ambitions for the presidency in return for control over the appointment of Judges to vacancies when they occur by reason of death, resignation, or retirement. It was power politics, pure and simple. The issue was not the betterment of our polity; it was about who would control the selection of Judges, with the sub-issue being the selection of Judges who would do what the pols wanted them to do meaning Judges who were team players. Matt, out of fear for his own ambition, was doing what the party leaders demanded.

Back in the early seventies, Matt and I talked about becoming law partners—we were that close. By the 1980's, we were worlds apart. I met him in Harrisburg in the early eighties when testifying about judicial reform to the House Judiciary Committee. Sitting in the old Capitol lunchroom, I outlined my feelings about the slide of the judiciary into the Dark Ages, a slide led by Justice Larsen. He agreed with me that "it was getting bad." I outlined some changes that would help. He refused to consider any suggestions for change. Because of his refusal to make any effort toward judicial reform, I ran a candidate against him in the next election and for the first time in years, he had to campaign to defend his seat. He held his seat and there was no reform. Again, out of fear for his own political well-being, Matt was not about to take on the powerful above him.

As time went on and Matt's power increased, he became a force for closing the legislative process to public scrutiny. It was only a matter of time until he collided with Sam Klein. The secretive dealings reached new levels when the leaders of the legislature closed the Caucus Room's heavy oak doors for budget horse-trading. It became de rigueur for the leaders of the legislature to wait until the eleventh hour before the deadline for the budget, go behind these closed doors, agree upon a budget, and with hours left, give the two-hundred plus page budget to the rank and file and call for a vote. Ninety-five percent of the elected representatives had no idea what they were voting for. Out of fear, the legislators did what they knew was expected of them. Common Cause became outraged at this process. Enter Sam Klein with his passion for openness in government. Common Cause, through Sam, tried to put an end to the flagrant nose-thumbing to the public by these leaders. Sam lost that battle. The Courts, not surprisingly, supported the legislative secrecy.

In 1990, Matt spearheaded Special Legislation through the House to modify the age seventy mandatory retirement in the Constitution for Judges. It was Special Legislation to benefit Commonwealth Court President Judge Crumlish and President Judge Catania from Delaware County which I outline in the chapter *The Pols Lose One*. *The Philadelphia Inquirer* wrote an editorial:

What's this bill for? It's unconstitutional and unneeded

Matt had lost his fear. He was part of the leadership and would do as he damn well pleased. The neutered *Inquirer* was irrelevant.

"Walking Around Money," known as WAMs, is taxpayer dollars that the legislative leaders squirrel away in the budget to do favors, without public scrutiny, for the locals in legislative districts. A new Men's Locker Room at Charlie Sexton's Springfield Country Club is a good example. These special favors would never pass in open session of the legislature but in the secret world of WAMs, it gets done. The leaders, such as Matt Ryan, put the money in the budget as a payoff to the back-bencher who kept his mouth shut and did as he or she was told, like voting "yes" on an unseen budget. This process was at the heart of Matt Ryan's ability to maintain his leadership position. He was now the one applying fear. In Harrisburg, fear and money makes the world go around.

When I saw Matt Ryan's obituary, I called Barry Kauffman, Executive Director of Common Cause, about the *Inquirer* editorial. Barry told me he really didn't know Matt. "For the sixteen years I have been Executive Director of Common Cause, Matt refused to meet with me.

He wouldn't talk to me except a hello passing in the halls." Here was an unquestioned leader in the legislature who refused to even listen to the only good government group that makes a difference in Harrisburg. He apparently feared a collision between his inner principles and his external politics.

In point of fact, my one-time friend, the political Matt Ryan, represented everything that is wrong with Pennsylvania and the upside-down political world in which we live. And the *Inquirer* knows this. That's why it didn't write that Matt was a fearless force for reform—a leader who left Pennsylvania better than he found it.

I am sorry for Matt's passing, sorry for Pat, his family and those he loved and who loved him. His private life was his private life but he chose to be a public figure and his record as a public figure is public. And in that public life he felt the fear that all lawyers feel when thinking about how his or their actions will be judged by the powerful.

I could go on and on with evidence of Matt Ryan's compliance with the status quo which, in Pennsylvania, puts us on a par with the Balkans. It is all there for anyone who wants to look. But who is looking and who will tell the people?

Here is the disconnect. Edmund Morris, in *Theodore Rex,* wrote about Pennsylvania over one hundred years ago:

> *Harrisburg was notoriously the most corrupt seat of state government in the nation.*

It still is, but to the average person, that corruption is invisible. Now, there is no one to tell the people. For a brief period, the Gene Roberts led *Inquirer* told the people but that fearless reporting has been crushed and the seventeen Pulitzers rendered meaningless. Even the *Inquirer* now feels the fear.

So we see that government works at two levels. There is the level that we all learn about in seventh grade civics. This is the level that the thousands of children see on a sunny Spring day when clambering off the buses and climbing the stairs to the state Capitol. It is the level that the public sees when a carefully scripted governor or president goes on television and wraps himself in the flag. It is the level at local political rallies when, with flags waving and bands playing, a candidate to political office stirs a friendly crowd with boilerplate rhetoric. It is the level that the lawyers see in the baroque Supreme Court chambers where the

Justices seem to be considering difficult questions. It is the level every lawyer who goes into a courtroom sees while wanting to believe in the system but knows deep down the system is broken. It is the illusory government we all want and need to believe in—and most do. It is politics without fear.

But the reality is far different. And this book, I hope, tells the story of that difference.

. . .

In the summer of 2004, three events occurred in the Pennsylvania legislature that says it all about morality in that body.

In the first, State Representative William Rieger, a thirty-eight year veteran of the House, rigged his voting machine by jamming a wad of paper or paper clip in the "yes" button and then drove to his home in Philadelphia where he remained while casting "yes" votes on the meaningless minor legislation scheduled for that day. It is a violation of written House rules to cast a vote when not physically present. **Let me repeat, it is a violation of written House rules to cast a vote when not physically present**. He accepted the $126.00 per diem for meals and lodging in Harrisburg even though he was at home in Philadelphia. Apparently a reporter noticed and wrote about it. The matter was referred to the House Ethics Committee. The Ethics Committee held a twenty-minute hearing behind closed doors and found that Rieger "did not violate House rules..." The Ethics Committee noted that ghost voting is a long-standing fact of life widely practiced by members in both parties. What I find most troubling is the atmosphere that this very obvious cheating on the rules and the per diem creates. All members of the House know it goes on. For obvious reasons they all turn their heads. The mentality "go along to get along" towers over the Chamber and encourages other abuses. It is part of the downward spiral that puts every representative's ethics and integrity in the moral basement where they seem to feel quite comfortable.

The second event involved the passage of landmark legislation on July 3, 2004, legalizing slot machines. The Bill introduced in the Senate, by none other than Senator Vincent Fumo, permitted legislators to own up to 4.99 percent of a new slot machine operation. Such a stake, which obviously would be a payoff from the owners to favored legislators, would have been worth millions of dollars, perhaps hundreds of millions of dollars. Even the pigs in the legislature knew that this was over the top so they settled on final passage for one percent ownership. On July 13, 2004, *The New York Times* editorialized about the evil of the nationwide explosion of slot machines and noted:

Perhaps the sleaziest new deal, however is in Pennsylvania, where Gov. Edward Rendell and the legislature have just agreed to allow as many as 61,000 slot machines at an estimated 14 locations across the state. . . . Tucked into the law was also a gift to the legislators who passed it. Pennsylvania will allow its lawmakers and other public officials to own up to 1 percent of any new slot-machine venture. . . .

Event number three was in the small hours of the morning on July 3, 2004, when the Senate Judiciary Committee, led by Senator Stewart Greenleaf, took advantage of a brief recess from the slot machine debate, to convene and kill the proposed Constitutional Amendment that would have led the way to caps on jury verdicts in medical malpractice lawsuits. Senator Greenleaf, demonstrating legislator dissembling that has become a way of life, claimed he opposed the Amendment because it did not "exclude catastrophic injuries." The Amendment in no way dealt with substantive issues about caps such as "catastrophic injuries." All it dealt with was whether or not a future legislature could consider caps legislation. But Greenleaf had to say something and this deceitful non-sequitur was the best he could come up with. By this action, the earliest tort reform could come to Pennsylvania now is 2007. PATLA money had prevailed and the crisis in the health care delivery system will continue for at least three more years. PATLA had taught the disorganized, fractured and unfocused medical community a very expensive lesson.

MAY I MAKE MY POINT

April 11, 2003

As previously mentioned, my parents were both journalists. Dad was City Editor of *The Philadelphia Public Ledger* and met Mom when she was hired as a reporter. I grew up around their irreverent and hard-drinking colleagues. More than once I listened to scornful derision about other journalists "who wouldn't spoil a story for the want of a few facts." It was almost mother's milk to me that you "get the story and get it right."

Reading my *New York Times* today, I, spotted an op-ed piece entitled:

The News We Kept to Ourselves

It was a mea culpa written by Eason Jordan, the Chief News Executive of CNN. He revealed that for twelve years, CNN had declined to inform the public about atrocities, atrocities with which he and his staff were personally familiar, committed by Saddam Hussein's government against his employees and the citizens of Iraq. He admitted he specifically knew of the torture of human beings that was going on around him. He admitted that CNN made a conscious decision not to report the truth. Let me repeat that. CNN made a conscious decision not to report facts in its possession while it was lobbying Baghdad to keep the Bureau open so it could continue misreporting the truth. He admitted to the conscious decision to abandon journalistic integrity.

Why did CNN do this? It did it for money. To keep the bureau open to attract viewers who would see it's advertising that paid the bills and enhanced the corporate bottom line. Let's be clear about what we are talking about. Time Warner owns CNN. It is a profit center. Time Warner is one of the global news conglomerates. Time Warner knew what Eason Jordan knew. It was more than compliant with the CNN decision. It was complicitous. The journalistic ethic was corrupted on a very large scale.

It should have been an earthshaking admission. It wasn't. Why wasn't it? Dishonest journalists, like dishonest lawyers are now a way of life. It is accepted conduct in this brave new world we have created. Let me be more specific about things that I know.

In a recently published book, *Art Held Hostage,* by John Anderson, a contributing editor for *The American Lawyer*, Richard Glanton, Thornburgh's Counsel to the Governor, is exposed for looting the Barnes Foundation of millions of dollars. Glanton, with the help of pals Vince Fumo, Charlie Sexton and others mentioned frequently in this book, spent and used Barnes money like it was Christmas every day. The *Inquirer* had most of the facts, and an even cursory investigation would have revealed a major scandal reaching into the legislature, the legal community, and other charitable trusts. The *Inquirer* chose to ignore what many saw as serious criminal activity. Why? Because the *Inquirer* was defending a libel suit brought by Judge McElree in Chester County referred to earlier in the book, and Glanton would be an important witness in that lawsuit. Perhaps more important, Senator Fumo was using Dick Sprague when media coverage got too close. The *Inquirer* was not about to risk another libel suit. Faced with a choice between self interest and aggressive journalism, the Inquirer, once again, ignored the path of honor and duty.

The Philadelphia Inquirer refused to print good and honest journalism by reporter Ralph Cipriano about the misdeeds of Cardinal Bevilacqua, the shepherd of his one-and-a-quarter million Catholic flock in greater Philadelphia. Why? If it angered some of the flock, they might not buy the *Inquirer*. Circulation would go down which reduces the dollars from advertising revenue. The decision, like the decision of CNN, was economic. It's money.

Similarly, the *Inquirer* has made the conscious decision to end investigative reporting on judicial corruption out of fear of libel suits. Libel suits cost money to defend and the settlements and verdicts cost real money. Is the *Inquirer* any different from CNN? The only difference I can see is that CNN, perhaps without understanding what it was really saying, admitted to a corruption of journalistic standards.

Having been close to the *Inquirer* on a personal basis and through its lawyer, Sam Klein, I could go on and on about *not the sound, but the silence,* from the *Inquirer.* The corporate bottom line now controls its journalism. And its journalism has been as corrupted as CNN's.

In a Sunday, May 11th 2003 seven thousand word article, *The New York Times* admitted:

A staff reporter for the New York Times committed frequent acts of journalistic fraud while covering significant news events.

The *Times* top editors knew staff reporter Jayson Blair was a pathological liar. They knew he was fabricating and those fabrications were printed as news. Nevertheless, they continued to assign him to important stories such as the Washington sniper and Iraq. Howell Raines, the Executive Editor and those under him corrupted journalistic standards in the name of diversity. When the story broke, it led to other reporters. On May 29th, 2003, the *Times* reported the Pulitzer Prize winning reporter Rick Bragg "resigned" after being caught using another reporter's work under his by-line. The "Newspaper of Record," as the *Times* likes to call itself, was imploding.

But it's not just CNN and the *Times.* On March 20, 2004, the *Times* reported:

USA Today Says Reporter Fabricated Articles Over 10 Years

Fabrication by lawyers, judges and journalists has become a way of life.

Further discussion of the trial lawyers is unnecessary. I hope the facts I have provided prove my point. So is further discussion of a Supreme Court that feels the need to solidify its power by silencing its critics. The facts speak for themselves. The Supreme Court and our

Judges eschew robust dialogue about the state of our judicial system, demanding instead a bar consisting of Stepford Wives who will do anything to avoid the truth for personal gain.

Years ago, I lost a dear friend over a drink on Anegada in the BVI when I spoke my truth about Matt Ryan. Similarly, when I showed the previous chapter to several selected lawyer friends in Delaware County, I was greeted by angry comments. Matt Ryan was everybody's friend. Two thousand people and four past or present Governors showed up at his funeral. Doesn't that prove Bob Surrick is crazy criticizing Matt? People I care about and respect will defend Matt to his death. It is part of what my son Craig calls the duality of life. On one level, almost everybody knows right from wrong. However, at the practical level, in what passes in today's society for probity, the window through which we gaze has become cloudy. The unvarnished truth becomes indistinct. What we need to see, what we want to see for our own well-being, becomes clear and that becomes our truth.

And now there are only a handful of older journalists, Judges and lawyers to show us the way back. The corrupt and the corruptors have just about extinguished the institutional memory of what was right. The light of now far-off integrity grows dim. We have truly lost our way.

MEDICAL MALPRACTICE VERDICTS WHERE IS THE TRUTH?

June 2004

During 2003 and the first part of 2004, I traveled Pennsylvania speaking to county medical societies, hospital staffs, senior citizen centers, service clubs, PAPA, and anyone else who would listen about the deepening health care delivery crisis. Sometimes I would share a platform with a representative of the trial lawyers. They would always mouth the Rendell mantra:

Jury awards were just a small part of the problem…

Well, here are the facts and you decide if Governor Rendell is telling the truth. In the early 1990's, a million dollar verdict in a medical malpractice case in southeastern Pennsylvania was rare to non-existent. Now, as reported in a revealing article in the *Philadelphia Business Journal* dated June 11, 2004, using facts compiled by the respected and impartial Jury Verdict Research, from 2001 to 2003, the following ten local law firms won over one-hundred and sixty million dollars in jury verdicts in the five southeastern counties with the lions-share coming from Philadelphia.

Klein and Specter (Arlen Specter's son)--------------51 million
Blank Rome--24 million
Beasley Firm ---19.1 million
Colleran Firm---17.8 million
Litvin, Blumberg-------------------------------------- 15 million
Lowenthal & Abrams-----------------------------------11.3 million
Abraham, Lowenstein and Bushman----------------- 7 million
Kolsby, Gordon-- 5.2 million
Brookman Rosenberg----------------------------------5 million
Duffy & Keenan---------------------------------------4.9 million

TOTAL-- 160.3 million

At the usual forty percent contingent fee, the above ten firms collected over sixty million dollars in legal fees. A lot of judges and legislators can be bought with that kind of money.

Bear in mind, these numbers are only for the top ten law firms. There are hundreds of jury verdicts garnered by other firms. More importantly the total aggregate dollars paid out in med mal cases, frivolous or not, which are settled, dwarfs the dollars from jury verdicts. And the size of the jury verdicts directly impact the amount of the settlements. The facts are that in this period hundreds of millions of dollars have been sucked out of the health care delivery system into the pockets of the trial lawyers, and the trial lawyers are using it with devastating effect to block tort reform by lavishly contributing to the Democrats.

You now have the facts. Are jury verdicts "just a small part of the problem"? Or has Rendell, a trial lawyer soul-mate of Bill Clinton, given new meaning to the word mendacity?

THE BARBARIANS ENTER THE GATES

July 2004

In 1998, John Edwards bought one of the two North Carolina seats in the United States Senate. He spent six million dollars to join the world's most exclusive club. Actually, his seat was cheap. Two years later Jon Corzine spent over seventy million dollars of his own money for a New Jersey seat.

Where did John Edwards, son of a mill worker, get that kind of money? He was a trial lawyer and one of the most successful in the United States. Edwards was ahead of the curve. Courtrooms would no longer be a place to merely settle disputes. They would become money machines and Edwards clearly saw the potential. In a brief twenty year career as a plaintiff's lawyer, Edwards piled up over forty million dollars in legal fees from over forty multimillion dollar verdicts. In a flattering article in *The New York Times* dated July 14, 2004, it was noted:

Most of Mr. Edward's biggest victories were medical malpractice cases, often involving claims against obstetricians. Mr. Edwards filed more than 20 lawsuits against doctors and hospitals in deliveries gone wrong, winning verdicts and settlements in just those cases of more than $60 million.

Note *The New York Times* spin. They write the verdicts resulted from "*deliveries gone wrong.*" The actual facts are that Edwards came up with the dubious theory that doctor error is the cause of cerebral palsy. He claimed that if the doctors involved had performed cesarean sections, the cerebral palsy would have been avoided. This theory has been universally rejected by medical experts today but it sure worked with juries in the 80's. One result is that in 2003, there were five times as many deliveries by c-section as there were in the 1980s. Doctors are practicing defensive medicine causing both the cost and risk to mother and baby to dramatically increase.

The national crisis from the use of this voodoo medicine to produce huge verdicts against ob/gyn doctors is just beginning to unfold. In 2003, only one graduate of the University of Maryland medical school and only three from Johns Hopkins Medical School opted for an ob/gyn residency. As I have noted elsewhere, women and babies will die when specialist care is not available for a problem delivery. And the availability of that care is decreasing at an alarming rate.

After four years in the United States Senate, the boyishly handsome Edwards set his sights on a higher prize. He would run for President of the United States. How would he do this? He would tap into the almost unlimited cash available to the trial lawyers. The nineties and turn of the century had not only been good to the trial lawyers in Pennsylvania, it had been Christmas every day for trial lawyers throughout the United States. Class action lawsuits got the members of the class very little on an individual basis but the legal fees were staggering. Forty to fifty million dollar fees were regularly awarded. The trial lawyers now had big bucks and were willing to spend it to enlarge the opening they had created into the bank accounts of corporate and professional America.

The march to the White House would not be easy. After September 11 and the invasion of Iraq, the nation was in turmoil. At various times, there were eight to ten other Democrats seeking the nomination. It became obvious early on that the liberal wing of the Party was in control and John Kerry, the most liberal Senator in Washington, was their choice. Edwards wasn't outspent but he was overmatched. Four years of undistinguished service in the Senate overcame his populist message. Kerry won the nomination.

Who would John Kerry pick as his running mate? There were those more experienced than Edwards. There were those brighter than Edwards. There were those with greater star power than Edwards. In the end, three things won the nod for Edwards. They were money, money and money. The trial lawyers deep pockets and their willingness to open those pockets would carry the day. Kerry needed that money and Edwards could deliver it. The Democrats, starting with Clinton, had made a deal with the devil when they sold the Party to the trial lawyers. The result is that innocent citizen taxpayers will pay the increasing cost of decreasing health care.

Never had a special interest group become so powerful so fast.

WILL YOU PICK UP THE TORCH?

In the summer of 1983, Justice Larsen filed a seventeen page complaint to the Disciplinary Board of the Supreme Court against me. I had become and would remain a target. Eighteen years later, in August, 2001, Sam Klein filed an appeal to the Court of Appeals for the Third Circuit from the bizarre and politically motivated decision of the District Court suspending my license to practice law for thirty months. The Third Circuit mushed around for sixteen months before hearing argument on December 18, 2002. Finally, on August 1, 2003, over seven months later, the Circuit Court handed down its Opinion. By a 2 to 1 vote it upheld the District Court's thirty month suspension. The majority opinion was written by Judge Roth. It was factually inaccurate and intellectually dishonest.

Judge Roth wrote that the decision of the District Court was by a "seventeen to nine vote". The District Court Docket reflects the vote was actually "14 to 13". Why did she misrepresent the record? A 14 to 13 vote would have sent alarm bells ringing to the other Judges on the Circuit Court who didn't have the record. She wanted to make it appear that it wasn't a close case in the District Court so she used Bashman's manufactured numbers.

The Opinion was intellectually dishonest in several particulars.

Judge Roth wrote that I should have anticipated that the Pennsylvania Supreme Court would adopt the "reckless" standard for an 8.4 (c) violation that was in existence in six other states but not

Pennsylvania when I filed the Motion to Recuse eight years earlier. In a blistering Dissent, Judge Cowen noted "(T)hat fact seems to prove only that forty-four states, or more than three-quarters on the nation had not extended their rule to include reckless conduct".

Judge Roth also picked up the misrepresentation in Judge Giles Opinion that I had admitted an absence of factual basis for my charges against Judges Bradley and Olszewski and that the Pollak Opinion for the first three judge panel had not found a due process violation by the Pennsylvania Supreme Court. As pointed out previously, no such admission by me can be found anywhere in the record and Judge Pollak's Opinion, in fact, states that the retroactive application of new standards by the Pennsylvania Supreme Court **"did not"** satisfy federal due process requirements.

Recognizing the dishonesty of Judge Roth's Opinion, Dechert's Jeff Weil heroically filed a Petition for Certiorari to the Supreme Court of the United States. That Court accepts about one percent of the Petitions filed. Not unexpectedly, the Petition was denied. As explained to me by a courtly gray haired lawyer at Dechert, the Supreme Court of the United States is unlikely to take a case just because one lawyer or litigant gets "screwed over" in the system. "They have bigger fish to fry".

What I have brought to you says it all. You have had an inside look at the way the system actually works. What happened to Bob Surrick doesn't happen every day in both the state and federal courts but it is all too frequent to ignore.. The system is broken and will only get worse.

I have not achieved my goal of leaving the system better than I found it. On balance, it is a hell of a lot worse. I don't know a lawyer who is enjoying the practice of law. The older ones want to get out. The younger ones are obsessed with money.

The crash you just heard was me dropping the torch. Will you pick it up?

The only success I might claim is heeding Ghandi that:

You must make the injustice visible

I hope I succeeded. And now, the blue water beckons.

EPILOGUE

Perhaps you noticed that the title of a prior chapter, FEAR IS THE FOOD THAT NOURISHES POLITICS did not end IN PENNSYLVANIA. That is because what I have written about is not unique to Pennsylvania. Pennsylvania just happened to be what I knew about from my own involvement. I suggest that many of the truths, the stories, the principles and principals recounted in this book are universal. The McClure machine in Delaware County didn't invent anything new. Justice Larsen was not one-of-a-kind in the judicial world. Politicians turned Judge like Franny Catania are straight out of *The Godfather*.

For more than half a century, New York had the infamous Tammany Hall. New Jersey had the Hague machine. Boston had Mayor Curley. Was "The Boss" in *All The King's Men"* really fiction? I could go on and on. But the point is, there will always be the corrupt and the corruptors. What the corrupt and the corruptors, in any state, in any city, in any hamlet, can't stand is exposure.

So I say to you, wherever you live, dedicate a part of yourself to understanding what is really going on around you. Become involved. Millions of your countrymen have died to give you the right to become involved. When you see injustice, and you probably will not have to look far, speak out. There is social injustice everywhere. There is political injustice everywhere. There is judicial injustice everywhere. Don't just go along to get along, make a difference. If you do, you and your world will be better for it.

I have a special message for my brethren at the bar. We have fouled our nest. As lawyers, we no longer receive respect anywhere except at bar functions where we give each other awards. Lawyer jokes proliferate and with good reason. Doing pro bono lawyering is fine but it doesn't make us a profession. Don't give another lawyer respect and stature because he or she makes big bucks. Go back to the basics and insist on honesty and integrity from those you deal with. Character counts and those without character deserve to be shunned. Pick your spot to improve our system and stay with it—make it paramount in your life. We have a long way to go to regain the respect of the community but if everyone takes a little piece and works at it, it just might happen. Grand gestures are not necessary. Insist that our leaders lead, not just enjoy the adulation of the office. Let's earn the respect we deserve and take back our profession.

About The Author

Born July 8, 1933 in Chester, Pennsylvania, he was the middle of six children. A so-so student in high school but a committed athlete, he discovered history, government and politics and philosophy at the University of Maryland under the guidance of Gordon Prange, author of *Miracle at Midway* and *At Dawn We Slept*, the definitive books on Pearl Harbor and the naval battle of Midway.

After serving two years in the U.S. Army, he matriculated at Dickinson School of Law in 1957 and graduated in 1960, sixteenth in his class.

Admitted to the bar in 1961, he began practice in Media. In 1979, he met Dick Thornburgh who appointed him, upon election as Governor, to the Judicial Inquiry and Review Board. It was there he collided with Supreme Court Justice Rolf Larsen, a classmate at Dickinson, when he voted to remove Larsen from the Supreme Court. His vote resulted in a twenty-year battle with the Disciplinary Board of the Supreme Court.

He was the recipient of the 1987 Public Service Achievement Award from Common Cause/PA for his efforts to reform the Pennsylvania judicial system.

In 1993 and 1995 he was a candidate for the Supreme Court and in 1997 for the Superior Court.

His passion is the law and his 37' sailboat Maverick on which he has raced to Bermuda six times, visited Cuba three times, sailed from Maine to Mexico and lived aboard in the Exumas.